"Peace is not founded upon disarmament; Peace is founded upon liberty and justice." O.K. Armstrong

"Life can be beautiful; It is bountiful, if not always materially, and it is brief. Everyone should try to fix his or her helm on gratitude for life and its blessings, but to do so takes a wakeful watch." Charles Lindbergh Armstrong

© 2018 Martin Capages Jr.

American Freedom Publications LLC

www.americanfreedompublications.com

2638 E. Wildwood Road

Springfield, MO 65804

www.themoralcaseforamericanfreedom.com

ISBN 978-1-64204-648-9   Hardback Version

ISBN 978-1-64204-649-6   Paperback Version

ISBN 978-1-64204-650-2   E-book Version

Cover Design   Christopher M. Capages

www.capagescreative.com

Manuscript Editor   Jordan Reilly Helterbrand

First Edition- March 1, 2018

Printed in the United States of America

DEDICATION

This book is dedicated to the memory of Dr. Charles Lindbergh Armstrong and in honor of the Armstrong Family.

Charles was a man of many talents with many accomplishments and with some left undone. This biography is intended to complete three of those left undone at his passing in 2017.

ACKNOWLEDGEMENTS

It has been my distinct honor to develop this biography at the request of the Armstrong Family. It could not have been completed without the direct encouragement and involvement of O.K. Armstrong Jr. ("Kay") and his brothers, Milton and Stanley Armstrong However, the most prolific contributor has been the subject of the biography, the late Dr. Charles Lindbergh Armstrong, through the many pages of written material and research that he compiled over many years.

I would also like to acknowledge the encouragement and prayers provided by my wife, Pamela, as well as her recollections of the Armstrong family as fellow members of University Heights Baptist Church in Springfield, Missouri.

TABLE OF CONTENTS

FOREWORD

By Martin Capages Jr. PhD

A member of my local Gideons International Camp, Mr. Orland Kay Armstrong Jr. approached me concerning a burden he had on his heart following the passing of his brother, Dr. Charles Lindbergh Armstrong in June 2017. Orland Kay Armstrong Jr. is the son of Missouri Congressman Orland Kay Armstrong Sr. Since his father went by the nickname O.K., his second youngest son, Jr., goes by the nickname "Kay".

I had known Kay for many years. Along with other members of my Camp, I had attended the military funeral of Dr. Armstrong and met Kay's siblings and other relatives at the conclusion of the service. Kay knew that I had recently authored a book, *The Moral Case for American Freedom*, and wanted to know if I could help him with some of his late brother's writings that Kay had accumulated over the past many years. He said he regretted the fact that his brother's work had never been published. Intrigued by the deep sincerity of Kay's request, I told him I would have a look at his brother's material and give him my opinion on its publication value. At the time, I had authored and published ONE book, a long way from being an expert on book publishing.

The material was presented to me in a banker's box. Three- quarters of the material consisted of a series of English word derivations from the original Latin. There were over a thousand pages of single-spaced typed derivations. I had two years of high school Latin, so, I was impressed, maybe in awe, but immediately bored. Latin in high school was not very exciting to me and still isn't today. But I kept digging through the box of written material. Then, in those many papers, I found a draft of an autobiography that Charles had written on his battle with throat cancer.

There was also a review of the early Armstrong family history and a remarkable description by Charles of his service as an Army Flight Surgeon in Vietnam. The typed material was in various stages of editing, and the page numbers no longer coincided with the flow of original thought. There were many editorial comments and suggestions by Kay Armstrong to his brother Charles. These were handwritten on the typed pages. You could tell there was a deep feeling of trust and love between these two brothers. Charles looked to Kay for guidance, and it was expertly given.

Included in the mix of papers was a set of guidelines that Dr. Armstrong had developed for submitting his creation to a publisher. It has been my intent to follow these guidelines as close as possible. His original work is presented in this book as almost an autobiography. The subject matter has been rearranged, but the bulk of the words are Charles' own.

In this book, you will be guided by Charles through his childhood of secure love and nourishment until his mother died, through an adolescence of change and insecurity, through an education which fostered his inquisitive mind, through a war which soured and saddened him, through a medical career in which he prospered and was gratified. Then, you will bear witness to a series of personal illnesses that rattled Charles' very being.

Charles has many heroes in his background, from his father, his father's famous friend, Charles Lindbergh, to his brothers and sister. He was blessed with a father who was a true crusader, a leader with rare courage and clarity of vision, who championed the cause of freedom, democratic government and human rights of peoples near and far. He was surrounded by American patriots in his siblings. All four boys wore the uniform of the United States. Milton and Kay in the Navy during WWII and Stanley and Charles in the Army during the Vietnam Era. Stanley would be an MP stationed at Fort Leonard Wood. Stanley would laugh about he and Charles sharing the same room at home for 16 years. Stanley played while Charles studied. Journalism was also contagious in this family since Stanley would be "recruited" to be the editor of the Base newspaper during his tour at Fort Leonard Wood. But I suspect that O.K. and Charles may have authored more print.

From the original material reviewed, to include handwritten editorial comments made by his brother, Kay, on Charles' typewritten text, this family was extraordinary in their love for one another. This is a story of American Patriotism.

I would be remiss if I didn't also note the Scottish heritage of this family as related to me by Kay Armstrong. The Armstrong Clan were the defenders of the Scottish Borders. They were an exceedingly rough bunch with a reputation for greatness in battle that was tarnished by a tendency toward brutality and criminality. The motto of the Armstrong Clan is, "I remained unvanquished," and their coat of arms is presented in a fitting manner on the cover of this book.

Charles had a wonderful way with words and phrases. One that I became particularly fond of relates well to this noble American family. *"Life can be beautiful; It is bountiful, if not always materially, and it is brief. Everyone should try to fix his or her helm on gratitude for life and its blessings, but to do so takes a wakeful watch."* It has been my privilege to be on the periphery of their story as seen through the eyes of Dr. Charles Lindbergh Armstrong.

Martin Capages Jr. PhD
Author of *The Moral Case for American Freedom*

PREFACE

By Charles Lindbergh Armstrong MD

Though influenced by experience, the most noticeable features of an individual's adult personality are on display upon arrival at the newborn nursery. That's the work of genes, even if her sister and brother display personalities alien to hers and probably to each other. My observation is that siblings are little more alike in personality than non-siblings picked at random. But genetic heritage is there, whether the heir is a tributary of the family current or a dry-bed rebel. The infant's basic personality is like the superstructure of a vessel. Its possibilities depend on constantly modifiable variables, such as its fitting-out (the spars and

Kay and Milton Armstrong

rigging of learning or training); physical maintenance (care, or neglect and abuse); and the extent to which its journey is within the appropriate medium. One's storm-tossed sea is another's tranquil pool. There are those who believe personality and birth-order are related. According to amateur authorities I have heard pronounce on the subject, the first-born are the conquerors, the last-born the rebels. I have been unable to find much analysis of my situation: several parents and a sibling.

When I was born, my two oldest brothers, Milton and O.K. Jr. (Kay) were 15 and 13, my sister Louise ("Little Sis" to my father) was seven, and brother Stanley was 13 months.

Louise Armstrong "Little Sis"

Throughout childhood, "Little Sis" was mature and strong for her age, qualities I first noticed by her guidance of her junior-high circle, that old gang of hers. Consequently, I grew up with one brother a year older and five "parents". Therefore, I'm impatient to see the results of organized research into whether and when an "adult-child" relationship between widely spaced siblings evolves into "adult-adult". My older brothers became less "parent" and more "brother" sometime during my twenties. My sister and I remained "parent-child".

Stanley (4) and Charles (3)

I usually referred to my father, Orland K. Armstrong, as "O.K.," his name to his friends. The same for my mother, "Louise," the better to maintain my sense of objectivity. O.K. exemplified that the fundamental personality is delivered with the baby and that individuals are alloys of genetic ore fused and tempered in the crucible of experience. For him, leadership was an inborn and life-defining trait, evident to all during his first decade of life, and a positive pole to the negative one of his father "Calvin's" personal weaknesses. O.K.'s relatives, friends, colleagues, acquaintances, associates and enemies were unanimous: They had never known a more natural leader. As one of them put it, "O.K. led, and if somebody didn't like it, he led anyway."

Sometime around puberty my learning began to advance from, "Life Is More Than the Comfort of Mother's Bosom", to "Life Doesn't Return What Is Due", a handle I was too weak to grasp at age seven. As an adolescent, when I became oblivious to that rule during an occasional cozy lapse, experience countered with a hard reminder. We'll revisit these precepts in their discovery phase, as they are crucial in understanding my behavior and my slow acceptance of such realities.

"Little Sis" with Charles and Stanley

Some of life's unfairness is the illegitimate child of chance--outside our command and indifferent to our orders. It's when the loose end of the leash around our waist is in our own hand that we earn life's load of "should have's." Casey Stengel's counsel, "When you come to a 'Y' in the road, take it," suggests why life is an archive of stalemate and hindsight, with all their health implications. Those, like me, who wash down every choice with a big gulp of doubt are going to believe lots of "should have's" stirring inside. My account reveals how illness amplifies the second-guessing that whispers in the ear and describes what ensues when the heart contends with its rival, practicality.

Congressman O.K. Armstrong

I'll delineate the paradox of my father, a crusader who never had much to do with doubt, but who more than once failed to seize the moment. We'll explore health and illness of individuals and of the greater arena: war and peace, the sickness and health of civilization and how they can affect the individual. We are all familiar with historical leaders-tyrants and demagogues-whose mental illness brought about conflict and carnage for their own people and often for the known world. This story expounds upon domestic and international conflicts, which cause personal disorders-physical or mental-and proposes that survival depends upon keeping a wakeful watch.

During grade school, I became growingly aware that my father was a commanding presence. I could sense the ambiance of authority about him and the respect it prompted from others. It was as if people speaking with him, or of him-all 5'9", 170 pounds of him-were looking up. How imposing he was to others became clearer to me as an adolescent. During my junior and senior years of high school, as soon as adults heard my name during introductions, more often than not, their next words were, "Are you O.K.'s boy?" An example from many years later: During our college summers, my brother, Stan, my cousin, Ed, and our girlfriends often spent weekends at Table Rock Lake, where we might rent a boat at the sleepy village of Branson, Missouri. During one of these excursions we dropped by School of the Ozarks at Hollister. O.K. had served as a Trustee and had written magazine articles detailing the methods and accomplishments of the unusual institution. The religious-based school provided education for Midwestern young people whose qualifications were financial necessity and the gumption to study and to work on the school's farm, cannery, or construction. I left a note for the president, M. Graham Clark, who was away: "Dear President Clark: We enjoyed our visit to your fine institution and were sorry to miss you. You may remember my father, O.K. Armstrong. Etc." A week later came this reply:

"Dear Charles: How could anyone possibly forget O.K. Armstrong? You are very lucky to have such a father." And so on. I always relished having some of this overflow of regard spill onto me, though I realized I was just in its way. My pride in having a father who habitually evoked that sort of response from people was unaffected by my realization that I did not have his gifts of leadership and strength. His was an exceedingly public personality, certainly not to be envied by a private one such as

Louise Armstrong in 1945

mine, nor by a proud son or daughter of any personality.

However, during my first few years my focus was quite ordinary--other than the usual early childhood self-absorption, it was on Mother. There were others raising me: my sister, my two brothers older than she, and, of course, my father. But I was in love with Mother; in love in the natural way of any healthy preschooler; and she was easy to love. Unlike Freud's Oedipus, I bore no grudges against Dad, but then, neither did the real Oedipus. In fact, during my first years I basked in the warmth and security of parental love, by which I mean their love for each other- their love for their children being granted. Theirs was romance, which is not a universal condition approaching the third decade of marriage. Therefore, at the age of seven I knew nothing of distress beyond an anxious hour or two of separation from Mother and nothing of sadness longer than the moment it took me to forget the trivial reason for it.

I knew very little of any maladjustment around me since any strange behavior was buffered by mentally healthy parents. Of course, there is always the tendency to fold early-life discord into an attic trunk, to which we then apply a memory-proof, lifetime seal. At that age, these darker dramas may be as over our heads and as fleeting as clouds. Or, if they have substance and edge, they might engrave an impression on our emotional plate-an impression not necessarily damaging, but lasting. As for my own pre-second grade years, the only distasteful side that lingered longer than a hurt feeling was an inhibiting shyness, especially with other children. I recall feeling much more comfortable and responsive with adult strangers than with other children, provided the company of mother or dad. That's not to suggest a mark of maturity. Quite the contrary, it was probably because I felt a clearer security with adults, an assurance not within reach with other children.

Some personalities are geared by nature to accept more readily life's unsavoriness as the natural course of things. I'm not one of those. During my first decade, my conditioning was that life's flow would be as smooth, warm and restful as my mother's love. My discoveries that life is not just warmth and security didn't come by graduation from soft to hard. In fact, one of the hardest came early, though I probably didn't feel it full- force at the time. During my first decade, I was as oblivious of death as a rich man of a mortgage. When I was introduced to death at age seven, I can't say I caught its name. Or perhaps I caught its name the way we do that of a stranger in a receiving line-more greeting than identity. At seven, the blow of death was cushioned by meager understanding and much naive trust, trust that life would always go as smoothly as it had. It was also

The Armstrong Siblings at "Little Sis" Louise's Wedding to Edmond Cattan

From the left Stanley, Charles, Louise, Milton, and Kay

cushioned by whatever ability a seven-year-old has to lay things away in that attic trunk, to which we shall return for a look in due time.

When I was almost 11, another toll of the bell made death's inevitability much harder to ignore. This time I didn't just greet death in a receiving line-it followed me around. My Grandmother Armstrong's funeral was a trauma that bivouacked in my brain and held its ground for months despite my every effort to evict it. As I got into bed each night its reveille would blow, rousing the encamped demon. It haunted not because of deep feelings for my father's mother, but because this actuality--human loss, especially through death-was revealed to me at an age when understanding was more at hand than at seven and would take much more psychic trickery to resist. But during the ages around 11 each year seemed an epoch, and the seeming remoteness of adulthood, much less of later life and death, helped restore some emotional ease. That process was accomplished by the next summer's travels, which with one stroke broke the year's routine and my obsessive funereal thoughts. What lingered after my "getting to know you" with death was the frustrated outlook of "just one century isn't enough to take it all in."

INTRODUCTION

By Martin Capages Jr. PhD

Dr. Charles Lindbergh Armstrong was a brilliant man, a genius with an IQ over 165. This became apparent as I read each page that he had composed. He was born of a line of heroes and was named for one as well. To see how this came about requires some background into this amazing family called The Armstrong's. We will begin with Charles' father, Orland Kay Armstrong.

One key to the Charles Armstrong story is the relationship of Charles' father, O.K. Armstrong, to the famous Lone Eagle, Charles

Orland Kay Armstrong

Augustus Lindbergh (or Lucky Lindy). However, Charles' father was a bit famous in his own right. The son of a southern Missouri minister, he graduated *summa cum laude* from Drury College in Springfield, Missouri. He was also a flyer and had served as a pilot during World War One. After the war, he earned his law degree at Cumberland University in Tennessee, and went on to earn a master's degree in journalism from the University of Missouri, studying under Walter Williams, the Dean of the University of Missouri School of Journalism. He then moved to Florida.

In Florida, O.K. Armstrong continued his string of successes. In fact, Walter Williams came to the University of Florida to install Armstrong as the first head of the University's Department of Journalism. The 1928 University yearbook, the Seminole, reported: "The College of Commerce and Journalism was established as the School of Business and Journalism in 1925. For the first year it operated under the College of Arts and Sciences with the Dean of the College in charge. Beginning with the first semester of 1926 a special director was appointed, and the School began to operate as a unit separate from the College of Arts and Sciences. In the Spring of 1927 the Board of Control created the College of Commerce and Journalism out of this unit with a dean and faculty of its own and made it co-equal in every respect with the other colleges of the University."

O.K. Armstrong had also worked as a freelance journalist for several newspapers and national magazines in the mid-1920s. One article, which gained him notoriety, was a rare 1927 interview with Charles Lindbergh for Boys' Life magazine. After that interview, the two aviators, both with Missouri ties, became close friends. They would work together as patriots with a vision to keep the United States out of another world war. In this endeavor they would be unsuccessful, but not due to their own actions. It would be History that would have the final say. The following order of events were chronicled in ANNALS OF IOWA, *Courtesy of De Moines Register and Tribune*. The following is a synopsis of the article titled "Verne Marshall in 1940":

"On December 17, 1940, at New York's Hotel Lexington, Verne Marshall, editor of the *Cedar Rapids Gazette*, announced the formation of the No Foreign War Committee. Like most other isolationists, Marshall felt that the United States should build an impregnable defense. While at times Lindbergh wanted isolationists throughout the nation to buck the America First Committee, at other times he thought that two regional associations might operate more effectively. Lindbergh reluctantly endorsed the appointment of Verne Marshall as chairman. Within two days after the organization of the No Foreign War Committee was announced, Marshall noted that Lindbergh had promised to "do everything this committee wants me to do." Plans were made for a mass meeting in St. Louis, where the official campaign would be launched.

Pacifists were scheduled to play an important role in the new organization. O. K. Armstrong called an Emergency Peace Conference in Washington on October 21, 1940, with his old friend, Colonel Lindbergh, as the featured speaker. Pacifists were there in abundance at the conference. Later, in a letter written to R. Douglas Stuart, national director of America First, Lindbergh admitted that he differed with the pacifists on what he called "strong military forces for American Defense," but claimed that "the agitation for war and the trend towards it in this country have been so strong that I don't think we can afford to alienate any groups who stand with us in opposition." [A take on "the enemy of my enemy is my friend".] Therefore, with his belief that all antiwar forces must coordinate their efforts, Lindbergh wanted Armstrong to merge his No Foreign War Campaign with Verne Marshall's No Foreign War Committee. But, to maintain some control, he pressed for Armstrong to direct the field organization of Marshall's new group.

At first, efforts to gain pacifist backing seemed successful. But within two months after its birth on December 17, 1940, the No Foreign

War Committee ceased major political activity ,and four months later it formally disbanded. Charles A. Lindberg withdrew his support, and O.K. Armstrong also withdrew support from the Committee.

At a supper at Lindbergh's home on January 4, 1941, Armstrong and the Lone Eagle discussed the possibility of forming still another antiwar group, one which would sponsor mass meetings throughout the country. After a trip to New York in a last-ditch effort to wrest control of the Committee from Marshall, Armstrong submitted his resignation. The death of the No Foreign War Committee had few mourners. Most of its backers were strongly opposed to the domestic reforms of the previous ten years and found even the America First Committee--by no means a radical group--far too liberal." Although many Americans opposed Roosevelt's interventionism, this would all change on December 7, 1941.

The Lindbergh-Armstrong friendship continued after the war. Lindbergh was supportive of Armstrong's political endeavors in Missouri. Armstrong was elected to the Missouri state legislature for several terms, but District gerrymandering would prevent another run for the Missouri legislature. He also made an unsuccessful bid to be the Lieutenant Governor of Missouri. However, Lindbergh's support, along with Armstrong's own considerable skills, may have helped Armstrong get elected to serve one term in the U.S. House of Representatives for Missouri from January 1951 to January 1953. He also received many other honorary degrees before he passed away on April 15, 1987, in Springfield, Missouri. "Until his health waned in his 90s, O.K. Armstrong would lead all sizes of crusades, with themes such as integrity vs. governmental corruption; peace-the health of nations and international relations, which he believed to be founded on liberty and justice; and moral strength--to him the rule of the road to be fulfillment in life." (Charles L. Armstrong)

Charles Augustus Lindbergh

Most people are familiar with the remarkable story of the brave "Lucky Lindy" and his solo flight across the Atlantic. And many know the tragic story of the kidnapping of his young son. But the friendship between O.K. Armstrong and Lindbergh is glossed over in the annals of History. The friendship develops just before the United States entered the Second World War. The background is as follows:

"At the urging of U.S. Ambassador Joseph Kennedy, Lindbergh wrote a secret memo to the British warning that a military response by Britain and France to Hitler's violation of the Munich Agreement would be disastrous; he claimed that France was militarily weak and Britain over-reliant on its navy. He recommended that they urgently strengthen their air power to force Hitler to redirect his aggression against 'Asiatic Communism'. In a controversial 1939 Reader's Digest article he wrote, 'Our civilization depends on peace among Western nations ... and therefore on united strength, for Peace is a virgin who dare not show her face without Strength, her father, for protection.'[1] Lindbergh deplored the rivalry between Germany and Britain but favored a war between Germany and Russia.

---

[1] https://en.wikipedia.org/wiki/Charles_Lindbergh

Following Hitler's invasion of Czechoslovakia and Poland, Lindbergh decried suggestions that the United States should send aid to countries under threat, writing, 'I do not believe that repealing the arms embargo would assist democracy in Europe' and, 'If we repeal the arms embargo with the idea of assisting one of the warring sides to overcome the other, then why mislead ourselves by talk of neutrality?' He equated assistance with war profiteering: 'To those who argue that we could make a profit and build up our own industry by selling munitions abroad, I reply that we in America have not yet reached a point where we wish to capitalize on the destruction and death of war.'

In his 1941 testimony before the House Committee on Foreign Affairs opposing the Lend-Lease bill, Lindbergh proposed that the United States negotiate a neutrality pact with Germany. President Franklin Roosevelt publicly decried Lindbergh's views as those of a 'defeatist and appeaser.' Lindbergh promptly resigned his commission as a colonel in the U.S. Army Air Corps, writing that he saw 'no honorable alternative' given that Roosevelt had publicly questioned his loyalty."

After the Japanese attack on Pearl Harbor, Lindbergh sought to be recommissioned in the USAAF. The Secretary of War, Henry L. Stimson, declined the request on instructions from the White House. [Roosevelt could really hold a grudge.]

Unable to take on an active military role, Lindbergh approached a number of aviation companies and offered his services as a consultant. As a technical adviser with Ford in 1942, he was heavily involved in troubleshooting early problems encountered at the Willow Run

6

Consolidated B-24 Liberator bomber production line. As B-24 production smoothed out, he joined United Aircraft in 1943 as an engineering consultant, devoting most of his time to its Chance-Vought Division. The following year, Lindbergh persuaded United Aircraft to designate him as a technical representative in the Pacific Theater to study aircraft performances under combat conditions. Among other things, he showed Marine pilots how to take off safely with a bomb load double the Vought F4U Corsair fighter-bomber's rated capacity. At the time, several Marine squadrons were flying bomber escorts to destroy the Japanese stronghold of Rabaul, New Britain, in the Australian Territory of New Guinea.

On May 21, 1944, Lindbergh flew his first combat mission: a strafing run near the Japanese garrison of Rabaul. In his six months in the Pacific in 1944, Lindbergh took part in fighter bomber raids on Japanese positions, flying 50 combat missions (again as a civilian). His innovations in the use of Lockheed P-38 Lightning fighters impressed a supportive Gen. Douglas MacArthur. Lindbergh introduced engine-leaning techniques to P-38 pilots, greatly improving fuel consumption at cruise speeds, enabling the long-range fighter aircraft to fly longer range missions. The U.S. Marine and Army Air Force pilots who served with Lindbergh praised his courage and defended his patriotism. Charles Lindbergh passed away on August 26, 1974, in Kipahulu on the island of Maui, Hawaii."

Charles Lindbergh Armstrong M.D.

Charles Lindbergh Armstrong was born in Springfield, Missouri, July 17, 1940, as the youngest of five siblings. His older sister Louise Armstrong Catton died of cancer in 1979, but his older brothers, Milton M. Armstrong of Maitland, Florida., O.K. "Kay" Armstrong Jr., of Republic, Missouri, and W. Stanley Armstrong of Galax, Virginia, are still living. There are multiple nieces, nephews and cousins but Charles was especially close to Kay Armstrong's daughter, Dr. Carol Okuda, and Kay's son, Dr. Lance Armstrong. Charles loved the beauty of the American West and took Carol and Lance on visits to show them these miracles of nature that

Carol, Lance and Charles out West

he so admired. He had discovered this love for nature while in the Boy Scouts.

Charles graduated from Central High School in Springfield, Missouri, in 1958. He attended Wesleyan University in Middletown, Connecticut, on a full scholarship and graduated in 1962. He then attended the University of Missouri Medical School and graduated in 1966.

Before completing his internship and residency, he joined the U. S. Army and served as a flight-surgeon in Vietnam in 1968-69 with a helicopter unit of the 3rd U. S. Army located at Can Tho Air Force Base.

Capt. Armstrong made many "rescue runs" and was loved by the flight crews. When the brass found out about it he was grounded. The brass felt that Flight-Surgeons were too valuable to be placed in harm's way. After returning to the States and leaving the Army, Charles completed his medical residency and started his own practice. Charles was married for a short while and then divorced.

Captain Armstrong in Vietnam

Henceforth in this book, I will refer to Dr. Armstrong as Charles. The material is presented by Charles in the first person. You will be amazed at the visual rendering of the times and places recorded in his memoirs of the Armstrong family. And you will also discover that this man had a hereditary command of the written word. It was in his genes.

Charles practiced medicine in Santa Barbara, California, Winter Park, Florida, and Atlanta, Georgia, before opening a family medicine practice in Alexandria, Virginia, which he operated for nearly 20 years. To know Dr. Armstrong as a patient was to know you were in the hands of competency and genuine care. According to his family members, Charles was an intellect extraordinaire and a humble, generous spirit. As his posthumous biographer, I can personally attest to that.

As discussed earlier, the preponderance of material in this book was written by Charles in the first person. However, at some points in the development of the material, Charles relied on tape recordings of interviews he had obtained from sources, some of which are now unknown. To the best of my knowledge, this material has not been presented in any other works. Charles' famous father, O.K. Armstrong, has been the subject of many articles, to include a University of Florida master's thesis, which is cited as appropriate.

When Charles passed away in June 2017, he was suffering from malnutrition stemming from complications that resulted from the false positive cancer diagnosis and the following operations on his throat. The publication of his story, *A WAKEFUL WATCH*, is a tribute to Charles and the Armstrong family, a family of remarkable dedication, talent and love for America and its gift of individual Freedom.

Martin Capages Jr. PhD
Author of *The Moral Case for American Freedom*

PART ONE-HERITAGE

11

Preacher's Kid, Patriot and Patriarch

O.K. was nearly two generations my senior. I was a child of mid-century. He witnessed its turn. I attribute my existence to parents who felt in mid-life that the way to stay young was to have young. My clan has displayed as much or more neuroses and maladjustment as the next, though O.K. and his eight brothers and sisters were, by and large, spared anything more serious.

There were certain matters, especially of sex and backsliding, that my Dad's generation of Armstrong's regarded as better left undiscussed. I did not learn until my late teens that my Uncle Angus's daughter, my cousin Karen, was the offspring of a second marriage following a—gasp- - "divorce", and that by his first wife, Angus had had a son unknown to me because of the hush-hush.

Most of my grandfather's (Calvin) and grandmother's (Agnes) children became missionaries, either officially (to Brazil), or by way of institutional leadership, as, for example, in the Women's Christian Temperance Union, charities, church, and politics from local to national level. But all of them knew that O.K. was the real leader.

By 1910 the family decided on Springfield as home because, as southern Missouri's largest town, its schools were better than the more rural ones. My grandfather, Calvin, would board the Saturday train to church, taking advantage of the clergy-discount, and return on Sunday evening. During the school year 1911-1912, a Professor McMurtry was sent by the administration of Drury College in Springfield to scout for good students. On the list proposed by the faculty at Carterville High were O.K. and his sister Delta. Delta should have entered college in 1909 but was obliged to sit out those years at home, holding books to her nose, until the family could save enough to buy spectacles. As Valedictorian of the Carterville High School Class of 1912, O.K. was awarded a tuition scholarship from Drury College of Springfield. The Assemblies of God gave him still another scholarship as the child of a minister [of any denomination]. These two grants covered O.K.'s tuition and some living expenses his first year, a favorable development since the cost of small private schools was out of range for his family:

O.K. graduated *summa cum laude* from Drury in 1916. Delta graduated summa cum laude from Drury the previous year. Southwest Baptist College immediately offered him a position teaching history. Having not yet heard a clear professional call, he accepted. At the sound of the opening bell in September, the college administration reasoned that O.K.'s baccalaureate degree in psychology warranted his teaching that subject as well. O.K. agreed with enthusiasm.

Soon thereafter, Dean Pike observed to O.K. in an aside that "someone was needed to teach the dozen or fifteen novice preachers in whatever else you want them to learn." O.K.'s response to this rather direct hint was the 1916 equivalent of "Oh sure, no problem." Part of "whatever else you want them to learn" was a survey of European-American history emphasizing the evolution of democratic government, with special emphasis on the U.S. founding. O.K., capable as he was, was not an expert in all those subjects at age twenty-two. But their less-than-fastidious observance of official credentialing (If you can teach something, then go right ahead) and their consequent acceptance of O.K. as an instructor in several fields speaks for the era's relative casualness of

13

academic structure, at least in small college America. "Oh, and by the way, O.K., would you mind taking charge as dean of the dormitory and the forty-five students housed there? We can't finance it, but you just apportion out your costs to the boys residing and boarding there, and charge them as much."

"Yes, I believe I can manage that readily."

And again, Dean Pike just a few days later, "Incidentally, O.K., we want to continue some athletics here at Southwest. Have you had any basketball experience?" "Oh, by all means," said O.K., "my brother and I were stars of the second string in high school, and I would be delighted." O.K. recruited six men, giving him always one reserve. They won some games that year against distant powerhouses, such as Buffalo (the one in Missouri), Drury College and Springfield's Normal College (later known as Southwest Missouri State Teachers' College, then Southwest Missouri State University and now, Missouri State University).

Two months into the semester, Dean Pike said, "Now, O.K., we have run out of money. We can't pay you, but can you stay anyhow?" O.K. appealed to his family in Springfield for survival-sufficient funds and stayed the year. He and the boys at the dorm ordered much of their staple foods from Sears and Roebuck, whose prices beat the local suppliers, wholesale or retail.

World War One: "The Great War"

On April 6, 1917, war was declared. The Armstrong boys' grandfather, veteran of two wars, had told them, "If war is declared by the United States, don't wait to be drafted. A conscript will be looked upon as a convict." O.K.'s younger brother Angus signed up on April 9,

Angus Armstrong

and was on the train to Jefferson Barracks in St. Louis that night. Four thousand young men had already gathered. The response had been too great to process. These men were inducted and sent back home to wait to be summoned for training. Meanwhile, Angus volunteered for civilian work as an electrician at the Ship Yard in Philadelphia. There the Navy was converting interned German passenger ships (ships in our waters when war was declared). Angus was assigned to a ship named the U.S.S. von Steuben in honor of the German General whose help was crucial to America's Revolutionary War victory. In August, Angus was ordered to basic infantry training at Camp Clark in Missouri. "We put those new khaki uniforms on and strutted around there like we were some-body. And when we were given our Springfield rifles we thought we were ready to whip the Kaiser right now. We rode the troop train to Camp Sill Oklahoma, a two-day trip because of stops at every town to pick up more men and more cars."

Upon completion of training in the spring of 1918, the men were notified that they would be the unit assigned a new weapon, the machine gun. This was an upsetting development. They knew nothing about the weapon, but this was an infantry unit, and they assumed this turn of events was equivalent to a demotion. How surprised they were to learn the contrary, that they had impressed some visiting brass enough to be awarded this prestigious duty and were no longer "regular infantry."

In May 1918, the well-trained men of Camp Sill started the six-day train trip to New York, and on to Camp Mills for fitting out with new equipment. Then a ferry to New York, where Angus and his 35th Division buddies boarded the steamship Carpathia, which in 1912 had picked up the survivors of the Titanic.

Their convoy of twelve troop ships crossed the Atlantic with anti-sub destroyer escorts patrolling a 180-degree arc before the transports. The sub threat was serious enough that the convoy detoured north of Ireland and came down the channel to Liverpool. "The English lassies welcomed us with open arms, but it was a hug and a goodbye." From Liverpool, they took trains to Southampton, where they boarded ships for Le Havre.

There to greet the disembarking men was a Scottish bagpipe and drum corps. It was the opinion of the high command that the best thing to instill the fighting spirit was the skirl of the Scottish pipes, the martial sound of the drums and the flourish of the kilted marchers. On the sides of the boxcars of the French trains was painted *Quarante Hommes ou Huit Chevaux* (Forty Men or Eight Horses). To quote Angus: "We travelled with eight horses and forty men. We didn't care. By then we were inured to military orders. If they said give, we gave."

On the way to Mulhouse the Americans were billeted in villages and farms close to the front, such as St. Mihiel and Thann in Alsace-Lorraine, mostly sharing barns with livestock. Angus and his buddies first came under fire at Thann, a few miles northwest of Mulhouse. They tried to shoot down the German planes that flew over dropping bombs but got no hits. General Black Jack Pershing's plan was to push back the Germans' St. Mihiel salient (50 kilometers northwest of Nancy), part of their thrust to take Paris. And that's what these men did with about two days of intense fire. They then expected some rest time, but it wasn't to be. Next was the annihilation of the Hindenburg Line. General Pershing assigned this task to the 35th Division on Sept. 25, 1918. Angus and his buddies trudged up Hill 285 and set up their machine guns as close side by side as possible in order to lay down a barrage (Angus's word). A naval Lt. Commander approached and told them he had a Navy 16" gun mounted on a flat car, and the signal for the artillery and machine-gun cover for the 'jump off' would be the firing of that gun. Angus: "We woke up with a start as the boom shook the ground at 0500 on Sept. 26. We made a dash for our machine guns and laid down our barrage for the infantry while they jumped off over their trenches and rolled on ahead. Later, our rifle-infantry comrades told us, 'With your machine gun barrage backing us up, we thought our brigade could thrash the whole German army.' Our push against that salient was a turning point in closing the war and forcing the armistice. By October 4, we had pushed their line back by perhaps 20 kilometers; we knew victory was at hand."

Meanwhile, at the close of the 1916-1917 school year, Dean Pike asked O.K. if he could stay another year, to which O.K. said, "No, I'd rather enlist than be drafted." In an act of wartime patriotism, the YMCA was offering its summer camps to the Army for training purposes. Before

17

O.K. could report to an enlistment station, the Army asked if he would like to be the civilian director of the Keystone National Guard Division, the 28th, consisting of Pennsylvania boys and officers, stationed at the YMCA camp in Augusta, Georgia. The camp was divided into "huts", one for each regiment of men. The 109th and 110th Regiments made up a brigade, the 111th and 112th a second brigade, with a Brigadier for each of those and a Major General over the Division. At these Army training camps and posts most of these young men heard their first Gramophone records, with such hits as "If I Were Huckleberry Finn" and "Let Me Call You Sweetheart" played on a Victor Talking Machine.

O.K. became restless at the National Guard camp. Being civilian and free to do so, he enlisted in the U.S. Army Signal Corps, Aviation unit. While in college, O.K. had learned drill as part of the athletic program. Within a day of reporting as an enlistee to his squadron in Memphis, the Sergeant Major chanted, "If any of you men has ever had military drill, step three paces forward." O.K. alone stepped forward and was promoted to sergeant a few hours later. O.K. began teaching drill the next day and continued to do so for some months. He was transferred to the University of Illinois for special training in administrative skills needed to organize the new branch of the army, the Aviation Detachment. He then returned to his squadron, which had moved from Memphis to Alabama's Taylor Field, now Maxwell Air Force Base but then just a converted cotton patch.

What a change of atmosphere from Champaign-Urbana, where the men went out at night to see the aurora borealis. Now it was semi-tropics balmy. Using shovels, hand scrapers and ox teams hitched to wagons, Negroes leveled the cotton rows into runways for biplanes. Generations

18

later, O.K.'s ear harkened to the singing of these laborers as one of the more pleasant and indelible memories of the Great War era.

Within days of returning from Illinois, O.K. was promoted to sergeant major. He was also assigned to edit *The Propeller*, the newspaper of army aviation. He then took required tests for promotion, passed them, and was commissioned a 2nd Lieutenant.

The Army had a need, a way of finding someone who could fill it, and an award of commensurate rank. Things were a little simpler in those days. The commanding officer at Taylor Field had further reason not to

Second Lieutenant O. K. Armstrong

be fussy about army protocol. He was busy inventing a silk cloth and rope device that flyers could strap to their backs to catch the wind after jumping from an airplane, crippled or burning after taking a hit. It was something of an irony for the General that he witnessed, a few days before the armistice, the descent by parachute of the only World War I pilot on either side who could thank the new device for his life--a German, who lost a dogfight to an American but won the privilege of describing this distinction. The General captured the pilot, perhaps a small consolation. Meanwhile, the British command refused to let their men use parachutes on the theory that the new contraptions would sap the flyers' defensive spirit.

With the assignment of rank, O.K. received a new order: report to Chanute Field, Illinois, whither O.K. headed by train. There, late October 1918, the Colonel interrupted O.K.'s preparations for flight training.

The command staff needed an assistant adjutant, someone who was good with a pen. As assistant adjutant, O.K. had access to all orders coming through the field headquarters. One order read, "Find forty-two junior officers to proceed to Kelly Field, Texas, to train the recruits in the aviation section." This meant a nation-wide canvas. I neglected to ask O.K. how this was done, and so close to the [new]millennium, I could find no World War I veterans to interview. The consensus of younger experts: The job was done "mostly by telegraph, perhaps some by mail. Any by telephone would have required a relay of at least four connecting 'central' operators for each call." O.K. and his senior officers mustered, by the first week in November, the quota of junior officers. Inductees from all over the country were set to take the train to Kelly Field for flight training. On the morning of Nov. 11, 1918, a telegram arrived from Washington: "The war is over. Dismiss your recruits".

Post-War Service

O.K. was discharged at Taylor Field in February 1919, but, perhaps in gratitude for his promotions, he kept the army informed of his whereabouts in case he was needed. Within a few weeks he received a wire inviting him to don his uniform and direct the Army's YMCA training camp in Springfield, Illinois. There was no more Great War, but there was still a modem army to maintain. As soon as he said "Yes", the army came back with another proposal, or more likely, directive. Go to France and oversee the Russian soldiers liberated from German prison camps and now under the custody of French officers who crave only the ease of nominal command and want someone to take de facto charge of these men. The Russians were freely encamped at Raon l'Etape, 75 kilometers southeast of Nancy. Most of them had been confined to German prison farms where they worked raising food for the German army. As soon as the armistice was signed, the Germans dumped them over into France. Having heard about Bolshevism, France's leader Monsieur Clemenceau inferred that keeping the Russian soldiers in France would be the only humane choice if the alternative was to turn them over to the Bolsheviks. The Russians stayed gladly.

While passing through to coordinate plans and orders, the ranking officer said, "Lt. Armstrong, you'll need to linger in Paris a couple of weeks. While you're here, take charge of this boxing tournament we're having for the entertainment of the men still tidying things up before going home." A few days later O.K. presented a token trophy to the winner of the tournament, a marine named Gene Tunney. Then on to Raon l'Etape, where three thousand Russian soldiers stayed under the coordinated auspices of the U.S. Army and the YMCA. The Army lent

O.K. a camionette, a stretch Model T Ford, that had been used as an ambulance during the war. Painted on the side of this little lorry was "American Field Service, Columbia University Class of 1886," the alumni who had raised the money to provide it. The Russians, "most of them big, burly fellows," were assigned to eight different camps. O.K.'s job was to tour these camps daily in his ambulance to make sure the men were properly fed, kept busy, entertained, and lodged as comfortably as possible given these conditions. The Army Corps of Engineers of World War I had not been called on to do projects of World War II or Vietnam scope, such as building comfortable casernes or barracks. One group of Russians, St. Petersburg cathedral singers quartered together in order to practice their art, was billeted in a barn, not a good likeness to their accustomed prewar lodging. In O.K.'s words, "Oh, what they could do with chords. And what magnificent dancers they were." They played balalaikas (a triangular Russian stringed instrument with a neck like a guitar) they had made from pine boards. To simulate more properly Russian dance by couples, two men of average size volunteered to dance the women's part with husky partners. Now they needed costumes "pour les Dames." Meanwhile, they called upon O.K. to round up more instruments. He filled both orders through Army-YMCA headquarters in Paris. The YMCA, despite the "M" and its military mission, provided some YWCA services and had women's costumes. Through proper channels, of course, O.K. liberated clarinets, flutes, a trumpet, a tambourine, a cello, two fiddles, and pretty frocks for the crossdressers. Nobody could have been more appreciative than those Russian music and dance men in an alien land.

The army sent to O.K. "flickers" (silent movies from Santa Barbara and Hollywood) with French subtitles. The Russian officers were all educated, which to a Russian meant familiarity with French. The movies were a delightful novelty for all and certainly for the Russians. Having been prisoners of the German army for an average of nearly three years, they also knew substantial German. But the Russian officers were still loyal to the Czar and, therefore, refused to speak German. The enlisted men were indifferent or hostile to the Czar and enjoyed practicing the German they had learned in confinement, a happy state for all since O.K. wanted to learn German. O.K. ate alternatively with the Russian officers and enlisted men, and so he had daily classes in French and German.

Florida Roots

Even before O.K. and Angus entered the army, their father had looked forward to alleviating his annual Missouri-winter "grippe" by moving south. This hope made him even more than customarily prey to the charms of an oily charlatan. A traveling land-shark named Alyea, peddling his worthless contracts mostly to preachers throughout northern Dixie and the mid-west, moved in on his prey. The Rev. Mr. Armstrong, as pointed out, never suspected anyone would tell him an untruth and was ripe for picking. The smooth-talking con-man depicted for Calvin the charms of some imaginary land on Crystal River at Homosassa on Florida's west coast. Mr. Alyea further "let Calvin in" ("Now Rev. Armstrong, bein' as it's you, tell ya what I'm gonna do ....) on a business deal promoted as if it would allow him, upon his arrival in Florida and with minimal effort, enough monthly income to semi-retire. On this, at least, Alyea had signed promissory notes.

And on that package Calvin blew their meager savings, including some of Agnes's portion of a modest inheritance that had been distributed to each child of Daniel Brockhaus. Included in the deal was the transference to Mr. Alyea of Calvin's Missouri property, which Alyea resold within days.

O.K., just back from France in January 1920, took the Southern Railroad from New York to Florida. He expected to find the family perfectly content in America's semi-tropical Eden. There was much about Florida in those days that was indeed close to paradise. In Crystal's words, "It was as primitive as when the Spanish found it. The rivers were brim with fish --they were jumping out at us. There were no roads. Unless

24

towns were important enough to be connected by railroad, you couldn't get from one to the next without an ox." But O.K. found the family far from content:

"When I arrived down there I said, 'Now Papa, what about your business arrangement? Are they paying you?'

'Well, no; Mr. Alyea says they'll get around to it when the chits come in.' My heart sank. I didn't want to scold my father, but I knew he had been taken."

O.K. tracked down the "skunk" who had pulled this enormity on his father.

O.K.: "This Mr. Alyea was smooth and knew how to worm around. You see, these land sharks would go to the court house and find out what properties' taxes hadn't been paid. I mean, who would want Florida land anyhow? The state capital was up north in Tallahassee because no white man would ever want to go farther south, where there was nothing but swamps, 'gators, mosquitos and Indians. So, they would let the land just lie there. But I was a little wet behind the ears. If I had known then what I know now, I would have taken the buzzard to court."

Ignorant of legal options, O.K. had to settle for telling the serpentine Alyea what he thought of him. For Papa Armstrong a pastorate at nearby-Lake Butler balm straightaway. And in time this dark interval yielded to a brighter outlook for Calvin's children, who, with one exception, met their betrothed in their new home, the South.

The Love of His Life

O.K. had elected to attend law school, but for the sake of filling in the time until the beginning of the next academic year, accepted an offer to become the first director of the Baptist Young People's Union headquartered in Jacksonville. This job meant travel throughout the southeast. O.K.'s memory was clear sixty-one years later:

Louise McCool

"On the second Sunday of August (1920), I had returned from business in Birmingham and was free to attend the First Baptist Church of Jacksonville, my headquarters town. During the service, I noticed a beautiful young woman, brunette, with bluish-gray eyes. I was too shy to approach her directly. At the close of the service, I left by the front door and was saying goodbye to an acquaintance on the lower step when suddenly she appeared. To my surprise and delight, she stepped up, extended her hand, and said: 'I know who you are; You're O.K. Armstrong, and if nobody's going to introduce us, I will. I'm Louise McCool.' I was elated. After several minutes of pleasant exchange, I said: 'I must meet you again.' She thought a moment and said, 'I have a little time tomorrow morning'. She set it for 10 am. Believe me, that was one engagement I was anxious to keep.

When we met the next morning, all I could do was just wonder 'How could anybody be as beautiful as this girl is?' I had business about ten blocks away, so I said: 'If you can take the time, I'd like you to walk with me to a publisher's office downtown (Jacksonville) where I must turn in some copy.' She said she'd be delighted, so we strolled together into town. After a dinner and a lunch or two with her that week, we both had out of town obligations to meet. We agreed to meet at the train station in Blackshear on Friday, a few days before she would finish visiting her family in Blackshear and leave for school in Louisville. Louise introduced me to her family, all of whom were there except her older brother, who had married soon after returning from the war in Europe. That evening Louise and I took the train the thirty-five miles to Jessup, where we would take the trolley for Jacksonville. She suggested we walk around Jessup for a while.

While we were walking along in the dusk, some young men walked by and greeted Louise as a longtime friend. We had some friendly back-and-forth, and then one of them said, 'Look, Louise, is this the man you're going to marry?' She said 'Yes, if he'll have me.' Although I didn't say so at the moment, I was smitten. I knew she was the girl for me.

During that school term, we corresponded every few days. In May 1921, we met at a student convention in Chattanooga. Meanwhile, I had heard by way of my sister Crystal, who roomed down the hall from Louise in the dorm at Louisville, that Louise had received more proposals than she could count from the student ministers at the seminary. We took the trolley car that ran from town to the summit of Seminary Ridge. The Civil War history of Seminary Ridge was not my interest of the moment; my mind was on this beautiful girl. There we sat on a big rock as the lights came out on the city below us. There I proposed, and she said: 'I've been waiting for that.'

Soon after that I resigned from my job in Jacksonville to enter the Cumberland University School of Law while Louise completed her studies at Louisville. Louise always thought of that as 'Our lost year.' On May 21, 1922, we were married at the church where we had met. The emeritus pastor who had baptized Louise and her father the Rev. A. M. McCool co-presided. We were happy for 26 years until she was taken from me and from us." O.K. and Louise were a good team. I felt secure getting introduced to life in the atmosphere of their mutual regard and affection. I was always pleased that others' accounts of their marriage reaffirmed my entirely positive memories. I idealized their sweethearts bond, though as an adult I became able to acknowledge my aunt Lois's earthbound observation, "Even your mother and O.K. had to work at it."

Louise and O.K. Armstrong in 1946

Back to Missouri

After O.K.'s graduation the couple settled in Springfield, Missouri, where he passed the bar exam and opened a private practice. As the months wore on it became clear to O.K. that he was uncomfortable in the legal profession, or perhaps uncomfortable with it. By late 1922, he knew law was not for him. "I was so unhappy and dissatisfied. Soon Louise said, 'Then let's do something else.'" But countering this restless drag were two forward thrusts: journalism and public service.

First and foremost, among the legitimate schools of journalism was the University of Missouri at Columbia, which O.K. entered the semester starting January 1923. Walter Williams, dean and father of modern journalism education in America, had never graduated from any college.

Later, the self-taught dean's career would be crowned as the President of the University of Missouri at Columbia. Academic protocol in those days was undoubtedly much like that of the military; a) Find the most capable person for the position; b) and then assign proportionate credentials.

In 1924, O.K. and his fellow students took a five-week field trip to Nebraska and the Dakotas to gain experience in investigative journalism. One story they compiled during the trip was about plan of the U.S. Postal Service to experiment with hiring aviators to transport the mail. The first air routes would be St. Louis to Chicago and St. Louis to Omaha and a few points farther west. The St. Louis-Chicago route would be assigned to a young pilot named Charles Lindbergh. Just outside Omaha at a field flat enough to serve as a landing site, the students witnessed and reported the nation's first touchdown of U.S. air mail.

O.K. graduated July 22, 1925, the day after the birth of their first child, Milton. After the conferring of diplomas, Dean Williams quipped, "O.K., this week both you and your wife have earned master's degrees," and then pointed out, "You are now prepared to teach journalism. There are two universities that want you to start a school: Washington and Lee, in Virginia, and the University of Florida." O.K. chose Florida.

During an address to the Florida Press Association convening in Gainesville in early 1925, Dean Williams emphasized journalism as an essential discipline for any school having serious pretensions of being a modern university. The publicizing of this speech bolstered the hopes of the University of Florida's president, A.A. Murphree, who wanted to institute a school of journalism separate from the College of Arts and Sciences. The University's Board of Control approved. Now President Murphree needed a dean for the new college. A tuition fee of ten dollars financed the hiring of Professor (of Economics) Walter Matherly from the University of North Carolina as dean of the College of Business Administration and Journalism. Dean Williams told President Murphree he had just the man in O.K. Armstrong as founding director of journalism education at the new school.

Florida Calls Again

In July 1925, O.K., Louise and their infant Milton made the two-week trip in their Model T to Gainesville, where O.K. and Professor Matherly founded the School of Journalism at the University of Florida. At the 50th anniversary reunion ceremonies [in 1975], O.K. reminded the guests that in 1925 there were fewer than 2,000 students total at the University of Florida, fewer than the number of faculty in 1975. In 1925, the university comprised fifteen buildings. Students paid a twenty-six-dollar student activity fee, six-dollar infirmary fee, eight-dollar registration fee (tuition), and, for seniors, a five-dollar diploma fee.

O.K. taught eight courses: History and Principles of Journalism; Editorials; Law of the Press; Feature Writing; Newspaper Production; News: Principles of Reporting; News: Practice in Reporting; and Agricultural Journalism. In 1926 O.K. was promoted to Associate professor. With the new title came new obligations (in addition to the usual courses). He would now teach the Writing of Special Articles; The Writing of Feature Articles; Newspaper Management; Industrial and Trade Journalism; Mechanics of Publishing; and a graduate course, Research in Journalism. Among his students was Fuller Warren, future governor of Florida. O.K. was also Fuller Warren's teacher at another place in Gainesville, his Sunday School class.

In 1924 the Florida legislature opened the university to women, provided they were at least twenty-one years of age, juniors, and taking courses not offered at any other Florida institution. In 1927 several women enrolled in the school, now called the College of Commerce and Journalism.

31

The Lindbergh Connection

In early June 1927, O. K. set an example for his students. He went to Washington to cover Charles Lindbergh's return from his famous flight. He described the occasion this way:

"President Calvin Coolidge sent the Navy destroyer Memphis to bring the young flyer, at that time the most popular hero of the world, and his plane back home. In New York there was the biggest ticker-tape parade ever held, before or since, down the streets of New York. Then Lindbergh was whisked to Washington to be the guest of President and Mrs. Coolidge at the temporary White House, known as the "McLean House," on DuPont Circle. (The White House was undergoing repairs at the time.) "I was teaching journalism at the University of Florida It was vacation time, so I took a train to Washington to see the big show. On the evening of June 9, I mingled with the huge crowd in a park south of the White House. We watched the Postmaster General, surrounded by all the cabinet, mount a wooden platform and present a special medal to the tall, handsome young hero in honor of his contribution to the new national service, the carrying of mail by air.

Standing near me was a young man who began complaining about being turned away from the McLean House when he tried to see 'Slim' --as he called Lindbergh-- that afternoon. 'But I'll be seeing him in the morning,' he said. 'Lindbergh has invited me and several others who taught him to fly or flew with him to come to the temporary White House at 9 o'clock.'

"I introduced myself. The man said he was Frank Robertson[2], from St. Louis. A few minutes of conversation revealed that he was an Army

Frank Robertson

aviator who had instructed the fledgling flyer Lindbergh. I said I wished I could join that select number, realizing full well that several million others would like that privilege. I explained that I was teaching journalism and wanted to take this rare opportunity for an interview both as an instructive example and for an article on behalf of the Boy Scouts of America. 'Why not tomorrow?', Robertson queried. 'I'll get you in. Meet me at the north door of the McLean House before nine.'

"I was there well before 9 o'clock. Thousands of men, women and children were pressing about the residence and being restrained by police. I edged my way to the entrance. It was guarded by two burly policemen. When Robertson appeared, he simply gave them a card and added: 'This man is invited too. He's with me.'"

"We were ushered into the spacious living room, where eight chairs had been arranged in a semi-circle around a single chair where Lindbergh was to sit. Another chair was brought in for me. Robertson introduced me to the small group as 'a writer from Florida'. Promptly at nine Lindbergh entered the room, smiling bashfully. Instantly all the men

---

[2] Frank Robertson, Cofounder of Robertson Aircraft Corporation, https://en.wikipedia.org/wiki/Robertson_Aircraft_Corporation

33

sprang to their feet. Their spokesman from St. Louis grasped the hero by the hand. 'Slim!' he said. 'So good to see you.' 'Thank you, Frank. So good of you gentlemen to come!' Lindbergh responded. The celebrity took his seat, and so did his guests, mostly pilots, of which most were mail pilots and a few were former instructors of Lindbergh.

'Well, Slim, you did it'! said Robertson.

'But you fellows taught me all I know about flying,' Lindbergh countered with a laugh.

'But we didn't teach you how to fly the Atlantic,' the spokesman said. 'Slim, everyone here wants to know what special preparations for the flight did you make after you got to Roosevelt Field (on Long Island)?'

'Well, I did some calculating of my weight. I decided to discard every item that might hold us (the Spirit of St. Louis and me) back. I took no clothes other than my flying suit, not even an extra pair of shoes. I planned to buy an outfit when I arrived in Paris. But by then the American Ambassador, Mr. Herrick, had already done so and presented it to me. I promised to pay him back when I got home, but he said he wouldn't take any money.'

'How about food for that 33 hours, Slim? We hear you did not have a box lunch.'

'No, that would have weighed too much. I took a sandwich or two, wrapped in light paper.'

34

One of the pilots asked, 'What were your fuel calculations?'

'Four hundred gallons to reach Paris. So, I put in 425,' Lindbergh explained in a matter-of-fact voice.

"Two or three of the men in the room were not pilots. One of them said, 'We understand you did not follow a map.'

'That's right. I flew by dead reckoning.'

'Dead reckoning?' the layman exclaimed. 'You flew the Atlantic by dead reckoning?'

'Yes, I charted the course with a piece of string, which I stretched from Long Island to Paris over a globe, a great circle route. I plotted it in hundreds of miles. There were thirty-six of them. When I had flown a hundred miles, I would turn right by --' he mentioned a certain number of degrees. It was clear that even the flyers present were deeply impressed by Lindbergh's skill at dead reckoning.

Lindbergh continued, 'But nearly halfway across I almost lost my chart. I got so sleepy I opened a window for fresh air, and a gust blew the paper almost out of the plane. I caught it just in time.'

Another asked, 'How did you stay awake all that distance? You hadn't slept for two nights.' 'When I got the report that it was clearing up over the Atlantic, and it was clear at LeBourget Field, I lay down for a few hours, but I did not really sleep. When you have a job to do, as you fellows know, you stay awake to do it.'

"The 'fellows' were silent for several seconds. It was obvious to me what they were thinking. Here was a young pilot, brave enough to risk the Atlantic alone, but also a precise engineer, coldly calculating what his plane would do, how much weight it would carry, how much fuel it would need, how long that Ryan engine would keep on whirling, and what he himself could endure as its lone pilot. After about half an hour Lindbergh thanked the men again for coming to Washington to see him. He stood and Robertson took me by the arm and led me to the guest of honor. 'Slim, this man would like a brief interview for the Boy Scouts of America.'

For the first time ,I clasped the hand of the man who became one of my closest friends in later years. He sat down, while I drew up a chair. For about ten minutes he answered my questions while men were still milling around, and Lindbergh began chatting with them. I could not help thinking that here was a chance for the White House to show some hospitality. At least some refreshments, if only punch and cookies, granted that that might have cost the President and First Lady a few dollars. I went into the hall. The curtains over the big windows had been drawn. I pulled them apart enough to peak out at the thousands of people, shouting and waving outside, hoping to land a glimpse of the man they so admired. Suddenly a private elevator opened. One man got out -- President Coolidge. He walked to the window and took a peek at the throng. 'A most enthusiastic crowd, Mr. President', I remarked. 'A great tribute to Charles Lindbergh?' Coolidge dropped the curtain and turned toward me. 'Yes.' That was all he said, and he turned on his heel to disappear down the hall.

O.K.'s was the only audience the aviator granted a journalist upon his return from Paris. "My brief interview with Lindbergh was published in the Boy Scout Magazine and republished many times. It won for me a request from Boy Scout headquarters that I write a new book of instructions for a Merit Badge: the first one in journalism to be included in the Boy Scout Handbook."

Lindbergh and some friends had attended a show in New York the night before departure. Cloud cover extended the width of the Atlantic and was not expected to clear for some time. After the show, word came

President Calvin Coolidge awards Lindbergh the Congressional Medal of Honor in 1928

that clearing had begun. Lindbergh was in a race and didn't want the competition to take advantage. What was left of the night was spent in urgent preparation with a gesture at napping. He was so sleep deprived at takeoff that he had to contend with hallucinations en route.

A retired commercial pilot recalls the psychological impact Lindbergh's flight had on America: "It's hard to conceive without having been there. It transformed everybody's thinking about aviation. But more importantly, it symbolized freedom in the sense that 'We Americans are free to do anything in the world'. It was a spirit of adventure like the Gold Rush days. Private enterprise got serious about building airplanes.

Some in the press tried to label Lindbergh as foolhardy, but he wasn't; he was very meticulous."

1928 was a busy year for O.K. In addition to teaching eight classes per semester, he wrote his first book, *The Life and Work of Dr. A. A. Murphree*, a biography of the University of Florida's president (in office 1909-1927). He collected material for another book, *Old Massa's People: The Old Slaves Tell Their Story*. He began a textbook on news-writing principles for high school students; wrote an article on Georgia Tech football coach John W. Heisman; collaborated with Melvin Lee, dean of the Columbia University School of Journalism to compile a Boy Scout pamphlet offering vocational guidance to scouts contemplating careers in journalism; and delivered the commencement address for the graduating class at Gainesville's Waldo High School.

Rae O. Weimer, an officer in the administration of the University of Florida while O.K. was there and later dean of the College of Journalism and Communications, characterized O.K. as "a self-starter, innovative and resourceful to developing something original. And he was a hell of a nice guy. If it weren't for him, we wouldn't have had the same kind of support. He was a little ahead of his time." And in a 1983 letter, Journalism School Dean Ralph Lowenstein thanked O.K. for being "the father of journalism education at the University of Florida. Whatever we have become is largely because of the seeds you planted almost 50 years ago... Thank you for the role you played in laying solid foundations for the college."

O.K.'s founding of the university's School of Journalism is more significant in the long run but less dramatic than another event of the time. In O.K.'s words, "The late lamented Florida real estate boom was on. There never was a boom like it, and I hope to the Lord there never will be again. We got there just in time to catch it. Everybody was as crazy as bedbugs making money in Florida land. Louise and I had saved a precious few hundred dollars. Here came a fellow saying, 'You need to invest your money in property at Orlando,' then a town of about twelve thousand citizens. I drove our Model T down to have a look. All I had to do was put down $500 on the $2,500 mortgage on lakefront property. My fine comrade of The War, Sergeant John Ross, who had an abundance of money, said, ' Let me know when you decide, O.K., and I'll buy in with you.' Ross and I each put down $500 on property on Lake Locano in Orlando. About three weeks later I got a telegram from a realtor asking if I would take $1500 for my part of the property. This illustrates just how deranged people had become. I remember that the news was full of how money was being made, particularly in a certain street in Miami the record had been broken: That property had sold at $40,000 per front foot. It was insane. People would simply quit work, put on silk shirts, knickers and a Panama hat and sell 'binders,' which were options, just paper exchanges. People wouldn't bother looking at the property. They would just buy and sell the option. They would show the next buyer an abstract of the property's location and make the exchange. Big buses would round up buyers and carry them to Coral Gables, a barren area of streets and twenty-five-foot lots and a huge entrance gate. There they would sell them binders to buy lots. It was a mill. People would buy multiple lots with thoughts of one big home on several lots, or several small homes, but a big profit either way. It was unregulated and wild.

"Under that sort of influence, I turned down the $1,500 offer. Everybody who bought lakefront property wanted to build houses on it, and Ross and I were trying to decide whether to join in. Then came the winter of 1926, and the boom stopped. Historians and economists have analyzed and written about this Florida boom and bust ever since. I don't know what happened, except that it had become entirely out of line with the actual value of the time. In February 1926, some light began to break on reality, and people began to realize they might not get their money back. Investors panicked, tried to unload, and couldn't. Ross was in fine shape and so took over my deed and held it for several years. I think maybe he broke even, but that's questionable. My father by then had become pastor of a church at the little town of Mims, near Titusville.

Two of his deacons, brothers (in genes, not necessarily in Christ), were worth millions in property at the height of the boom. By late February they were penniless. A few survived, simply because they were already using the land, such as for small farms, and did not need to unload regardless of their property's theoretical worth. And many of those were able to sell for handsome profits years later when things regained some sanity. Meanwhile, the bust affected not just Orlando, but the entire state. A professor at the University held the first mortgage on our home in Gainesville and was now insolvent. Creditors were pounding on everybody's door.

The Lure of the Ozarks

In July of '27, O.K. Jr. ("Kay") was born at Gainesville's only

medical facility most resembling a hospital, the University of Florida Infirmary. By May of 1928 the School of Journalism was strong enough to make a go of it, so O.K. said to Louise, "Let's get away from this madness. Let's move back to Missouri." "Louise and I packed our worldly possessions and our two-year old infant son into our Model T for the two-week trip to Missouri".

Kay Armstrong 1928

In 1992, Anadarcia Sirianni, a University of Florida graduate student, completed her master's thesis titled "Orland Kay Armstrong: Writer, Educator, and Public Servant. A Thesis Presented to the Graduate Council of the University of Florida in Partial Fulfillment of the Requirements for the Degree of Master of Arts in Mass Communications." Her abstract begins: "With the encouragement of University of Florida President Dr. A.A. Murphree, Orland Kay Armstrong, a recent journalism master graduate, launched the journalism department at the University of Florida. The results of this study indicated that Armstrong was a spokesman for the rights of the underdog and for equality for all through his lifestyle of integrity and honesty." Chapter One begins: "A prominent Orlando attorney (J. Thomas Gurney) who knew Orland Kay Armstrong for more than half a century, once described him as 'an unusually talented writer of high moral sense who was devoted to the American principle of government and honor, a pleasant and entertaining companion and, above all, a gentleman of the first order."

Ms. Sirianni continues, "Armstrong was responsible for articles that helped chronicle history and intriguing events, but no one has taken a comprehensive look at this crusading Scots-Irishman. Even if it meant a sacrifice of income, if there was a purpose or direction that he thought was worthy and urgent, he would devote himself to it. Armstrong had a vision of a peace-filled future and a willingness to lead the people toward that future. He used his writing and political activism to warn people of the consequences of not meeting a particular problem or to call them to an opportunity that was being missed."

O.K., looking back upon their return to Springfield, "If I had had the sense of a goose, I would have filed for Congress in 1928. I could have had the nomination because the man from Sedalia who finally announced was reluctant and on the outs with the party anyway."

Freelance Journalist

Instead of seizing the day politically--his first of three watershed failures to do so--O.K. launched a career as a magazine writer. Freelance journalism was a hard living, but a living. He wrote for the Saturday Evening Post, Country Gentlemen, Colliers, The American Legion, This Week, Nation's Business, Saturday Evening Post, Harpers, Christian Herald, and many others. He had only just heard about the Readers Digest. His first published article, about the American Legion Hospital for Crippled Children in St. Petersburg Florida, appeared in the November 1929 issue of American Legion Magazine.

O.K.' s second book, published in 1931, was *Old Massa's People: The Old Slaves Tell Their Story*. The Dedication reads, "To My Wife, Louise McCool Armstrong, Fair Granddaughter of the Old South, I affectionately Inscribe This Story of Slavery Days." O.K. spent years researching this portrayal of the culture of old Dixie by interviewing, in every state of the Confederacy, more than twelve hundred former slaves in their ninth to eleventh decades of life. "Armstrong was skilled as an interviewer, making his subjects feel at ease. He was at home with any group without regard to its members' profession or to their current or ancestral culture. The purpose of the book was to depict the Old South as the Negro saw it. The book compiles the stories of those brought into the sphere of cruel traders and owners and of those more fortunate, of whom Mammy in *Gone with the Wind* is a reminder, brought into the inner sanctum of the owner's family. He wrote it in their vernacular and did so with a respect which bespoke a fondness of, even a kinship with, those he interviewed, which wasn't surprising in as much as he knew a thing or two about humble circumstances. He wrote in the margin of his 1930 notes for the book: "What they need: 1) Justice; 2) Education; 3) Special industrial training --Make the Negro an asset."

The Dream House

In the Introduction to her thesis, Ms. Sirianni wrote: "O.K.'s heritage built into him a generous and optimistic spirit, which was matched by Louise's. He was forever willing to share what he had, and on many occasions through the years of his life he would provide

Mom Louise with Kay and Milton

housing, education and sustenance to relatives." By late 1932, Louise's brother-in law, married to her sister Bernice, had lost his job as a tobacco auctioneer in Raleigh, and thereby became still another victim of the Great Depression. O.K and Louise invited them to come to Springfield and share their small, two-bedroom, one-bath house with them and the two small boys.

In February 1933, "Little Sister" was born, and they named her for her mother, Louise. With two couples and three youngsters, the house was becoming crowded. Early in 1934, O.K. drove his car around the streets of Springfield, searching for a larger but affordable house. He noticed a huge, vacant house with the front door standing open. He walked into the house and admired the woodwork, the spaciousness and the seven ornate fireplaces. The twelve-foot-wide hallway was paneled in walnut, front to back, which extended up the massive stairway and throughout the upstairs hallway. The dining room was paneled in butternut or, perhaps, cherry, and had a bay window overlooking the

45

broad lawn with thirteen oak trees. Each of the four big bedrooms upstairs was trimmed in a different wood: oak, cherry, mahogany and elm.

When O.K. walked out, the gentleman next door, Ed V. Williams, a department store owner comfortably surviving the depression, rushed over to greet him.

"O.K., would you like to buy this house? Over ten thousand square feet-plus basement, 50-foot-wide attic and 1870s servants' area. The Sigma Nu's couldn't keep up the payments and moved to the dorms even after I lowered the rent."

"Ed, I don't have the money to buy a house like this."

1307 Benton Avenue, Springfield, Missouri

"I'll rent it to you for $35 per month."

"Well, it's more house than we need, but maybe we can get our money out of it if I can turn the servants' quarters into an apartment." O.K. and Louise were renting the house for $35 when Mr. Williams died. Williams's lawyer called. "O.K., we've got to do something with that house you're in. We've got to sell it. I've been authorized to sell it to you for $5,000 plus four hundred for our agent if you can come up with a hundred down." It took O.K. twelve years to pay it off.

The Great Depression

Those of us who did not experience the Great Depression but want to envision it must put to the unaided eye a lens that will fix on a world not our own. A few other signs of the times might help: O.K.'s sister Delta began teaching high school in Lake Butler, Florida, not long after her family settled there in 1919. In 1930, she was notified by the Lake Butler school district that all teachers would be paid with "warrants," promises to pay when cash was available. Sometimes cash became available, sometimes it didn't. In 1932, their brother Noble, with his PhD in education from Duke, got a job teaching Education at Columbus

Crooked River Club

(Mississippi) College for Women, the nation's oldest state supported college for women, for $60 per month plus board in the dining hall. During the late 1920s, my mother's brother Dennard McCool established the Crooked River Club, a lodge for "sportsmen" wanting to take advantage of Nature's bounty in the river and the surrounding marshes and forest. The club was near the town of St. Mary in southeast Georgia.

It was a lush setting, semi-tropical and sensuous, the evening breeze carrying in the smells and warm weather sounds of the river and swamp. He went into sizeable debt to build the big $20,000 inn. During the mid-thirties, their profit margin narrowed to the point of failure. When they raised the price of their nightly seafood banquet from 50 cents to 65, they took a barrage of complaints from their patrons, mainly professional people and those whose inherited wealth

End of the Hunt

survived the 1929 crash--the only folk who could entertain thoughts of recreational travel.

Getting Political

In November 1932, O.K. was elected to the state legislature and re-elected in 1934. A letter to the editor of the Springfield News-Leader by one A.C. Hayward after the 1932 election read as follows:

"To say I am glad Greene County kept enough head to send to the legislature that brilliant young chap, Orland K. Armstrong, is putting it mildly. O.K. is a brother Ozarkian-Hillcrofter of mine. He is a writer, a statesman and an orator of the first water" (a favorite superlative of the day). "His Old Massa's People is one of the great regional books of the hour. He is one of the coming sons of this grand old state. Aside from these marks, he is about the most human, lovable character you ever knew."

In April 1933, O.K. received a letter from a former colleague, Elmer Emig, Professor of Journalism at the University of Florida. After describing changes that had occurred on the campus and throughout Gainesville since 1928, Professor Emig ends with: "O.K., your slavery book was a good one, and well done. I hear reactions to the prison-camp article in the *Herald-Tribune*. Keep up the good work. How does it look for Congress? I hope things will shift the opportunity to you; You deserve it, and you can handle it with glory."

Back to Big Time Writing

But by the mid '30s, times were too lean for divided labor, so O.K. dropped elective politics to focus on writing.

A bit more Depression lore is O.K.'s outreach to the freight-train hobos. He let it be known that he would provide them with meals and pay for work. They would jump off the boxcars at the Frisco station and go to certain homes that had "codes," penciled notices posted on front doors of homes to let the hobos know whether or not they were welcome and what they would get for work. O.K. would let them paint or rake leaves for a meal and maybe a dollar, which would buy enough food for a couple of days. He also tried to motivate them to reform their bad habits and learn a skill.

In 1935 Harry Truman entered the U.S. Senate. In 1941, he was named chairman of a committee serving as watchdog over the treasury. Believing Truman's work deserved recognition, O.K. wrote an article for the *Saturday Evening Post* titled "Billion Dollar Watchdog." The article made a big impression on the media, hence on the citizenry. It brought Truman to the attention of President Roosevelt, and O.K. to that of Dewitt Wallace, founder of the *Reader's Digest*. Wallace's later opinion was that the impact of this article greatly influenced Roosevelt's decision to bring Truman onto the ticket in 1944. After reading "Billion Dollar Watchdog," Mr. Wallace invited O.K. to join his small staff of permanent writers (most *Reader's Digest* articles were condensed from other sources; Only one or two per issue were by The Digest's own). For O.K. it meant finding in Wallace one of his life's closest friends, and no more free-lance frazzle.

51

Government, world and American history, and politics were the dominant themes of O.K.'s more than 120 articles for the Digest; Other themes were the scope of human experience. For example, his first story for Wallace was titled "Barriers Between the States Must Go!" about interstate trade taxes.

The sight of that first *Reader's Digest* paycheck brought Louise to tears, primarily for the recognition it meant for her husband. His interviews and writing reached freed former slaves to main-event figures, including Herbert Hoover, Richard Nixon, Republic of China President Chiang Kai-shek, Admiral Richard E. Byrd, Orville Wright, Louisiana Governor Huey P. Long, John D. Rockefeller, and non-politicals such as football coach John W. Heisman. As Darci Sirianni points out on page two of her thesis, whoever faced him, whether interviewee or public audience, was at ease regardless of origin, station, accent or education.

The articles he wrote about the American Indians, a series during the 1940s and another during the '50s, are typical of his use of the pen as a crusader's lance. Here's an excerpt from his 1945 article "Set the American Indians Free!"

"Few know the shameful story of the present status of the Indians. Although all native Indians were declared citizens of the United States by act of Congress in 1924, the act made no provision for the details of their emancipation. In three important respects, they have never been emancipated: They are restricted in property rights. They live under conditions of racial segregation. And they are subject to special limitations and exemptions because they are Indians. Despite government outlays, most reservation Indians live in poverty. Until war work came, not more than 2 percent of reservation families averaged more than $500 income per year. Disease is prevalent and infant mortality is high. Edwin Stanton, Lincoln's Secretary of War, said, 'The government never reforms an evil until the people demand it.' When this reaches the heart of the American people, the Indians will be saved."

In his 1948 article, "Let's Give the Indians Back to the Country," O.K. proposed a five-point plan: 1) Congress should close the Office of Indian Affairs; 2) Abandon federal control of Indian reservations; 3) Grant Indians all rights of citizenship; 4) Transfer Indian education to the states, and 5) Assist Indians to become self-supporting. In an address to Congress O.K. said: "Certainly those Indians who want to retain their ancient culture and ways of life should be permitted to do so, but they can do that without the supervision of a Federal Bureau."[3]

I know of at least one article by O.K. on a lighter subject. In 1955 the *Digest* published his story, "The Funniest Football Game Ever Played." In 1922, Georgia Tech dispatched Cumberland University two hundred twenty-two to nothing. Cumberland fielded a "rag-tag, bob-tail" team of eleven men. Neither team made a first down during the game. Cumberland's best play was a three-yard loss. At halftime, with the score 115-0, Tech coach John Heisman said to his players, "Now be careful boys, be on the alert. We don't know what they've got up their sleeve." After the game, Heisman kept his men on the field for a scrimmage workout so they wouldn't miss a day of practice.

---

[3] Congressional Record 4378

When home, OK's time was ours for every needed father thing, but he tried to make every other minute productive. Favored descriptions of such behavior include "disciplined," "compulsive," "workaholic," "dedicated," and "broke". For O.K. I'll favor the last two, since "dedicated" really means "love of job". He would write at home and at the interview site, of course. But he would write on the card table at the back of a train coach and on the lunch tray of an airplane. He would burn a pound's worth of tallow staying up to get the job done.

While on "vacation" at Uncle Dennard's sportsman's paradise on the banks of Crooked River in south Georgia, he wrote in the boat on a briefcase on the keelson board next to the tackle box. In the evening he would write by kerosene lantern at Uncle Dennard's clubhouse, a pleasant setting for Work. If at a clan gathering on the Florida coast, he would write on the beach under the shade. Even his daily exercise had to be productive--building a shed or a wall or chopping wood.

In September 1940, O.K. and Louise invited their nephew Dennard McCool, son of Louise's big brother, to come live with them and attend high school with Milton and Kay. Southern Georgia at the time provided only ten grades of

Milton, Charles, Louise, Stanley and Kay
(Milton headed for Navy Flight School)

54

school. In late 1941, a news bulletin interrupted one of Dennard's favorite radio programs. He bolted into O.K.'s study and exclaimed,

"The Japanese have attacked Pearl Harbor!" Much later, O.K. looked back: "Before that, FDR was spouting his fibs, for example, during one of his radio talks he said, 'I pledge to you parents that your boys will never have to go into any foreign war'. I called downstairs, 'Louise, did you hear that? I'll make a prediction: Before these boys are grown, they'll all be in uniform.'" And he was right.

Kay Armstrong 1945

A Crusader for Peace

I am not an expert on Lindbergh's position or that of the America First movement, but I believe I can speak with some authority on my father's ideology of war and peace. It includes these principles: The good must remain stronger than the aggressor. Peace is not just the absence of war, but it must be built into the character and lives of our many leaders and few statesmen.

His canon was that peace is predicated upon freedom and international justice. After the Great War, he became increasingly concerned about the spread of totalitarianism--National Socialism (Nazism), Communism and Fascism. And although his theology might not have been rated orthodox by all (but whose is?), he believed that Christianity's emphasis on the sanctity of the individual–as opposed to any collective power--provided the moral force by which the Western world civilized its culture and protects its citizens from tyranny. He believed that the principles of freedom and justice that evolved through Western Civilization, the Christian moral compass, was the ultimate answer to totalitarianism and aggression.

Before December 7, 1941, O.K. had vigorously protested the U.S. blockade of Japan's oil imports, warning that it would provoke war. As for the war in Europe, O.K. and Charles Lindbergh teamed up to oppose an early American entry. To them, allying with one totalitarian power over another was arbitrary, short-sighted and counterproductive, a mistimed involvement of America. In short, an alliance with a totalitarian power was an alliance with iniquity. They believed it wiser to let Hitler and Stalin, whose regimes were the two greatest evils of the middle-aged century, go at each other, after which the U.S. would pick up the pieces militarily and politically and construct a stable peace free of totalitarianism. O.K.'s thinking was that Stalin and Hitler would likely fight to a draw. Then the United States could step in and provide leadership with the peace and reconstruction. If, on the other hand, one totalitarian regime should begin to gain the upper hand over the other, then America could intervene and quickly prevail over a debilitated foe.

O.K. enlisted Charles Lindbergh's help, hoping Lindbergh's prestige would be influential. A letter from O.K. to Louise, June 6, 1940, letterhead: Hotel Astor (not the Waldorf-Astoria) Times Square, NY, reads: "My Lover, It is eleven o'clock. I have just left Lindbergh. We were nearly four hours talking. He's heart and soul wrapped up in my plans. He said he would help--would raise money, speak, do anything to keep this country out of war. I really enjoyed him. I showed him the pictures. He got a laugh out of little Stanley trotting along the walk. I'd phone you if it didn't cost so much."

O.K. remembered: "I was up to my neck in the keep-out-of-war campaign. We knew Roosevelt desperately wanted to get us into war. We knew he would if he could, and he could, and he did." In early October 1941, the Japanese embassy's top attorney [there's a special word for it], knowing of Lindbergh and Armstrong's effort, called O.K. from Washington to request a meeting. In O.K.'s words: "I went to his hotel. He sat on his bed, and if you ever saw the face of dejection, this was it. I said, 'Mr. Terasake, what has happened?'

'Something terrible, Mr. Armstrong. Prince Konoye and the Peace Party in Japan have fallen. Admiral Tojo, the new Premier, is in total

57

charge of my country and is a war hawk bent on breaking through Mr. Roosevelt's oil embargo. This will undoubtedly mean war'.

The politics of it was that FDR knew the Japanese would make war on us if we cut off the oil. Roosevelt could have supplied it, but he convinced the British, the Dutch, and so on, to join an embargo, knowing this would go far and probably all the way to incite war. Later we learned that FDR had tried to get Hitler to attack by sinking some of his submarines, which he ordered our Navy to do during 1940 and 1941. Hitler knew what that meant and wouldn't take the bait."

Integral to this history is the Kimmel-Short affair. After the Pearl Harbor disaster, civilian leaders in Washington needed cover. Rear Admiral Husband Kimmel and Maj. General Walter Short, the ranking officers at Pearl Harbor on the Sunday morning of December 7, 1941 -- the Day of Infamy -- were blamed for the success of the Japanese assault. Shortly after the U.S. declaration of war, Kimmel and Short were accused of being derelict in their duties and were relieved of their commands. Their request for courts- martial [with which] to clear their names was never granted. Upward of a dozen hearings, investigations and conferences were held on this issue over half a century. Dereliction of duty charges were repudiated by these investigations. The two top naval combat commanders in the Pacific Theater during World War II were Admirals William F. Halsey and Raymond A. Spruance.

Adm. Halsey wrote: "In all my experience, I have never known a commander-in-chief of any United States fleet who worked harder, and under more adverse circumstances, to increase its efficiency and to prepare for war; Furthermore, I know of no officer who might have been in command at that time who could have done more than Admiral Kimmel did."

Adm. Spruance wrote: "I have always felt that Kimmel and Short were held responsible for Pearl Harbor in order that the American people might have no reason to lose confidence in their government in Washington." Defense Under Secretary Edwin Dorn's report, subsequent to the Senate's final (1995) investigation, disclosed officially that blame should be "broadly shared." Dorn's report confirmed that members of the high command in Washington were privy to intercepted Japanese messages that in their totality...pointed strongly toward an attack on Pearl Harbor on the 7th of December 1941, and that the intelligence was never sent to the commanders in Hawaii. Vice Admiral David C. Richardson criticized the Dorn report for not specifying those who should "share the blame."

In January 1941, our ambassador to Japan had reported that in the case of a break with the United States, the Japanese were planning "a surprise mass attack on Pearl Harbor." In July 1941, the chief of the Navy War Plans Division named Hawaii as the probable target of a Japanese air assault. At the same time, Navy Secretary Frank Knox wrote to Secretary of War Henry Stimson, "Hostilities would be initiated by a surprise attack on Pearl Harbor." By August 1940, American cryptographers had deciphered the Japanese diplomatic code. On Nov. 22, 1941, they intercepted a message from the Japanese government to their envoys negotiating with the Roosevelt administration, notifying them that in about a week "things are automatically going to happen." A few days before the aerial raid the FBI reported that the Japanese consulate in Honolulu was burning its diplomatic papers. In spite of these warnings, there were no special guards on any of the ships at Pearl. The fleet was on its loosest alert. Only 25 percent of its anti-aircraft guns were manned, and half the officers were on shore leave. As a cost-cutting measure, weekend reconnaissance flights were canceled. At the airfields, planes were lined up wingtip to wingtip, making them perfect targets for aerial bombing. The setting at Oahu was ideal for Captain Mitsuo Fuchida's Nakajima-97 bombers, Aichi dive bombers and Zeroes –142 planes in all.

An article in the May/June reissue of "Naval History," the magazine of the United States Naval Institute titled "Advance Warning? The Red Cross Connection" by Daryl S. Borgquist presents evidence that President Roosevelt ordered a secret shipment of surgical supplies to the Red Cross in Hawaii in anticipation of the attack on Pearl Harbor. The article is persuasive that Mr. Roosevelt summoned Don C. Smith, director of the War Service for the Red Cross, to his office to inform Smith of the news of which the President's intelligence staff had informed him, that an attack on Pearl harbor by the Japanese was pending, that supplies should be sent to a port-of-entry on the west coast, and that no one, including military and Red Cross personnel in Hawaii, was to be informed. Roosevelt countered Smith's protests with a description of the Presidential motive: The American people would never agree to enter war short of an attack on U.S. territory.

O.K. continues: "Lindbergh and I were convinced that without U.S. intervention the Nazis and the Allies would come to a draw, at which time we could step in and make sure that the whole lot of totalitarianism was swept away, and with minimal loss of American lives. Hitler's thrust was to the east: Drang nach Osten. He was afraid of drawing America in.

After his aggression in Czechoslovakia I think he would have stopped at a line short of drawing in the British. Hitler wanted to make peace with England partly because of his perception of German-English kinship as Nordic races, partly to get England's help to defeat Russia. Dunkerque closed that door. If the Japanese had had the oil they wanted, they would have settled their hostilities with China, and I think they would have been neutral toward the United States.

"The first week of November, E. Stanley Jones, an influential missionary and pacifist who was close to Mr. Roosevelt, phoned me to ask if he could join our effort. [Stanley Armstrong was named after E. Stanley Jones] I arranged a meeting to include Mr. Terasake, Mr. Jones and me. Mr. Terasake was terribly agitated with the possibility that his government was preparing an assault. So, I went to the Japanese embassy as soon as I could schedule a meeting with Admiral Nomura, the special ambassador sent in just before Pearl Harbor. On November 30, I told him I would do everything I could to prevent war between our countries. The ambassador shook his head and said, 'I'm afraid it's too late.' He either already knew of the plan or suspected the carriers were due to sail within days to blast Pearl Harbor if they could.

"Seven days after the blitz, on December 14, while in Washington doing research, I went by Mr. Terasake's apartment. He was not there. He had been interned. He had been separated from his American wife and their six- year-old daughter. I slipped by the secret service men guarding the apartment. Inside, I asked Mrs. Terasake: 'Was my correspondence saved?' 'No, every bit of paper was burned.' All Japanese diplomats were herded down to White Sulfur Springs, Virginia."

From the modest lectern of a state legislator, O.K. vigorously denounced the post-Pearl Harbor internment of Japanese Americans as a cynical propaganda maneuver designed to stir war hysteria. "The Japanese-Americans had been here for decades or even generations. They were industrious, and they were as good Americans as those who said, 'off with their heads.' The state with the most Japanese was California. Governor Earl Warren should have stopped the incarceration but didn't--that's how great the pressure was. During wartime, the pressure is difficult to resist. But that didn't rob some of us of our calm sense. I knew what was going on.

"I promptly got a call from the (Springfield) News-Leader: 'O.K., what do think about this Pearl Harbor situation?'

I replied, 'Well, it means we're at war, and we'll have to win it. But I'm convinced the Japanese people knew nothing about Pearl Harbor, and I'm also convinced the Japanese people did not want war with America.' Pretty soon some of the hotheads in our American Legion post had a meeting at Judge Fairman's office at the Landers building in Springfield to debate what to do about O.K. Armstrong, who 'has spoken treason.' Since 1929 I had been in charge of the Legion's child-welfare program and a member since shortly after World War I. They said, 'Well, let's just return his dues and expel him from our post.' That hit the newspaper. Immediately I had calls from three other posts asking me to join."

Charles Lindbergh postponed the publishing of *The Wartime Journals of Charles Lindbergh* until a quarter century after the war, the better to attain "the objectivity that comes with years and the eyes of a new generation." His 1969 Introduction to the book provides a worthy retrospective: "We won the war in a military sense; But in a broader sense it seems to me we lost it, for our Western civilization is less respected and secure than it was before. In order to defeat Germany and Japan we supported the still greater menaces of Russia and China --which now confront us in a nuclear weapon era. Poland was not saved. Much of our Western culture was destroyed. Meanwhile the Soviets have dropped their iron curtain to screen of Eastern Europe, and an antagonistic Chinese government threatens us in Asia. More than a generation after the war's end, our occupying armies must still occupy, and the world has not been made safe for democracy and freedom."

PART TWO-GRIEF AND GROWTH

Louise Armstrong Passing

While I was an adolescent, several older relatives and family friends shared with me their observation that my relationship with my mother had been in one way noticeable. While other pre-or early-school kids might have been more diverted by an expanding world, I was content simply to sit and be with her for hours on end while she did her ironing and sewing. As a first grader, I didn't make much of my teacher's periodic comment "How is your mother?" I took it as a greeting or friendly conversation rather than an inquiry. If l had recognized it as a question, I still wouldn't have known what to say. I answered, "fine." But I noticed that other adults were visiting mother with increasing frequency and paying her more than the usual attention. And I had noticed that she seemed physically uncomfortable much of the time. But I didn't ponder these facts, or draw conclusions, or even try. At six years, my experience had been that if adults were doing something, that something was the normal course of things. If they said it, it should be done or was true. My bouts with measles and chicken pox had taught me sickness was something that passed quickly. I took the behavior of a prolonged illness as just another experience.

But by the time of my September entry into the second grade, Mother had seemed uncomfortable far too long, even to my beginner's mind. The situation was troublesome to me. If her condition was normal, it was certainly an unpleasant sort of normal. But my observation that "something is wrong" was still just "something", not a formed idea about serious illness. I knew next to nothing about such things and certainly nothing of sickness not followed by wellness. Mother leaned on a chair when she walked about friends or couples. One woman or another seemed always to be with her, even while we were at home. Nobody had tried to explain to me or to eight-year-old Stanley that our mother had breast cancer, that she had already had surgery, and that she might get well but might not. I say "tried to explain" since they may have anticipated my response to be, "Cancer?"--What's that?" One might wonder, why not an age-appropriate clarification? My parents saw no reason to explain things in any thorough way to the boys who were off to college, so it's not surprising they kept the six and seven-year-olds in the dark. My parents were probably as open about personal matters as befit the time. But I think the reasons that they were not at all forthcoming was because they were in the dark. My brother Kay attended college and boarded at home, so it was obvious to him that mother was ill. But he was at a loss about its seriousness, at least for the first year. By the time I entered second grade, Kay suspected the truth. That's clear, for he offered my first intimation of mother's condition.

At bedtime one night, he told me she might not be with us much longer, so I must be sure to kiss her and tell her I love her. Whatever his wording, that was its drift. And whether fresh to the world or in denial, I had only the weakest grasp of the significance of what he said. It's not surprising that some of our most vivid memories are of first-time, "what's-going-on-here?" experiences. I include in this species my first audience with a magician or a ventriloquist, first visit to a funeral home, first seeing an immersion baptism, first meeting a retarded person, and seeing "The Wizard of Oz" before I knew there was such a thing as fiction.

In each of these instances I knew something was mysterious indeed, and its strangeness paralyzed any capability I had to express my curiosity. So, it was with my mother's illness.

That year Harold Dryden, son of mother's sister Lois, was the second of our first cousins to come live with us. This time it was only for his senior year since by then the southern Georgia school system provided up to grade eleven. Harold seemed eight feet tall to me, though he was a foot and two-thirds short of that. I watched Harold, summoned from football practice, help turn mother in bed, but I still didn't allow such particulars into my seven-year-old head as a threat to my world.

A few weeks after school started, Harold's mother, Lois McCool Dryden, left her Waycross, Georgia, home to be with us. Dad was away on work assignments about as usual during mother's illness.

Later I would connect the pieces of O.K.'s emotional puzzle enough to find "denial". "My beloved wife might die of breast cancer?" Not a thought. Most likely, O.K. supposed her previous year's mastectomy the end of the matter. It is highly improbable that there were false assurances by her surgeon and long-time friend Dr. Durward Hall. There were so many influences weighing on my father's mind that I can only speculate as to which was heaviest. His family's doctrine had emphasized keeping or regaining health by right and proper living--health as a life path.

This creed had always served O.K. well, and from his vantage there was no reason to imagine that the outcome for his wife would be any less providential. The image of his sweetheart preparing to shuck her mortal coil was simply not coming and for many reasons. There was the comparative medical ignorance of the time. I think it likely his attitude was, "Now is not her time to leave." But if that is so, I don't know how much was "conspiracy of emotion without reason" and how much was calling upon his religious faith. He was not given to simplifications regarding intervention by the Lord, but when it came to his adored wife he may have considerably qualified his world-view on ultimate and final matters.

Whatever his mental processes, I think they distilled into a refusal-to-believe on the part of someone as much in love as on his wedding day. Much of the time he was away on research trips as customary. He had no savings and could do his assignment without first going to the source by traveling to Europe. On a normal day, nothing suited him better than to lead a quest to or from the headwaters of a journalistic stream, thereby gratifying with one effort two passions, crusading and writing. With all these factors, he was a man whose vision was distorted enough to justify going off to right the wrongs of a foreign continent while his life's only emotional intimate was in peril. The truth was invading the borders of his vital realm, so he strafed it from the fort he had emplaced around his consciousness.

In September O.K. departed for Europe to research material for a *Reader's Digest* series that would stoutly protest some of the U.S. government's post-war policies in Europe. He was expected to report to a Senate committee upon return. One of those policies was the destruction of Germany's industrial capability.

O.K.'s attitude was: "The Nazis are gone. Revenge against the German people, who never were our enemy, helps no one and burdens our already heavy commitment to help reconstruct a despoiled Europe."

Another policy O.K. deemed entirely insane was the destruction of prime-of-life American aircraft following a four-power Allied agreement designed to please Berlin-based Soviet officials who had "insisted" on it. At an Allied airbase in Bavaria 2,000 fighters and bombers had been destroyed, and at another base the same fate for hundreds of P-47s. Some of these planes had seen only a few dozen flights or had only been flown a few hours. O.K. questioned the bureaucrats at the Office of Military Government in Berlin about the matter and got only a few evasions and (what the diplomats call) "untruths." A civilian-surplus worker questioned O.K.'s credentials for the probe. O.K. responded with a withering refresher course on the rights of citizens and taxpayers to know the fate of their property. O.K. then befriended a corporal, who drove him to an airbase outside Meierhausen. They arrived in time to witness the blowing up of a mile-long, wing-to-wing line of B-17s. In a newspaper article O.K. wrote: "The sight of these blasted airplanes is not stimulating to American pride or to our sense of security. Would any Congressman like to inspect about half a billion dollars (a lot of money in 1947) worth of sabotaged American glory? I can tell him where to look."

Boyd and Julia Dicus, among O.K. and Louise's best friends, became alarmed over Louise's declining condition. They found O.K. Junior as much in denial as Senior. Mr. Dicus wrote and showed Kay a preliminary cablegram to O.K. that read something like: "Louise failing; come home." Kay said, "But he would be horrified." Dicus replied "He needs to be horrified." The cable reached O.K. in Italy. He took the next

70

train to Paris for the first flight home, only to face a strike by the Overseas Airline Pilots Association. He went on to London and with some calls to Washington got priority for the next transatlantic flight. He arrived at her bedside and clasped her hand. His loving voice roused Louise from a coma, and she mumbled her love to him. In minutes, she was gone.

The next day there was much bustle, with more than the ordinary number of visitors and relatives at work at home, all moving quickly about. An ambulance came and left. Mother was not home. I asked my sister Louise where mother was, and at fourteen years of age she can be excused for saying "downtown," but it left me all the more confused. The next day Dad took Stan and me "downtown." After he parked the car, we walked along a broad avenue where business and residential districts merged. We paused in front of what looked like a manor. We sat on the waist-high wall while Dad talked to us. "Mother has gone to heaven."

The truth came early in his speech, which he tailored carefully for two who were still "strangers to the world." The significance of his speech didn't register fully, either as expected of a seven-year-old or because I resisted the message. To say I was baffled or befuddled may be to exaggerate my state of mind, or to miss it entirely –I can't say for sure because the back-looking is by adult eyes. I can't re-live my seven-years-old grasp of death and its finality, but I know it was inadequate. If I had any thoughts close to, "What's this all about," I certainly didn't have the initiative to say, "Daddy, please explain this again." From that day forward, I knew mother was dead, but I still didn't get it, certainly not the finality or permanency of it. At the funeral, I didn't know what to do or say. I felt entirely lost, inadequate to the grief around me.

By the time of mother's death my two oldest brothers had been discharged from the Navy and had entered college. My sister Louise was fourteen and mature, but not enough to assume the keep of two little brothers and her school attendance. Dad would have had to call in help even if he had not been away on business about half the time. His mother volunteered immediately. She had been widowed some months earlier, and her coming into our home was symbiotic. But life's interplay of sorrow and fulfillment isn't bound by a rule that sequel to every setback is desert and vice versa. Within months my grandmother fell, fracturing a hip.

Our Own Mary Poppins

Now there were three to care for. Total hip replacements were an image inside some orthopedist's head. But fortune's wheel would now turn so that the point fell on favor. Dad found Mrs. Holsinger, a widow who would probably have given her age as "three score and ten." Her language was as much Elizabethan as it was pure down-home Arkansas. Mrs. Holsinger's faith was Assembly-of-God. She read the Bible daily. She was warm, patient and in control. She understood children, partly because she was the matriarch of a populous clan. She had every quality one could want in a foster mother. Her only negative habit was to repeat the punch line of every story at least twice beyond the first telling (a habit perhaps more cultural than quirk). While interviewing Mrs. Holsinger, O.K. took board and room so much for granted, beyond her modest fee, that he didn't bring up the subject. He simply said, "Now, let me show you to your room." Her board and room were more our benefit anyway, as she was quickly a member of the family by Act-of-Sentiment. Without her, those interim years could not have been as pleasant.

O.K.'s strength and warmth went far to make up for his frequent research and crusade absences. Until we children were well into the grades, he told us funny, attention-holding bedtime tales. He improvised these stories as he went along, sometimes recycling those told to the older children but restructuring just enough to entertain himself, often with satire on the current political scene. The personalities of some of the starring animals were consistent with caricature: clever, conniving Fox; conniving Buzzard and sassy Wolf, comrades in lying and thievery; the disoriented Professor Owl, who tended to forget whose side he was on; Skunk, who protested wrongdoing in a manner only his kind could, hard-

73

working Gopher; and confused but plodding Harry S. Donkey, that is until he took the alias of Jackass, the scheming politician. Some were original: Unlike Bugs Bunny, O.K.'s Rabbit was humble and shy and had to be brought out by the fostering leadership of the gang's patriarch, Ole Man Bear; and the stalwart, resourceful, clean-living Dudley Do-Right Hero, Florida Gator, who would subject himself to risky missions and save the day with the help of his loyal, trustworthy Lieutenant Hound. The plot and inevitable moral of each story were O.K.'s own, as were the ever-changing names, usually of politicians, he assigned to Fox, Wolf, and Buzzard depending on up-to-the-minute news of the world. We were too young to understand why he would go "Ho, ho, ho" after giving 3 news-maker's names to that night's buzzard. He always kept the stories light, the worst transgressions by Fox, Buzzard and Wolf being their bungled attempts to deceive and trick their fellows of the kingdom. There was no villainy mean enough to keep us awake. Justice prevailed at story's end (unless it was a serial installment), and the right-living animals would celebrate by sharing some of "Ole Skunk's Firewater." After the story, we would sing songs such as, "My Old Kentucky Home", "Way Down Upon the Suwannee River", "When It's Springtime in the Rockies" or "We Are the Boys of Old Florida, Down Where the Ole Gators Play". It included "Where the boys are the squarest and the girls are the fairest of any old state down our way..." In those days "square" didn't mean nerdish or prudish, it meant honest and truthful. (After hearing "Remember the Red River Valley" at a Gene Autry movie I asked Dad to teach it to us, but he said the story was too sad.) After a song or two, the Lord's Prayer and lights out.

The Changing of the Guard

Somewhat less than two years after mother's death, in May toward the end of my third grade, Dad brought home a guest, Marjorie E. Moore, editor of the Southern Baptist Convention's religious journal, *The Commission*. O.K. had known Marjorie since 1939. Soon after returning from Antarctica that year, Admiral Byrd asked O.K. to direct his public

Marjorie (Moore) Armstrong

relations. O.K. already knew of Marjorie by professional reputation, so when he wrote an article titled "Peace Statesman" about the Admiral's adventures he called upon her to do the editing. In Marjorie's words, "Our friendship grew like the Constitution: article by article." I liked Marjorie. In fact, when her weekend visit was coming to a close, I asked her in Dad's presence if she might arrange to return within, say, a month. "Splendid idea", responded O.K.. Mrs. Holsinger was entirely gracious to Marjorie (and Marjorie to her) and seemed accepting of this development. Her feelings weighed heavily with us, certainly with me. On any matter of consequence, including that of Dad's courting a woman who might join the family, I regarded Mrs. Holsinger's opinion to be as legitimate as anyone else's excepting Dad's. That's because I had learned to respect her judgment, and because by then she and my family had made a substantial mutual emotional investment. I doubt that I was analytic about the matter at the age of eight. My response followed feeling more than it did thought: I was relieved that Mrs. Holsinger liked Marjorie. My mother was gone, and after an interval of nearly two years Dad was bringing home a pleasant visitor. The marital potential of this new circumstance may have occurred

75

to me, but that issue played second-string to the simple, good feeling that Dad now had a nice companion, and all of us had someone who seemed to make the scene more complete. Maybe I had a new companion too, but I certainly didn't try to put Marjorie on the balance opposite mother. I didn't think, "Here's a new mother," nor did I think, "Nice, but not a new mother." I didn't deliberate the matter. It felt appropriate; it felt good. It didn't take analysis to feel a void in the family. Stan's void, the same as mine, was partially but comfortably filled by our adored Mrs. Holsinger. Dad's was filled only by work until Marjorie came along. I entered the fourth grade that fall, and soon thereafter the plans for their wedding began.

After Louise died, O.K. didn't try to find another "true love", probably for at least two reasons. He may have written it off as too unlikely, too far-fetched. It is more likely that he didn't want anyone to replace his "first and only and always love". The intimate place in his life had been taken; the body left, but the spirit stayed. One small illustration of this was his ritual with letters to family. (Letter writing was the way of the day: To most, but especially to a Scottish journalist during the Great Depression, telephoning was an expensive indulgence compared with typed correspondence.) As the fifth child, I would receive the fourth carbon, so there was no reading it in dim light.[4] Until his last years, Dad enclosed in these "Dear Children" letters a little sprig of Lilies-of-the-Valley, mother's favorite flower, which he would pick from our back yard. At any pretext, slight or grand (such as a meaningful date on the calendar), he would make a loving reference to her in the letter. Marjorie must have had occasion to notice these unrelenting reminders.

---

[4] See Letter to Kay Armstrong in References

76

But back to the time of mother's death. With his real mate gone, his intention was to find someone to meet practical needs. His emotions would adjust to realities. He wanted someone highly efficient and competent. O.K. was continually traveling the country and the world on political crusades and *Readers Digest* research missions. His life lacked organization. He would forget his hat, make it to the airport just in time, misplace a bill, and never shop for clothes. In Marjorie, he saw system and order to the needed measure and beyond. And, he knew, with her comparative youth (late thirties, nineteen years his junior), she would keep things organized. And organize she did. Within weeks of Marjorie's joining the family the talents sought by Dad were on display, including some reforms he did not foresee, and at least one he almost didn't notice: Marjorie bought O.K. clothes for him on the sly. He wouldn't spend for himself--on clothing or much of anything else. He also wanted nothing he wore to draw attention by quality (too cheap or too fine), color or style. There was accordingly a sameness to his outfits. This allowed Marjorie to buy clothes for him, clip the tags, and slip them into the closet where he would reach for them without a thought and none the wiser.

Mrs. Holsinger was impressed by such clandestine goings-on. She had always been entirely adaptable to Dad's almost literally fly-by-night schedule--off on a political crusade here, a research trip there. Marjorie wouldn't try to change that, but she would arrange pertaining circumstances and the home milieu to fit.

Marjorie's diligent efforts to keep O.K. to his schedule, home and away, were generally successful. While she couldn't rescind Murphy's Law, she made sure departure preliminaries didn't overlap departure time. No more arriving at the airport while the DC-3's props are already whirring.

She bought him a bigger desk and a proper typewriter. She learned and remembered names. At a convention, for example, Dad and Marjorie would come across an acquaintance. Marjorie: "O.K., you remember Robert and Jane Remington ...." O.K.: "Yes, of course ..." Her skills at editing were such that the experts at the *Reader's Digest* left O.K.'s manuscripts at her word and bothered only with Digest-style condensation. Most of her organizing efforts came off much more predictably when Dad was out of town, his presence being something of a disruption of the rhythm. An example was afternoon tea, which she dreamed up as a home-from-grade-school greeting for Stanley and me. Dad wasn't opposed to it, but when he was home it often didn't fit. By the time Stan and I reached later grades, with other things to do after school, it never fit.

PART THREE-POLITICS AND WAR

Back to Politics

Pretty soon there was much ado, some organized, some hurly-burly, because Dad was running for Congress. By then, at age ten, I had learned (my understanding of it was rudimentary) of his several terms in the Missouri Legislature. Later I would learn more: that many of his legislative colleagues had routinely come to him for help with the wording of legislation. I learned that in 1938 Governor Stark had called upon him to serve as one of two secret agents with the assignment of investigating and undermining the Pendergast machine of Kansas City. The Governor was familiar with O.K.'s work as a legislator and with his syndicated 1934 exposé titled "Feed 'Em and Vote 'Em," which uncovered Boss Tom Pendergast's vice network in Kansas City.

In a cover letter to the publishers, O.K. wrote: "My greatest difficulty was keeping the length down. A book could be written about this most powerful city boss in America (Pendergast was a political boss, not so much into the violence of the Capone type underworld mobs). There is no doubt about this coming election doing just what I say in the story --it will clinch his control of the state to an absolute degree. His control is quite different from that of Huey Long, as you know. We hit it squarely with the Long story, and I hope, hereby, to keep up my reputation for prophetic revelation."

Pendergast's political machine owned a huge cement enterprise. The Kansas City sidewalks became six feet deep! He picked and trained police officers who would arrest motorists at random and run them through the courts to shake them down for imaginary transgressions, and he appointed judges who would kowtow to these proceedings. Another shakedown was to force city employees to "donate" two days' pay per week to the machine. Purchasing agents would rotate the take. One competing vendor of food for the jail would play the game by bidding absurdly high and 'lose' it that month. Another vendor, whose turn it was to be "it", would be low bidder that round, but his bid would be high enough to allow a kickback to the political machine. Bidding would be restricted to those firms who agreed to play the game, each in its turn every fourth month.

Dewitt Wallace of the *Digest* reminded O.K. that a politician or two in very high places on the other side of the fence owed his job to Boss Pendergast and to brace himself for an I.R.S. hit at some point.

In a speech to the U.S. House of Representatives in May 1952, O.K. said: "It was apparent to me that unless an aroused public worked against this machine it would continue to rule and to spread its corruption."

In January 1939, he testified on his findings to a Jackson County grand jury, Judge Allen Southern presiding. In 1947, O.K. wrote for the *Readers Digest* "Kansas City's Boss-Busting Editor," about the newspaperman with the courage to reveal the gangster activities in print.

Governor Stark warned O.K. that, in revenge for his crusade, the Kansas City branch of the I.R.S. now or later would go after him. Especially if he ran for Congress. At age ten I didn't know such details. Soon after the candidates announced, I got up the nerve to ask Marjorie, "What's Congress?"

The most time-consuming phase of the campaign was driving through the rural seventh district of southwest Missouri in our "sound-truck," an old car with megaphone-shaped speakers mounted on top. While the Marine band played from 78 rpm records, we would pull up to the town square, a crowd would gather and candidate Armstrong would

On the Campaign Trail

Kay, Charles, Stanley, O.K., and Marjorie

give his stump speech. In her graduate thesis on O.K., Ms. Sirianni wrote: "He was an encyclopedia of knowledge in many different fields. His oratory could stir the blood of ordinary farm folks, or he could speak in front of the most educated people." And at a convention or banquet he could hold forth after no more than this notice: "O.K., do you mind offering a few words; say, twenty, thirty minutes' worth?" O.K.: "I'd be delighted. When do I go on?" (The time is 7:40) "How about 7:45?". O.K.: "Excellent."

He always invited follow-up questions, and on the campaign trail these pertained to such issues as the Marshall Plan, the Soviet Union, inflation, debt, farmers issues and so on. A group of college students supporting O.K. heard that Will Rogers Jr. was coming to Springfield to make a speech in behalf of Dad's opponent, the incumbent. They contacted Mr. Rogers and urged him to debate Mr. Armstrong, and to do that with the media present. Of course he would. But when the incumbent's managers heard about this, they contacted Rogers and reminded him that he had never heard Armstrong at the lectern, and they told him they were cancelling the debate. Meanwhile the incumbent Congressman made the mistake of agreeing to a series of debates with O.K., but, after the first debate in which the incumbent was humiliated, he failed to show for the second debate and cancelled the remaining. O.K. won the election.

After the election, there was an interim while Dad and Marjorie searched for a home in the Washington area. By January they found a small house in Westham, nearby Bethesda.

Members of the U.S. House of Representatives were allowed staffs of three: two secretaries and an administrative assistant. I remember seeing in the Congressional office-supply store a "robotyper." This innovation was quite a leap. With the robotyper, one could punch a bunch of selectable paragraphs into a magazine.

There were as many magazines as points to make or topics. The first magazine of the semi-form letter would have a "Dear Constituent" opening and introductory paragraph. A separate magazine provided the closing paragraph on each issue. The center paragraphs could be magazine or individualized. After punching in those magazines, the robotyper would type out your letter except for the tailor-made portion. Wow.

The Korean War

By the time the 82nd Congress opened in January 1951, Congressman O.K. had become thoroughly disgusted with the direction of the Korean war since the entry of the Communist Chinese. The Chinese had invaded South Korea, and instead of meeting them with a mailed fist, the Truman administration was extending them a limp wrist. The conflict was being waged with a "stalemate or defeat" strategy, featuring unprecedented engagement restrictions ranging from the bizarre to the absurd. These restrictions resulted in maximizing allied casualties and precluded success. In their effort to fathom this baffling policy, some believed that certain U.S. State Department leaders were beholden to special European economic interests who did not want to offend Communist China and, thereby, compromise trade. Others speculated that the administration simply didn't want to offend Communist China, period. Whatever the reason, it was clear to O.K. that the war was being run by civilian fools.

O.K. provides a fair scan of his world view in this section of his book, *The Fifteen Decisive Battles of the United States* which portrays American history from General Oglethorpe's defense of his Georgia colony at Bloody Marsh in 1742 to the Battle of Midway. The Foreword is dated 1961:

"I resumed this study after World War II had ushered in the new and terrifying era --the atomic age, which quickly mushroomed into the thermonuclear age. It is still my purpose to honor those who bore the battle, whether their cause triumphed or not; to show how the brave met the brave; and how the skill of commanders, the steadfastness of officers, the courageous obedience of armed men on land or sea, led to victory or, by the turn of fortune, met defeat. But another and more compelling purpose prompts me to present the accounts of the decisive battles of American arms: It affords the opportunity to point out the stark fact that war is now completely obsolete. As a method of resolving differences between governments of sovereign nations, which today means between entire populations, war is the ultimate in futility and absurdity.

The author shares the profound conviction of people of good will everywhere that the supreme task of humanity is to prevent war in the present and the future. The great challenge of this age for those who believe in the preservation of a way of life in which people may enjoy liberty and the pursuit of happiness is to make war impossible. It can be done -and it must be done. It will mean abandoning fear and appeasement of the evil force that, through the mistakes of the victorious powers in World War II, allowed the worldwide domination of the countries of eastern Europe and allowed the Communist menace to spread from the Soviet Union to mainland China, Manchuria, the northern parts of Korea, Vietnam and Tibet; and to eventually threaten millions more peoples with its aggressive designs in every area of the globe.

The task will mean meeting the present challenge of a regime based on atheistic materialism, dedicated to stamping out all freedom of the individual citizen and his collective liberties, with our determined announcement that this world cannot endure half-slave and half-free, and that those of the free world will never cease their efforts for human liberty until all the world is free. It will call for the steadfast endeavors of those who, with courage and initiative, will fashion the new tools needed to build a lasting peace.

The peace that humanity seeks must replace the international anarchy of the mid-twentieth century with order under law. It must improve upon the United Nations, reshaping that organization into an instrument whereby its high aims and objectives can be realized instead of thwarted by the enemies of peace, a forum where simple truth can prevail over vicious propaganda, a parliament whose constructive action cannot be vetoed by aggressors who thrive upon conflict and disorder.

The structure of peace that we must build, if we are not all to perish together, must be based upon these four great foundation stones of liberty, equal justice under national and international law, collective security to prevent the rise of lawless aggressors, and a brotherhood of those who recognize and utilize for the common good those spiritual and moral values without which all else will fail.

If, in addition to building a protection for our own lives and for those of future generations, we desire to honor those in the past years who were willing to pay their 'last full measure of devotion' to the country asking this bounty of them, we will assume without delay our responsibilities in this great task."

Of O.K.'s precepts, a most pointed one was, "Peace is not founded upon disarmament; Peace is founded upon liberty and justice." A derivative principle was to rid the world of totalitarianism. South Carolina Congressman William Jennings Bryan Dorn shared O.K.'s view that the Korean War could be won with proper military appliance, including the use of Nationalist troops. O.K. recalled a meeting with the House Foreign Affairs Committee during which Dorn needled Secretary of State Dean Acheson with, "Mr. Secretary, are we going to win that war?"

The following are comments by Major General John K. Singlaub[5] that I transcribed from tape. General Singlaub would later command U.S. Forces in South Korea:

[Singlaub] As early as 1927, Chiang Kai-shek knew that Soviet adviser Borodin was there not to help China but to help Mao Tse-Tung and the Communists, and for that reason threw Borodin out. Chiang needed means to resist the revolution which had been started by Sun Yat-sen. Our State Department refused financial support, and on that account, Chiang had to make deals with the bankers of Shanghai.

General Singlaub

The U.S. State Department was actively supporting Communist China and had been doing so since before the end of World War II. President Truman sent General Marshall on the "Marshal Mission" to China to bring the Communists and Nationalists together.

[J. M. Roberts] The 38th parallel (dividing North Korea from South Korea) was conjured up in 1945 as an administrative boundary to divide the responsibility of disarming Japanese forces, to be done by Soviet forces north of the line, by American troops south thereof. Plans for

[5] See Singlaub in References

reunification were referred to the United Nations. Efforts were made to hold elections for Korea as a unit. These failed, so the United Nations. recognized a government established in the south as the legitimate government of the Republic of Korea. But by then the Soviet zone had a government claiming general sovereignty. Russian and American troops withdrew in May 1949. [Johnson 447-448] In January 1950 Dean Acheson, in a speech to the National Press Club in Washington, declared, "Taiwan Indo-China and Korea to be outside the American 'Containment' perimeter.' Acheson implied that he did not see a Communist China as worrisome since China and the Soviet Union would be rivals. After all, the Russians had taken the Chinese provinces of Mongolia and Manchuria. So, why antagonize China by protecting Taiwan, Indo-China and Korea? Acheson was unaware that negotiations were underway leading to the Soviets returning the Manchurian railway and Port Arthur to China. [Johnson] Stalin dealt with Mao's new government by taking advantage of Acheson's green light on Korea. Stalin reasoned that a war in Korea would teach Mao who his true friends were and establish Chinese military dependence on the Soviet Union. Stalin signaled North Korean Communist Dictator Kim Ill-sung to start a limited aggression across the 38th Parallel.

But on June 25, 1950, Kim invaded the south, not with Stalin's probe, but with full force. President Truman, acting on behalf of the U.N., responded immediately. We were able to get the U.N. force committed because the Soviets had walked out in 1950, and weren't there to veto. MacArthur's perspective was that all Korea was open to Allied military operations. [Summers] In July the U.S. and its allies fell back into defensive lines along the Naktong River, a strategy designed to buy time until proper forces could be mobilized. By September the buildup was complete, allowing the allies to assume the strategic offensive with MacArthur's brilliantly planned Inchon invasion. The Eighth Army, breaking out from the Pusan perimeter, forced the North Korean Army into retreat. Within three months Allied forces under MacArthur had pushed well north of the 38th Parallel [Johnson] and had retaken Seoul. [Summers] On October 19, 1950, North Korea's capital Pyongyang was captured. On Oct. 21 the 17th Infantry Regiment of the 7th Infantry Division, U.S. X Corps, reached the Yalu River on the Manchurian border in eastern Korea. In the west, the U.S. Eighth Army was also nearing the Manchurian border. At the time, Col. Hany Summers was a sergeant in the 24th Infantry Division's 21st Infantry Regiment 18 miles from Sinuiju, on the Yalu River. In his words, "North Korean forces were surrendering in droves."

When American-U.N. forces closed in on the Manchurian frontier on the Yalu, the Chinese intervened. [Singlaub] A half million Chinese troops had crossed the border and were   in the mountains of North Korea. [Summers]: On Nov.1, the 130,000-man Chinese XIII Army Group struck the Eighth Army, destroying the 1st Cavalry Division's 8th Cavalry Regiment and forcing the entire army into retreat. [Singlaub]: With a major offensive in November and December, they overran our Second Infantry Division on the northern west coast close to the Yalu. [Summers]: On Nov. 25, in the east, China's 120,000-man IX Army Group attacked X Corps, destroying the 7th Infantry Division's 31st Infantry Regiment and [in December] forcing the 1st Marine Division into its famous fighting retreat from the Chosin Reservoir. [Singlaub]: They hit the 10th Corps located in Hung-Nau north of the big port of Huan-San. That Chinese offensive forced the 10th Corps to withdraw all their troops from North Korea back to South Korea. The 8th Army, located up near the border, did an orderly withdrawal of its forces from the west coast. [Summers]: By Jan. 1, 1951, the U.S. and its allies had been forced out of North Korea. On Jan. 4 the South Korean capital of Seoul once again fell to the enemy.

[Singlaub]: General Walker was killed during this offensive against Seoul. General Matthew Ridgway was sent in to replace him. Ridgway developed a plan to stabilize the attack and to blunt it south of the Hann River south of Seoul, which he did in major battles.

Then when the Chinese reached south of Seoul, General Ridgway started his U.N. counter-offensive. Ridgway worked wonders with the Eighth Army. By the end of January 1951, the U.N. forces were on the move again. Seoul was recaptured in March. Ridgway drove the Chinese back close to what is now the Demilitarized Zone. Soviet U.N. representative Malik offered to negotiate.

[Summers] Allied forces were ordered to fall back into a tactical defensive and a strategic defensive as well, giving up any plans to drive north again. The best one can hope for in a strategic defensive is a stalemate --victory was ruled out. This prospect induced General MacArthur to write House Minority Leader Joseph Martin a letter with the famous "In war there is no substitute for victory."

Major General John K. Singlaub states: "When we entered the Korean war, the administration assigned to our command senior Army officers who had spent their careers in quartermaster or staff assignments and had never seen combat. The Chinese Communists "ran circles around them." Everything we did seemed as if ordered by the

Communists. The Communists had quickly made the 38th Parallel into a boundary, which colored all thinking in the U.S. State Department. Anything suggestive of adjusting that line to make it more defensible was vetoed. The Truman administration established numerous other disabling restrictions: The Truman administration denied the U.S. Navy the authority to interdict vessels going from China to the port of (sounds like) Ab-doo. I was deputy commander of the Joint Advisory Commission of Korea, the CIA's covert action unit, and I had a maritime unit. We made it very unpleasant for the Chinese to try to make that crossing. We captured a lot of their cargo ships and hurt the North Korean economy. That had to be done as covert action. But the Navy could have easily closed off those ports in North China. By that time, we knew the Chinese were in. Chinese propaganda would have it that these troops were volunteers, but they were not. The excuse for some of our restrictions was that the Chinese delegates to the United Nations claimed that their troops had no connection with the Chinese government.

There was a restriction prohibiting any amphibious end run. We had done that in the initial attack. After Inchon, we pulled out a couple of divisions, including Marine divisions from Inchon, and moved them to the East Sea (the Sea of Japan) and landed a force of marines and the 3rd Infantry Division from Japan, landing at Huan-San. We had the 7th and 3rd Infantry Division and a Marine Division. Two Korean divisions were under the 10th corps and pushed up to the border, surrounding and neutralizing large numbers of North Koreans. That was the situation when the Chinese intervention occurred in Nov. 1950. The restrictions against going north were placed on the commander so that after we withdrew all the forces from North Korea in late Dec 1950, we were not permitted to contemplate an encircling movement. We had the

91

amphibious advantage; Amphibious landings on the west coast are very difficult because of the World's second largest tidal action, at 31 feet, second only to Canada's Bay of Fundi with 32 feet. This exposes miles of mud flats over which vehicles have no mobility. The Inchon landing was an engineering miracle; the force had to land at high tide, and then wait until the next high tide for reinforcements.

MacArthur's Inchon invasion was a major victory for the U.S. U.S. forces were prohibited from attacking the Chinese airfields north of the Yalu River, mostly in Manchuria. An-Dung was a port city at the mouth of the Yalu. Immediately to the north and west of An-Dung were three of their principal airfields. There were many others, but the most important were there close to the border at the river. We were prohibited from taking out those airfields, thus providing sanctuary for the forces killing our troops, when they certainly offered us none. These airfields were in China, but the aircraft were flown by Russians. Stalin had sent an entire aviation corps, consisting of an air-defense division and two Mig-15 air divisions made up of Russia's best pilots. Most of these pilots became Stalin's heroes by fighting Hitler's remnants after the Luftwaffe had been reduced to old men and teenagers with experience far too meager to put up a decent dogfight. In Korea, our Saber Jet pilots shot down nine of these Russian Migs for each U.S. aircraft lost. The North Koreans and Chinese had access to China; If they were pushed anywhere near the border, all they had to do was step over the border and make faces at our troops.

MacArthur was never allowed to make division-sized attacks. [Singlaub] Meanwhile, Taiwan's forces were eager to join the effort. They recognized that the Communists were a threat to all Asia, not just Korea.

We refused to allow Chinese Nationalists to pursue them. MacArthur objected to this and to these restrictions against going north and to sanctuary in China. President Truman had made a clear-cut decision about that, and MacArthur went around the President to Congress in hopes they would change the restriction policy. MacArthur spoke openly about the matter.

In April 1951, Congressmen O.K. and Dorn flew to Korea to design a plan to win the war and keep Korea free and unified. O.K. intended to return to Congress and "hold their feet to the fire."

In her thesis, Ms. Sirianni capably reports on the scene: "Congressmen Armstrong and Dorn forfeited their Easter recess and paid half the airfare to see the conflict in Korea for themselves and report to the American people. According to the 1951 Congressional Record, Armstrong and Dorn made a good team. Dorn was young, aggressive and gregarious. Armstrong was older and more reserved, a former university professor, an accomplished author, lecturer, and byline staff writer for the *Reader's Digest*.

Thirty years later, at the age of almost 88, O.K.'s memories were fresh. "Fellow Congressman Dorn and I were not at all satisfied with what was going on in Korea. This was April 1951. We had had a briefing on the war by Secretary of State Dean Acheson. The best he could do with it was to say that 'We're in this war with allies, and we have to cooperate with them, in particular the British.' Acheson's idea was not to win the Korean war but to hold the Communists to a stalemate at a battle line, World War I style.

Acheson was also loyal to British motives, which principally centered about trade. The British wanted to trade with Red China. They wanted to trade with anybody willing to trade with them, regardless of politics or principles. And I think the British then, as of now and forever, were for trade over all else. Also, I think that it was so fixed in Acheson's mind that we should not win a war --that would be bad for our image. But if we hold them, they'll get discouraged and stop." That disastrous theory was picked up by President Johnson and Robert MacNamara during the Vietnam war.

"In any case, I attended this briefing. At the close of the briefing, a young man introduced himself to me as William Jennings Bryan Dorn of South Carolina. He was as exasperated as I was. So, he and I decided to give up our Easter vacation in order to go to Korea, see the war in person, and draw up a plan if we could. I had already drawn up my own outline of the fundamentals, which I considered to be: the removal of sanctuaries; the destruction of the bridges along the Yalu; destruction of all enemy airfields; authorization for offensive action against Communist troops; and authorization to ignore artificial boundaries such as the 38th Parallel.

Now bear in mind, we paid our own way. We flew to Japan and then to Korea. The Air Force showed us every courtesy. Dorn had served in the Army Air Corps. I had helped to start the Aviation Section in World War I that developed into the Army Air Corps and then into the Air Force. The man in charge of the Far East Wing of the Air Force was General Stratemeyer of Orlando. He assigned a plane to us, and we were flown all over South Korea, and we saw the fighting clear up to where they were dropping the napalm bombs."

Addressing the House of Representatives on May 3, 1951, O.K. recounted his visit: "For a little more than three weeks, Congressman Dorn and I were privileged to inspect most of our military installations in Japan, the bases, camps, the fighting front of the Korean war and the strength of the Nationalist Chinese forces on Formosa. Right on the battle line, we had the unique privilege of talking to the commander of the Eighth Army in Korea, General Matthew Ridgway. The war was real as we stood at the front-line north of Seoul and observed the engagement between our doughboys and enemy troops just across the river. We talked to scores of high ranking officers of all branches of the service, including Generals McArthur, Stratemeyer and Ridgeway. We also talked to scores of American GIs. We gained an accurate cross-section of their opinions.

We are not here to debate how we got into the tragic war in Korea, although it is quite clear that there would have been no Korean War had it not been for the vast mistakes in our foreign policies since the victory of the free world in Europe and the Far East in the Second World War.

The people of our nation are asking anxiously, "Are we doomed to perpetual war, with all its costs and losses? Can we never have peace as past generations knew it?" Certainly, if this Nation and the world are ever to have a just and lasting peace again it will be because of new, firm, workable policies based on justice and honor instead of expediency and appeasement. We should formulate and announce those policies now.

Three things struck us square in the face as we saw the grim fighting in Korea. First, the losses in this war are the greatest for the number of men engaged of any in American history. Second, our boys are fighting bravely in the hope they might speedily win the war, despite the handicaps forced upon them by our short-sighted policies. Third, in this undeclared war military strategy is subordinated to political expediency.

"Many of our allies are dealing in war materials with the enemy. Members of the United Nations that have branded Red China an aggressor before all mankind are still carrying on a lucrative trade with those who kill our men on the battlefield. Strange as it may seem, our own soldiers, those who fight and die for freedom's cause, are not permitted to strike the enemy at his bases and centers of transport and communication beyond Korea. And most astonishing of all, our allies, the free Chinese, those who fought the Communists long before we did, are neutralized and not permitted to help win the war against the tyrants that oppress their own country. Although the Nationalist government is still the recognized member of the United Nations, and a permanent member of the Security Council, the military forces of that government must stand idle in Formosa for fear of offending some of the appeasers of the criminal regime. Bear in mind that the announced objective of the United Nations when we went into Korea was not to stop the fighting at the 38th parallel; it was to unite Korea as an independent nation.

"I submit that there are three things we can do in Korea and the Far East.

First, we can withdraw from the war, thus turning Korea and eventually all of Asia, including Japan, over to the Communists. This would mean the utter defeat of our first at collective security. Such an action would be branded as dishonorable in the eyes of history for all time to come.

Second, we can end the war by negotiating with the aggressors. We can sit and talk and wait and talk some more. We can dicker with 'these underlings of the Kremlin.' This is what Stalin and his stooges would like for us to do. But the 'peace' they would promise would be false, and the price they would demand would be too high. This seems to be the course the British Socialist Government would have us take. On the very day I arrived in Formosa, the day on which General MacArthur was recalled, Mr. Shinwell announced in Parliament that his government would insist upon three conditions: That the Red Chinese be given a seat in the United Nations; that Formosa be turned over to the Communist Chinese; and that the Communist regime be permitted to help write the treaty of Peace with Japan. To seat the Red Chinese in the United Nations would be to denounce every ideal of its charter. To turn Formosa over to these enemies of freedom would mean that all the Nationalist Chinese, military and civilian, would be slaughtered. To allow these international outlaws to help write the treaty with Japan would be to throw away what is left of the victory in World War II. That such suggestions could come from any official of a once proud and powerful nation is unspeakably tragic.

When I conferred with Generalissimo Chiang Kai-shek, he asked me: 'Does the discharge of General MacArthur mean that your government is ready to adopt a policy of abandoning us?' I assured him that whatever the administration policy might be, there would be those of us in Congress and among the people of this country who can never forget the historic friendship between us and China and who will never turn our backs on those who fight for liberty and justice. Yes, we can end the war by shameful retreat, or by compromise and appeasement. Or, our third option, we can go ahead and win the victory free men deserve.

I tried conscientiously to find the answer as to whether we can win the war in Korea promptly and finally. I say to you that we can. We can win if we adopt a new program of firm, vigorous, intelligent action to establish a just and lasting peace in all the Far East and ultimately in all the world. In order to bring the fighting in Korea to an end, we must apply pressure on the following categories -- political, propaganda, and military. We must utilize political pressure that brands Soviet Russia an aggressor for sponsoring and supporting this war and that warns her enslaving regime that it must stop the war in Korea or be ostracized by the breaking- off of diplomatic and trade relations. Propaganda pressure should start with the announcement of the willingness of free people to work constantly for the liberation of those now enslaved by the communist world.

Militarily, we and our allies must do four things: First, we must enforce a blockade against the entire mainland of China. This should have been done long ago. It should have been done on the day the Red Chinese entered the war. Instead, most of our allies have continued trade with Red China as usual.

You were shocked, and the whole country was shocked, by the announcement a few days ago that since the beginning of the Communist aggression in Korea last June, 120,000 tons of rubber have passed from British Malaya into Red China, all of it to feed the Communist war machine and much of it passing right on into Soviet Russia. This was just one item in a long list of strategic war materials being supplied our enemies. Tin, steel products, machine tools, airplane engines, motor vehicles --numerous such commodities are imported regularly into Red China by ships flying flags of the free nations.

In Formosa, I was given the information by Chinese intelligence officers (and doubtless such information is in the hands of our government) indicating that some time ago the Soviet government began construction of an atomic bomb plant in northwestern China, near the Soviet border, and that nearly all the material needed for that plant has been supplied by our allies who are supposed to be fighting aggression. This is a shameful betrayal. It will not be enough for an aroused public opinion to force a halt to the shipment of war materials. We should blockade the entire Chinese coast. We should cut off all communication and trade. We should make the embargo so tight that not even a fishing smack can get through. If we do that the armies of Communist General Mao would face starvation. This is our first step to make them lay down their arms and quit the fight.

Second, we should permit and encourage use of the Nationalist Chinese troops now idle on Formosa. On this recent trip, I visited and inspected thousands of these troops of all branches. They are marking time, eager to get back into the fight. How long are we going to send our boys to slaughter while able and willing Chinese soldiers are not permitted to fight for their own country's freedom?

General MacArthur advocated use of these troops. He did not advocate engaging our land armies on the mainland of China. He did not want the weakening of the defenses of Formosa. He pled for utilizing Generalissimo Chiang and his troops in any practical and effective way.

For this he was denounced by our administration. Yet, MacArthur is right --this is a logical step in ending the Korean War in victory.

Third, we should encourage and support the guerrillas within Red China, to offer every possible resistance to their oppressors. According to intelligence given me in Taipei, there are more than a million of these loyal Chinese underground fighters for freedom ready to harass the Reds, to foment rebellion and to assist in the overthrow of the Soviet-dominated government. Let us encourage them in every way possible. Let us promise them arms and ammunition. Let us assure them they will be supported.

Fourth, we should permit United Nations forces to bomb military targets in Manchuria and China. Note that I said military targets. I shall never advocate bombing of civilian peoples. For the common people everywhere are the victims of war. It was so in past wars, and it is so in this one. I watched the dropping of napalm bombs in Korea. The bombs are made of jellified gasoline, and upon exploding they literally burn up everything within range. It is utterly tragic that in this war of attrition we are having to destroy so many Korean people-- and their homes and workshops. What a way to "liberate" people. We can stop that by bombing the railroads and supply lines and military bases of Manchuria and along the China coast. The war is being fought from Manchuria, where the heavy arms industry is manned partly by Japanese prisoners of war that Russia refused to repatriate. From Manchuria, the war implements are brought into Korea.

Congressman Dorn and I heard from Allied soldiers of all ranks, including our Canadian friends. They know that if it were not for the build-up in Manchuria, if it were not for the plants where those MIG planes are built and for the tanks and for the guns manufactured there, they could not carry on the war in North Korea.

Soldiers cannot fight without food and ammunition. The Communists cannot fight in Korea and at the same time fight the guerrillas and stave off invasions at every point on their coast. They cannot fight without bases and supplies. With their transportation lines, bases, and airfields destroyed, it would be impossible for the Red Chinese to mass again and cross the Yalu River for another offensive.

Congressman Dorn and I met with General Ridgway near the battle line. As he stood with his battle map in his hands, I asked him the question, "General, can we win this war under our present handicaps?" He answered, "We can hold them, I feel sure, and we can drive them back. But we cannot win a military victory this way." That statement was supported by every high-ranking officer and by every GI that we talked to. I could quote by name many other generals who expressed the same opinion as Ridgway. I could--but I shall not, for I do not want any more generals fired. Not one of them said we could win this war of attrition – by this operation "meat grinder."

Look what we have to gain by a positive program. Not only may we win victory in Korea; we can overthrow the Communist regime in China. And that would be the greatest victory over the world-wide conspiracy of Soviet communism since our misguided leaders began their policies of appeasement and collaboration in 1943. It would be the Kremlin's first significant setback since the dismal betrayals of the rights and interests of free men at the conferences of Tehran, Yalta and Potsdam. With all steps in this program taken, the war could be ended in a few months. I tell you, we and our allies can end this war–in victory.

Such can be our immediate program for victory and peace. But let us not stop there. Let us make clear to our fellow Americans and the whole world that we stand for a continuing program of peace through strength and honor. It is essential that our allies carry more of the load of combatting Communist aggression.

We must insist that they devote more of their manpower and resources. There must be less sitting on the bench. Let us use in this struggle not only the Chinese Nationalists, but other people willing to stand up with us. In Europe there are those ready to help us strengthen the Atlantic Pact and prevent the threats of Soviet aggression breaking into active war. Let us call to our banners the military forces of Spain, of Greece, and of Turkey. Let us use any willing to stand with us and furnish troops. And remember--those troops will take the places of boys we are forced now to draft and send to fight on foreign soil.

America's long-range program should include the strengthening of collective security. To accomplish this, we should vigorously advocate reforming the United Nations. We should make it an organization truly capable of preserving the peace. We must give it the power to define and prevent aggression before armed conflict starts.

Let us revive again those great moral and spiritual values that made and preserved us a great Nation. When Abraham Lincoln said, 'This country cannot exist half slave and half free,' he turned his back upon fear and compromise and took up the torch of freedom and unity. Let our government be courageous enough. 'This world cannot exist in peace and justice half slave and half free. We are determined that all people shall someday be free.'

Let us be courageous enough to declare that it is our purpose to work for a world in which there shall be no more concentration camps with their torture and death, that our crusade shall never end until mankind is blessed with those inalienable rights for which our forefathers fought and died. I say to you that the whole world is waiting for firm, intelligent, and vigorous leadership. With the principles that our nation has espoused since its beginning, with a program to fit the needs of this modern day, and with the election of candidates who will stand fearlessly for what is right, we can give the people of the entire world the leadership they need.[6]

The jeep General Ridgway was driving got too close to the fighting, and a shell blew out the windshield. Ridgway hustled the Congressmen out of the line of fire.

Ms. Sirianni's thesis includes the following: "Armstrong believed that President Truman would secretly offer the island of Formosa, now Taiwan, to China, and the United States would withdraw support (to end the war). In 1951, Formosa was governed under the Constitution of the Republic of China by President Chiang- Kai-shek. To make it difficult for President Truman to offer such a concession, Armstrong called a press conference in Korea and announced that 'the rumors about the United States giving up Formosa were all lies. The United States would

---

[6] Congressional Record 4812 and 953695

never do such a thing.' This stirred up the ...press corps. The State Department had to deny that there was such a plan."

O.K. continues: "We talked to American officers and enlisted men, who confirmed what we suspected, that the policy of the United States government under Acheson, and of course under Truman, was to simply hold the Communists, not to defeat them --the first non-victory war policy in American history. Well, anyhow, we spent about two weeks over South Korea. We got up to the Hahn River, the border with North Korea. While interviewing General Ridgway I asked him this question: 'Can we win this war fighting it under the handicaps imposed on our forces by the United States government? And he said, 'Positively no.' The handicaps were the following that they would not permit the U.S. army, when they permit our planes to fly to where they could hit the air fields and ammunition depots either in North Korea or in Manchuria. It was a dastardly way to fight a war, compelling our men to fight with one hand tied behind them.

The Acheson policy, adopted soon after World War II, was simply to hold the enemy--don't try to win. After Dorn and I had seen all we needed to see, we went in with Gen. Stratemeyer and Brigadier Gen. Nuckles, who handled publicity for the Air Force. We wanted to see General MacArthur. MacArthur had heard of me through an article I wrote about his fleeing with his wife from the Philippines to Australia and vowing, 'I shall return.'

"MacArthur pointed out to Dorn and me a picture of his wife on the wall and said, 'That's my boss.' We all smiled at that. Now, we learned very quickly from MacArthur that he was under severe pressure. He felt

104

that it was unfair to be restricted in what he was trying to do. He had written a letter to one of the Republican leaders in Congress, Minority leader Martin of Massachusetts, who had written the General to ask, 'Will you tell me how the war is going?' MacArthur expressed himself to Martin as dissatisfied with the Defense Department and with the way the war was going. That letter, unfortunately, hit the newspapers because Congressman Martin released it. That aroused considerable criticism of MacArthur. Now, while I was sitting next to MacArthur conferring on a plan to pull this thing out, he smacked my leg with the back of his hand and said, "After General Stratemeyer briefs you, I want you Congressmen to go down to Formosa--he called it Formosa; He meant Taiwan, of course, although Formosa had been the Portuguese name for Taiwan. It had been owned by the Japanese for half a century. Then after the war they lost it to the victors. In any case, he said, 'I want you to go down there, and I want you to learn a plan we have approved.' Dorn said, 'I'm sorry General, I have to get back to South Carolina for an engagement, and then back to Washington?' Now, our leave of about three weeks was about to expire, but in spite of that I said, 'General, I'll go to Formosa and confer with your men on this plan'. And he said 'Excellent.'

I was immediately ushered into the office of General Stratemeyer. He had a map as big as the whole wall of Japan, Korea and Manchuria. He took a pointer and said, 'We know the location of every airfield and ammunition dump; We know everything about the enemy in North Korea and in Manchuria. There are five roads coming into the Manchuria capital. We know where they are. We could blast them out, and that's what we ought to do. The plan is to utilize Chiang Kai-shek's army. We should have been doing this all along.' Bear in mind, Chiang had been forced out of China in 1949, two years before. But his army was still

105

intact, totaling 450,000 men just waiting and loafing around in Taiwan. Stratemeyer went on: 'General MacArthur has agreed that Chiang Kai-shek will divide those troops. One half of the units will be deployed to Korea.' That would be Asians fighting against Asians, which we didn't have. They were depending on America and British and Turks, Australians, and few other of the allies. General MacArthur and the commanders of the Chinese would plan strategy in Korea. Stratemeyer: 'The other half would make a diversion against mainland China, and that would make a pincher movement'. I am firmly convinced that Red China would have fallen. I don't think they could have withstood a pincher, a simultaneous movement, from Korea and from the mainland, starting from the Pescadores Islands off the coast of Taiwan. We would have had to furnish the equipment they needed, but they would have made a landing, and I think it would have succeeded, especially with U.S. Air Force cover, including what the Air Force needed to do in Manchuria. So I said, "I will go to Formosa."

General Chennault

I cast around to find a regularly scheduled airline only to find none. But there were occasional flights by Major General Claire Chennault. Gen. Chennault, who had been in World War I, had helped with victory in the far east. He had married a Chinese and had considerable clout with those who knew aviation in the far east.

Before I left, they had a reception for Army Secretary Pace there in Tokyo. I went to that reception. That was on Monday night. I went to Secretary Pace and said to him, "I've been concerned about the criticism

106

that I've read about from Washington. Senator Kerr of Oklahoma has criticized General MacArthur, saying maybe it's time to re-evaluate General McArthur's leadership. These criticisms were based on Acheson's opposition to MacArthur's wanting to win the war in Korea. Secretary Pace said to me, "Well, don't worry about anything that Senator Kerr might say. I know there is some friction about General MacArthur, but if there were anything of merit in any of these criticisms, I'd know all about it." This was on Monday night, two days before MacArthur was discharged. At any rate, I found that a military plane was leaving for Taiwan early evening, and so I asked one of the pilots if I could book passage, so to speak. He said, "We don't have any passenger flights, but we'll be glad to put a chair on one of our freight flights and we'll fly you down there." Well, it was unheated, and it was cool weather and nearly froze. We stopped in Okinawa where I warmed up, as did the pilots and the sergeant accompanying us. Just before dawn we reached the airfield at Taipei. I looked out of the window, and in the early morning light I could see that Gen. Chennault had come down to meet me, as had the Assistant Ambassador with a contingent of three or four Americans. One of those fellows grabbed me and took me to a hotel up on a high hill in Taipei, the Grand Hotel, and there I opened my suitcase and was about to crawl into bed for some sleep when the phone rang, and it was this Assistant ambassador. He said, 'Well Congressman, my mistake. The Chinese say they also have a Blair House (President Truman was at the time residing at the Blair House during White House renovations), and it's ready for you. The reason the Chinese officials didn't meet the plane was that I could not convince them that a Congressman would fly on a freight plane. They are acutely embarrassed, their faces are red, and they are coming to get you. So I got dressed quickly, and here came a car with one of the biggest Chinese I ever saw, a Lt. General; I used to know his name very well. He said, 'We have a Blair House, and you're supposed to come and stay with us. The General has ordered it.' Well, there we went. And that house, I learned, had been the Emperor's headquarters every time he came down from Japan during the fifty years that they owned Taiwan, and Okinawa, incidentally. But anyhow, they had a press conference set up for the next afternoon. That night I was entertained by the (sounds like) 'Newan,' they called it, the parliament of the Free Chinese. The next day I attended the press conference at 3 o'clock.

Incidentally, present there were several Chinese graduates of the University of Missouri School of Journalism. They had scattered all over the far east, and I recalled that there were several Chinese students at the University of Missouri School of Journalism when I was a student there. I stood up to speak and had barely introduced myself when the door in the back opened and a Chinese messenger came trotting up the aisle and handed the chairman a telegram. The chairman read it and simply handed it to me. It said, 'President Truman has fired General MacArthur.' I looked at that telegram, and I said, 'Now gentlemen, this is sad news, and I can't believe it. I don't believe that a president would discharge a general

Chiang Kai-shek

as important as MacArthur without a hearing, with no pre-notification of it whatever.'

Everybody scattered to scout out any later news. I had dinner that night with Chiang Kai-shek and his aids. The vice president was there, his chief of military staff and one other general. I sat next to Madam Chiang Kai-shek opposite "the Old Man." Chiang was shocked. He kept asking me questions. 'Does

108

this mean you have abandoned us?' 'No, I can't believe that. I think that the American people still wish you well and want to go ahead and win this war in Korea', and so on. He asked several other questions, and then, 'Does this mean that your government has adopted the British plan'?' Well, I knew enough about the British plan to answer, but I thought best to hedge by saying, 'I don't believe America will ever adopt a plan of no victory.'

General Douglas MacArthur

I stayed there another two days, doing the best I could to assure the American embassy that, while I didn't know enough about the firing of General MacArthur, I hoped to go back to Tokyo and learn more and find out if I could be of any help to the general. When I got back to Tokyo, General MacArthur was already on his way back to Washington. So, I just took the next plane on back home to Washington myself. Now, General MacArthur came to Washington. He had shucked off his uniform and was in civilian clothes. He addressed a joint meeting of Congress. I think when the great speeches of American history are compiled, that speech will be among them. I saw men sit there and cry when he spoke. He told about how he had tried to uphold the honor and security of America.

The only insubordination even cited by President Truman was that he answered Congressman Martin's letter without going through channels, which meant the War Department and the President of the

United States. They never could find any order that he disobeyed because he never disobeyed any. He simply was wedded to the idea that 'We must fight this war to win it,' a predisposition contrary to the Acheson plan. Now, I did some inquiring when I got back to Washington. And the nearest I could learn was that Acheson had decided that the time had come for him to convince Mr. Truman that MacArthur had been disloyal or had disobeyed, or whatever it took. But at any rate, it was said that they held a midnight meeting at the White House, Acheson and several others of the clique around Acheson. Now I can't prove this, but I suspect enough drinks were had by all so that Acheson could effectively say, 'Well, fire the son of a bitch!' and Truman replied, 'Well, I guess I will.' That was 1 am, 3 pm Taiwan time, the very time I was preparing to speak to the reporters in Taiwan.

About two weeks after Dad's return from the Far East I had the privilege of witnessing, in the House of Representatives, General MacArthur's Old-Soldiers-Never-Die valediction. MacArthur's dismissal was the end of any end-the-war plan. A half century later American troops are still sentry in Korea. O.K.'s summary comment on MacArthur's role in the Pacific phase of World War II represents faithfully his regard for the general: 'After his dismissal, General MacArthur made no public mention of what should have been done in Korea because there was nothing he could do about it; that was a closed chapter. He did confine himself to a plea that he be recognized for doing his best. And believe me, he deserved credit for winning the war in the Far East, the Pacific. I doubt very much that the war in Europe could have been brought to the speedy conclusion it was without the victory in the Far East. That was to the credit of MacArthur. Of course, there are critics who say that he loved power. Well shucks, so did every other great general who accomplished anything.'

The Cold War

"The United States must now take a firm stand upon principle in the cold war against communism. The new policy of liberation for the peoples now enslaved by the Soviet Union could prove as far-reaching in its effects as did the Monroe Doctrine in its day. Its implementation by America and our allies would send a wave of hope and faith among peoples behind the Iron Curtain. The aim of liberating captive peoples emphatically does not mean plunging the world into another major war. If the internal resistance of these peoples to communist control is encouraged and properly utilized by the free nations, it will add up to such strength that Stalin and his Kremlin tyrants will not dare launch all-out war. It will mean that we shall have a bold new program dedicated to replacing totalitarian tyranny with free and democratic regimes throughout the world.

"If we continue to follow the futile policy of attempting to 'contain' communism in areas it now enslaves, the Soviet masters will continue to digest their gains, liquidate all free elements and gather strength for more attacks upon free peoples."

"Therefore, the policy of liberation can mean the difference between constant aggression and war. The very weapons used by the communists to destroy our resources and liberties; or a lasting peace, based on human rights, equality and justice. We in Congress, of both parties, who have supported a policy of liberation, hope that it will be based on the following:

1. There must never be any compromise with aggression. We should make it clear at once that we will never permit forced repatriation of prisoners of war; we will never admit Red China into the United Nations; and that we will never cease our efforts for a unified, independent Korea.

2. A strong general foreign policy, casting aside all the tragic agreements such as those of Yalta and Potsdam that hinder freedom and peace.

3. Improving and strengthening the United Nations as an instrument for preventing aggression and war and as a more effective agency to combat the world-wide communist conspiracy.

4. Strengthening of resistance movements within the Soviet orbit to bring about corresponding weakening of totalitarian grip.

5. A vigorous program of truth, which will constantly counteract the false propaganda of the Communist regime.

If we are to win the Cold War, we should seize the initiative for peace. The communists have appropriated the very word "peace." Yet their idea of peace is submission to their slave regime. We should convince the world that we of the Free World are ready to join in the inspection and control of all armaments, and only the aggression of the communists prevents this step. We should take the initiative for peace by offering just treaties of peace to Austria and Germany.

We should launch a great propaganda initiative that should be built around a crusade of truth to counteract the lying propaganda of the

113

communists. It should include a campaign of liberation, which will give hope to those behind the Iron Curtain that someday they shall be liberated. It should call for desertions from the Red Army and from all the satellite forces.

We should utilize all our allies willing to stand with us in the Cold War. In the far east, we should enlist the Chinese Nationalists and the guerrillas on the mainland; we should set free all Korean prisoners and permit those who desire to fight for the liberation of their homeland to do so. In Europe, we should enlist the strength of a new and democratic Germany to stand against the Soviet threat.

Finally, we should revive the moral and spiritual strength of this nation so that its leadership may be effective. If these moves are made quickly enough, the Moscow rulers will not be able to take the offensive again.

We can win the Cold War and thus prevent a shooting war. And we can go from there to build a just and lasting peace."

And in a speech to the Women's City Club of Washington and submitted to the press on March 8, 1953, Armstrong said: "In this period of uncertainty caused by Stalin's death, the United States government and people should move quickly into a crusade of psychological strategy to win the Cold War against communism.

Stalin's name struck terror in the hearts of millions the world over. He is the last link to Lenin and the original Bolshevik regime. His successor will not have that advantage -a fact we should capitalize upon

114

at once. An all-out offensive to win the minds and allegiance of peoples now dominated by the late Communist dictator's regime would prevent the outbreak of another war and lead to the downfall of Communism all over the world.

Malenkov and his fellow tyrants in the Soviet Politburo are more afraid of internal resistance on the part of the people now enslaved by the communist regime than they are of all the military weapons of the free world. If we people of the free world take advantage of the burning desire of these people for their independence, we can drain away Communist strength to such a point that the Red regimes can someday be overthrown.

The first task of our psychological crusade must be to win --and thus end-- the war in Korea. Up to now, because of what General James A. Van Fleet has called the 'sit-down tactics of our own choosing,' we have lost the Korean War. In the eyes of millions of the Far East, the United States and our allies have not been able to make good on our promises to run the aggressors out of Korea and unify the country in peace and freedom. Having disposed of that hot war, we can move to win the Cold War, and thus prevent further aggression on the part of the late tyrant's followers by a program which includes the following items:

1. Liberation for all enslaved peoples. This emphatically does not mean the encouragement of 'Titoism' among the satellites. Breaking away from Moscow is not enough. Communism, with its death to liberty and justice, is the enemy of mankind and not any one regime. Nothing short of replacing communism with liberty and freedom will ensure peace on earth.

115

2. We must take the initiative for peace. The best place to start would be to write treaties of peace with Germany and Austria, regardless of what the new Russian dictators do. It is nearly eight years since the close of World War II and still no treaties of peace. By this move, we could put a new and democratic Germany in her rightful role as the keystone of peace in Europe.

3. We must move to cut off trade in war materials with the Soviet Union and all her satellites, and if they do not consent to help establish peace, we must cut off all diplomatic relations with them. It is of the utmost importance that we should make clear to the captive peoples that we do not accept their captivity as a permanent fact of history. This is the new policy of liberation, which will give hope to all peoples behind the Iron Curtain that someday they too may be free."

On Nov. 29, 1953, O.K. took part in a panel discussion of "Freedom and Peace through Liberation" on The Georgetown University Forum. Appearing also were other leaders in the movement, including Michael A. Feighan, Congressman from Illinois; James D. Atkinson, PhD., Head of the Department of Political Science, Georgetown University; and Dr. Slobodan Draskovich, author, lecturer, and the former member of the Institute of National Defense, Yugoslavia. The narrator was Mr. Matthew Warren. The evening`s discussion included these points:

Mr. Warren: Congressman Armstrong, I would like to ask you first if you would define the term "Liberation".

Congressman Armstrong: Mr. Warren, I believe the term "Liberation" can be defined as a policy that holds that the people now enslaved by the communist regimes, wherever they may be, are not represented by those regimes rightfully, that those regimes have taken away their liberties and that our policy of liberation holds that we should advise those people in gaining their freedom and establishing democratic governments.

Dr. Draskovich: Congressman Armstrong, do you mean in the same sense that America has treated Japan and Germany-helping them to help themselves?

Mr. Armstrong: Precisely, a good comparison in that our aim is to support those who have been devastated by totalitarianism or are now being oppressed by it.

Mr. Warren: Dr. Draskovich, could you elaborate on the significance of the title of your policy?

Dr. Draskovich: Yes, Mr. Warren. I believe the title is justified for the simple reason that there cannot be peace without freedom. We are facing a highly dynamic hour with an ideology, from Marx to Malenkov, from 1917 and, especially, from the end of World War II, of global domination. In view of the progress of communication and in terms of human and political relations, the world has never been so small as it is today. It is too small for both freedom and slavery. So one or the other has to win, which means that unless communism is destroyed, there can be no peace in the world.

Congressman Feighan: Mr. Warren, may I add that everyone who seeks freedom will accept help from wherever they can. There is a wonderful exhibition of that when the Nazis went into the Ukraine, the Ukrainians were looking for freedom, liberation and an opportunity to resurrect their own government. Of course, they were fooled by the Nazis and went back with the communists because they were forced to do so.

Mr. Warren: Dr. Atkinson, the Soviets express an interest in "co-existence." What would you say about co-existence?

Dr. Atkinson: The term "co-existence" itself is a Soviet term used especially by Stalin and Malenkov. It has been used by them very cleverly when they want to reassure the Western World just as perhaps a gangster uses soft language in order to assure a future victim. Let us think perhaps of Emerson's statement, "What you say speaks so loudly that I cannot hear a thing you say."

Dr. Atkinson: May I say, in reference to terms such as co-existence and aggression, their use illustrates the tendency of the communists to use our own language to defeat us. As for "aggressions", in 1940 when the Soviets invaded Finland, they charged that Finland had committed aggression against the Soviet Union.

Again in 1950 when you have the invasion of South Korea by the North Koreans. This was trumpeted all over the world and is being trumpeted at the present time as an invasion of North Korea by South Korea.

That lie is being repeated by Soviet Ambassador Vishinki in the United Nations and by every Soviet propagandist throughout the world. So, no matter what we do, they are going to say it is aggression. That is a constant cover-up for their own aggression.

Congressman Feighan: We should attack this problem in a two-fold manner: First, by arming ourselves and the free nations of the world to such a military state that war would be prohibitive to any aggressor. In addition to that, we have to let the subjugated peoples realize that the forces of the free world are in their corner. Those forces should be brought vividly to bear in the fact that we, the free people of the world, are advocates of religion, enlightened nationalism, free labor, private property and enterprise.

Congressman Armstrong: May I pick up this phrase that Congressman Feighan so well used here? That is, the forces of the free world. I would go a step further and say that in my opinion if this policy, this ideal of liberating the people behind the Iron Curtain is carried forward by this new Eisenhower administration and by members of Congress united in a bipartisan manner, it will be a deterrent to war instead of provoking war with the Soviet Union. They will see these forces of the free world united in such strength that they will not dare attack. I would like to point out also that our ideal of liberation rests on moral principles. As you have said, Doctor, "This world cannot exist half-slave and half-free."

Dr. Draskovich: A great majority of the people behind the Iron Curtain are our allies, allies of the free world. There are six hundred million people who have been enslaved since 1945. If we don't do anything about it, those people who are idealists, who have fought, who are fighting, as we have been in Berlin and Czechoslovakia will stay enslaved.

Poland-- very recently, we have seen the wonderful example of the former prisoners of war in Panmunjom-and so on. Those people who believe in freedom, if their slavery lasts very long and the free world doesn't help them, they will lose faith in us.

To believe that our refusal to accept their dictatorship means war is to ignore the interrelationships between war and policy. Remember that Clausewitz, the well-known strategist, said that war is nothing but the continuation of policy by other means. The Soviets have reversed the order, and for them policy is nothing but unceasing war against us. To embrace the policy of liberation is not to provoke war but only to answer the aggressions of the communists.

Mr. Warren: Congressman Feighan, besides a strong defense, what other tools are there to implement effectively this policy of liberation?

Mr. Feighan: Psychological strategy. We have been on the defensive. We the people of America and the peoples of the free world generally have been on the defensive in the psychological struggle with communist regimes. The crusade for liberation, for freedom, is for the minds and hearts and the allegiances of the people. We should use broadcasts to the fullest measure, even though we have difficulty with the jamming of our programs.

Dr. Draskovich: Pertaining to the question of liberation is the unfortunate experience of the enslaved peoples during and immediately after the Second World War. They fought valiantly during the war. I remind you of the Warsaw uprising and the struggle and the participation of the Polish troops in the liberation of Italy and the struggle of the national guerrillas of General Mikhailovich and so on. All these people were deceived, they were let down and their communist counterparts were helped. Then, if we think of the conferences of Yalta and Tehran and Potsdam, we realize that we need quite a strong action in order to restore the faith in America of those peoples. Because as things now stand, it is not enough to tell them, "We haven't forgotten you." They already know that the United States wants to help them to run their own affairs and to establish an order that corresponds to their situation and to their needs. Successful propaganda can only be part of a successful policy. If the free world limits itself to saying, "Well, we morally disapprove of your slavery" and do no more, it won't work. The oppressed peoples must see that the propaganda of the West is a supplement to a policy of liberation. Active political warfare has to be carried out in the territory of the communists. By 'active political warfare' I am referring to people who are willing to live and die for freedom. Those people from Romania, Poland, and so on are willing to return there and do anything necessary for the liberation of their people. They will have the support of at least 95 percent of the population that now is oppressed by communism.

Mr. Warren: Congressman Armstrong, what else can we do?

Mr. Armstrong: Behind the iron curtain, in every country there is a well-defined, well-organized underground movement. We should assist the members of that underground movement in their resistance to the communist regime. This phase of our strategy would be coordinated with political-psychological action. I would like to ask Dr. Draskovich, what would you think of the formation of what we might call an army of liberation, to be part of the European Defense Force, made up of such men as General Anders of the Polish Force, refugees and those who escape from behind the Iron Curtain who are willing to join the defense, not simply of the West, but of the entire free world?

Dr. Draskovich: I am definitely in favor of that. Their work would come in a final phase after that of those who would subvert from the underground as mentioned by Congressman Armstrong. So that when the armies come, more than half the work would already be done.

Mr. Warren: Dr. Atkinson, do you really believe now that it is impossible for the Free World to live side by side with communist imperialism?

Dr. Atkinson: To answer that, we must consider the writings of Lenin and Stalin's interpretation of Lenin. As well as Stalin's own statements of policy and study what Soviet chief Malenkov said to the 19th party congress in October of just a year ago. Add to all that theory the past 17 years of Soviet practice, then we see that while they may occasionally toss out a few goodies, a few crumbs in the hope that they can buy a certain amount of necessary time, that is when we see those tactical things for what they are. I can see as the only answer in the long run, no. We cannot live with it.

Mr. Warren: Gentlemen, thank you. Ladies and gentlemen, you have attended the weekly discussion program of the Georgetown Radio Forum, broadcast of which was transcribed in the Raymond Reiss Studio on the campus of historic Georgetown University in Washington D.C.

A Slap at Russia

If anything, O.K. was not shy as a freshman Congressman. In Sept. 1951, he attended a diplomatic conference in San Francisco for the formal receiving, by the Allied Powers, of the treaty with Japan. All of the top diplomats of the Allied Powers were present.

Armstrong and Gromyko

Kay Armstrong recalled that his dad made quite a commotion at the conference. According to Kay, "During the conference, my dad tipped off the TV cameramen and reporters, telling them to focus on the Soviet Foreign Minister, Andrei Gromyko and one of his advisors, Sergie A. Golunsky. The two Soviets seated themselves at seats on the aisle at the beginning of the conference. Dad (Congressman Armstrong) walked up to Gromyko with a big smile on his face and said, 'I bring greetings from the peace-loving people of the United States.' Gromyko responded with a smile and handshake while the cameras rolled. Then Dad unfolded a map he had previously obtained from the AFL-CIO and said, 'I present you with a map detailing every slave labor camp and gulag now in operation in the Soviet Union.'

125

The visit jolted the Foreign Minister as he glanced at the map of the gulag just long enough to verify what he had heard, and with photographers' bulbs flashing, crunched it up and dashed it to the floor. Dad picked it up, turned it over, and announced, 'On the reverse side is an account of the population of each slave camp and deaths to date.' Each camp and gulag was marked with the Soviet hammer and sickle. He then handed the map back to Gromyko. Gromyko's composure changed from 'delighted to meet a comrade to a scowl'. Gromyko's aide, realizing how agitated his boss was, took it upon himself to grab the map and hide it while Dad and Gromyko scowled at each other."

It's important to know that the motto of the State of Missouri is "Show Me." The next morning, the *Chicago Tribune* ran a top of first page headline: "Missouri Man Shows Gromyko," with the picture of O.K. presenting his gift to the Soviet minister and another a few seconds later of the disgruntled face of Gromyko.

On Oct. 5, O.K. made the following remarks to the House of Representatives: "Mr. Andrei Gromyko, chief Soviet delegate, came to disrupt the conference, to delay its proceedings, to divide its delegates into waning factions. They sought to block any effective action by peace-loving peoples to create... peace with Japan. I presented a map of Russia to Gromyko, showing the Soviet slave labor camps, but he would not comment. What comment could he have had? He had been hit by the strongest weapon in the hands of free peoples --the truth. Confronted firmly and relentlessly with the truth, the lying propaganda of Communism falls flat on its face."[7]

---

[7] Congressional Record 12726

PART FOUR-LEARNING CURVE

Back to Grade School

The transition from small town Missouri to a Bethesda fifth grade class was a jolt for me, and not just because it was mid-school year. Whether the school system I was leaving was more or less than middling, it was not up to the snuff of my new neighborhood, in which many diplomats and bureaucrats who could afford to send their offspring anywhere stayed with the public schools.

I sensed immediately that my new fifth-grade friends were ahead of me. No meetings were called to discuss my problem. In fact, my new teacher didn't seem particularly concerned. But I felt uneasy and disorganized. An inkling of intimidation seemed to paralyze me. My initiative was stifled, as if I were walking through molasses. I couldn't call up enough punch to voice my concern to my teacher or my parents. I needed to recognize the logical steps to escape this trap, but immaturity or a sense of helplessness prevented me from shaping them, much less expressing and acting on them. I should have mentally said out of the following: a) "My new friends know things that I don't; b) I'm not familiar with some of the methods in my new school, especially this novel (practice) of 'homework;' such being the case, c) Let's have a meeting, my teacher (Mrs. Hays), Marjorie, and me to make a plan; d) Act on it daily; and finally e) Ask Marjorie to watch me awhile to make sure I get it." I think both Mrs. Hays and Marjorie would have been attentive and gladly involved.

My sixth-grade year was somewhat better but worse in respect to a highly traumatic episode. One morning I was late for my patrol-boy assignment directing other kids with street corner stop-and-go before school. I had to come up with an explanation for this transgression to the entire class, but since any story I could run through my mind was ridiculous, I was reduced to tears.

Meanwhile, having a crush on one of the audience, classmate Felicia, compounded my agony. To prolong the ordeal, I was not rewarded that quarter's emblem of duty fulfilled and had to spend the rest of the year with my Patrol Boy's belt sporting one less star than the others.

The better instructors in Montgomery County's fine public school system of that era would have graced any prep school. My sixth-grade teacher, Mrs. Ridgley, was a member in full standing of that club, so the year had potential. Some of that may have been realized, but my fifth-grade mindset of timidity and disorganization prevailed. I had a vague suspicion that my classmates knew better than I how to proceed, especially with homework, which presupposed untutored organization and initiative.

It was my seventh-grade English and social studies teacher Mrs. Cornelia Hurd who changed my heading. Under Mrs. Hurd's influence, I became less alienated and more involved, less intimidated and more enthused. She blew away the fog of my fear and gave me resolute bearing. I speculate about whether the other students had more than an embryonic appreciation of the quality of their instruction, since as natives of Bethesda they had been witness to the contrast that I had experienced. My parents' appreciation was not embryonic, it was fully mature. O.K. distinctly acknowledged the high standing of these teachers. They were of the Old School. They believed in teaching the fundamentals of language, math, history and science. They knew how to hook students on learning, how to get the hands shooting up during drill. Not all were this order of talent, of course, but most were, and Mrs. Hurd represented the best.

After more than a year at sea, it was Mrs. Hurd who brought me about. But with all her talent, Mrs. Hurd's influence on me was more a matter of academic technique than the personality behind the skill. It was her perspective, her attitude, that changed mine. I see her as one of those old-time telephone operators switching the circuits: When I called, she pulled out fear and qualm and pushed in the wires of nerve. Now school was fun.

Boy Scouts

Our Boy Scout troop 54, which met at the Chevy Chase Presbyterian Church, was led by Scout Master Dick Ellinger, who was of the opinion that once his scouts had set up camp, no weather should set it down.

In the wilderness, no troop in the National Capital Area Council should ever outlast or outdo Troop 54. Not that I was one of his better campers: I wasn't. I may have lived up to most of the Scout Laws as well as the others, but the motto "Be Prepared" too often found me lacking. I was always having to borrow somebody's flashlight or flint or matches. During night encampments, my feet were cold; sometimes my everything was cold.

The Ellinger dress code was not as strict as that for camping --he would tolerate a floppy shirt tail. But he held to a structured behavior code. He expected the older scouts, the Explorers, to be an example for us by living the scout laws. "Enthusiastic" might be too strong an account of my disposition toward scouting, and the same for my brother Stan, because our vision was becoming too peripheral for the Ellinger focus.

Stan was becoming more interested in politics and within a year would become a Senate page. The summer I turned 13, I was a willing enough scout to join the N.C.A. Council troops on the cross-country expedition by train to the National Jamboree at Irvine Ranch in California.

The impressions left on me by the Jamboree, with its 50,000 international scouts, could not match those of the journey itself with its

compressed two-week introduction to our western National Parks and the glorious spaciousness of the land between. Eastern mountains such as the Great Smokies and Pennsylvania's Poconos (where Troop 54 built a cabin made of twisted pine – "Twisted Ellinger," we called it) may be the match of any for beauty. But for grandeur and variety, I had never seen anything like the West.

Charles at the Jamboree in California

At Yellowstone, geyser blasts instantly formed white, gray and sunset-colored clouds (depending on the angle of the sun) --a new experience for me. The steam lazily floating atop the hot springs and Morning Glory Pool; the blue-gray fog drifting above the fumaroles (volcanic vents in Norris Geyser Basin); the mist-enshrouded bison and elk grazing beside Firehole River; the funny faces made by the bubbling, spitting mud of Fountain Paint Pot; the purple gentian flowers: all were new to me.

So were the colors, such as the merging earth-tones of Grand Prismatic Spring or the brilliant yellow of the volcanic rock (the Grand Canyon of the Yellowstone). At Bryce Canyon in Utah, the aroma of the aspen, the pink sand, the sculptured ravines and canyons containing colors that changed with the weather and time of day --all set off against the deep green of the aspens-- were a fresh-faced universe for me. The cliffs, each named after its characteristic color determined by geological age; the other-worldliness of Utah's Canyonlands; and at Zion: the Eden-like calm and placidity of the Emerald Pools, and the massive, chiseled chasm of its Narrows, and the rock faces of the Three Patriarchs blown sheer by the winds. My only chance to take a first impression of all this was a charm. Looking at a mountain in the distance from the train, and looking up every few minutes for an hour and a half and nearly a hundred miles to say, "Well hello again Friend, glad you aren't rushing off." Vistas of this scope were registering on blank pages of my mind. The stateliness of the natural towers, rock formations and domes, the splendor of the mountains, canyons, mesas and buttes, with their infinite variations in color were all stored away. The majesty of the wilderness presented the illusion of an unspoiled wildlife: all lodged for keeps in my impressionable 13-year -old head.

Upon returning from the Jamboree, Mr. Ellinger declaimed eloquently to me on the subject of my earning Eagle Scout. I listened, but it was too late. The boys in Troop 54 held nowhere near the fascination of the other model of 13-year-old. The scouts had nothing like the others, whose fine lines and curves flaunted a conspicuous superiority of design, whose faces were utterly captivating (a quality the boys were denied entirely), whose hair smelled good, and whose language was incomparably more intriguing. The scouts' behavior could not compare in allurement. Thirteen-year-old girls were manifestly a marvel of composition --a wonder to behold. Troop 54 was a lost cause, defeated by budding hormones.

Family Complexities

Within a few years, O.K. and Marjorie's marriage grew troubled. My early judgment was that Marjorie was the source of conflict. As my perception improved over the year, I would see that judgment was an oversimplification. A greater reason for my change of perspective was my growing recognition that Dad had a few quirks of his own. A great one is that he was still in love with my mother, apparent to anyone who would pick up the clues. In conversation with acquaintances and friends in Marjorie's presence, Dad would refer with detectable fondness to "the children's mother." Many years after the fact, Marjorie related to me an incident of their engagement. After O.K.'s summertime proposal, Marjorie suggested a certain day in November for their wedding. O.K. was not comfortable with that date since it was too close to the day he and Louise had married. Marjorie then proposed a time later in November. He then, perhaps embarrassed and clearing his throat, specified that as Louise's birthday. This might have signaled most women to have a talk with this man about his readiness to move on emotionally! Marjorie and O.K. agreed on a day in December.

O.K. was not looking for romance, or even love--not this time. He was looking for a problem solver, an organizer. Much later I would learn from Kay that as he, Dad and Milton were walking from their hotel to the church for the wedding, O.K. said: "Now, believe me, boys, I know what I'm getting into." Although Marjorie later maintained that she was in love within weeks of the start of their "courtship," she must have sensed O.K.'s sentiments to be more pragmatic than romantic. Certainly, she would have preferred romance. But she had admired O.K.'s reputation long before she met him, so when the opportunity arose, her thought may have been, "Better to go for respect and adventure than hold out for a future much less sure."

Under those circumstances, when Marjorie married O.K., it is not likely that she was not under any illusion about replacing Louise McCool. She said as much a few years into their marriage with a magazine article titled "I Married a Man and Five Children," wherein she referred to "my husband's beautiful and beloved first wife." But what at the outset she had taken as a manageable island loomed increasingly as an archipelago. It would be a most unusual woman, I think, who would find satisfaction in a marriage established on her gifts of order and arrangement. And resentment of a man who tendered her less love than respect must have entered into making their marriage as complex and disconcerting as it was systematized.

When it came to her husband, Marjorie's dealings and sentiments seemed in contention with themselves and with him all too often. Of this duet, number by number, Marjorie seemed to any audience on-first-listening to be the member out of tune. If one steps back to see it, the big picture suggests that the problem was shared. That's a matter of speculation because two material factors are unknowns. One is the degree of O.K.'s honesty with Marjorie about his feelings, which my guess is he expressed less than fully. The other is the question whether Marjorie would have been "this difficult person" had she been happily married? Most of their disagreements impressed me, and I think most bystanders, as reaching for provocation. Except that when O.K. said something that seemed headed for conflict, it often could be somewhat excused as a component of one of his compulsions, such as to save a penny in still another counterproductive way. But Marjorie seemed more consistently game for contention, going a stretch to be at variance with her husband as an almost daily and sometimes hourly ritual.

If the forest of this marriage were a problem for Marjorie, wouldn't it have been more fruitful for her to deal with it than to peck at it tree by tree? She would disagree sensibly when his penny-wise proclivity was sure to be pound foolish. On most other issues Marjorie seemed to turn as if to make sure their purposes would cross. When my brother's divorce gave his ex-wife an opening to change their son's name (born O.K. Armstrong III), Marjorie ordered for her grandson's birthday a plate with the new name and made much ado to her husband of her enthusiasm for this, as if compounding the insult would give her a one-up. And Marjorie would contrive scenes, as if for role-playing. She would repeatedly undercook certain dishes so that O.K. would, again, have to suggest tactfully that "maybe we should have left it in the oven a little longer." I always suspected that in this little madness of Marjorie's was method -of which she was at most only vaguely aware-- namely a game of frustration. Her middle name was Competence: if this kitchen number had been anything but a play, she would have had the details nailed on the second or third go, even if cooking was not her idea of recreation.

Even though Marjorie's resentments were bred by her early disillusionment and provoked by continuing frustrations, they always seemed superseded by respect for O.K. and perhaps by her own kind of love (even if not expressed in a manner readily detectable by others). That respect and love engendered a loyalty that seemed to grow paradoxically with her internal conflicts. For example, in O.K.'s absence, or in the one instance of his incapacitation by illness, she was ready with loyal and even devoted leadership. If O.K. was already at the helm during a storm, she served as reliable and efficient mate.

Marjorie was not only full-strength during crises, it seemed as if she got a charge from them. Frustration of being thwarted reached others, and eventually, affected her dealings with everyone she touched. She would obsess over trivia, as whether someone was eating ice cream with too big a spoon. She was not comfortable with young people and had little understanding or tolerance of their shortcomings, a characteristic O.K. attributed to her having had no children of her own. I can hear her exclaiming, "Small child!" A belittlement she pressed into service occasionally when Stanley or I would do something about as clumsily as expected for a 9 to 14-year-old. Although, words as accurately in conversation as in formal writing, she could be rather blunt, even with friends, associates or acquaintances. This peculiarity considerably chagrinned O.K., who weighed every word before releasing it.

Despite or perhaps because of all this, many adults connected with her personality and found her downright charming. She would pique her husband with points designed to goad, and then weep over him in his absence. Her marriage became an arena in which her devotion and resentment jousted to a draw. An occurrence illustrates devotion on the offense: For some weeks when I was 13 Dad went through his life's worst case of depression. For him, the blues were always situational, and in all but this instance, something to surmount within hours or days. Even when mother died he was able to internalize his pain convincingly enough to wage life bearing that cross, heavy to him but barely noticed by others. For O.K., the stress of this occasion weighed close to the burden of the loss of his lover. His Louise's death was a miscarriage of justice, but of such is the Kingdom of Earth. Her death was not at the hands of human villains, whom Dad had always judged to be subject to the arm of righteousness, provided that arm extended from a straight back. His faith in this code was being challenged as never before. His depression was clinical and had been dragging out for weeks. During this critical interval Marjorie and I were driving through the North Carolina mountains toward Ashville. Suddenly she pulled over at an overlook, which I took to be the subject for her next photo.

But she led us in prayer for Dad. She prayed aloud, trying to blend a theme of "Have Thine Own Way" with tones of petition, consistent with her lifetime credo (All things work together for the good of them that love God, and to them who are called according to His purpose). Her voice told me her credo was now wedged into the straits of the moment. I could sense the emotional load of this self-baring to the Almighty, its delivery carefully paced so her composure would hold. But in the content and spirit of this prayer, her love --as fierce as it was frustrated for her husband --was as evident as the mountain scene before us.

Falsely Accused and Vindication

The prophecies of Dewitt Wallace and Governor Pete Stark had come true. This was the headwaters of O.K.'s bad humor. Wallace had given O.K. and Marjorie a wedding bonus of $5,000, and the Kansas City IRS indicted O.K. for income tax evasion stemming from that gift. They threw in an accusation of tax evasion over a three-year period, 1947-1950, on an amount of income (not amount of tax: amount of income) which had to be less than his lawyer's fee. O.K. wrote to a friend: "You may recall that I am the one whom Governor Stark sent in to help break the Pendergast crowd. They have been after me ever since. They fought me in the legislature; they fought me when I ran for Congress. I was warned that if I ran, my income tax returns would be investigated. A colleague in Congress told me they did him that way. Anyhow, about three weeks ago, one of the D.A.'s assistants phoned my attorney and told him they wish they could get rid of this case; they still do not have the guts to toss it out the window." O.K. was found guilty on tax evasion charges in April 1955. Soon after the trial, seven members of the jury came forth to say that they knew Armstrong was not guilty of fraud; he was guilty only of poor record- keeping (that is, during the years before Marjorie came aboard, after which no more log-keeping negligence).

Three jury members signed affidavits stating that the verdict was a compromise whereby several who declared Armstrong not guilty would agree to vote guilty if the others would recommend leniency. As for those holding out for guilty, there was persuasive evidence that the prosecution was very careful in appointing a political jury.

In a statement to the Springfield News-Leader, O.K. expressed his sentiments: "The bitterest pill in the whole story was being knocked out of public service, in which I hoped to fulfill an ambition to help build world peace. After I left Congress when my district was joined with that of Congressman Dewey Short, I campaigned for General Eisenhower for President. My friend, the late John Foster Dulles, as Secretary of State authorized my appointment as director of public relations for the State Department in March of 1953. Soon after the news of my appointment came out, I was informed that the Kansas City office of the IRS had filed a request for criminal action against me. That ended any appointment."

In 1963 the U.S. Court of Claims ruled that O.K. Armstrong had never engaged in any fraud. The Court's vindication announcement was 65 pages long. The IRS was ordered to pay back $21,000 to O.K. Early in this story I recognized the moral "Much of what life offers is not due." To paraphrase President Truman: "If you can't stand the heat, stay out of the boiler-room." A crusader's venue is the boiler-room, and there's where O.K. spent his adult life.

I don't know how O.K. would have done as public relations director for the State Department. That was not his goal. His goal was to use his vision and skills to set the world on a course toward peace, in his view achievable only through world-wide freedom and justice. He knew that if you're going to direct the orchestra you must first secure the baton, at the time in the hand of Mr. Dulles. O.K.'s regard for Mr. Dulles was greater as a friend than as a Secretary of State. He looked upon Eisenhower and Dulles as weak, indecisive and irresolute, not up to dealing with the Machiavellian wiles of Sino-Soviet totalitarianism. He saw the Kremlin oligarchy as a shell that could be cracked with cunning diplomacy and psychological warfare. From the beginning of the Cold War, O.K. had seen the Kremlin bosses as canny men of realism, who knew they would lose all in a confrontation with U.S. power. He became virtually sick with disgust and frustration when the uprising of June 17, 1953 in Germany and the 1956 revolution in Hungary found Eisenhower and Dulles passive. In O.K.'s words: "There we missed two rich opportunities to liberate eastern Europe."

Highschool Begins

During the ninth grade, I caught sight of one of my passing infatuations running laps around our junior high school's extended athletic field. Maybe she had decided it would make her a more competitive soccer player. Maybe she reasoned that if a little exercise made her feel good, a lot would make her feel even better.

Whatever the process, it was unacceptable to me, a male adolescent, to let Barbara make me feel the lesser physically, especially when I needed to impress her. I didn't see anybody else running, aside from the assigned laps before or after softball, soccer or track. But Barbara told me she was running for fun, so I had to run, fun or no fun. And so I did and added laps daily until I was convinced I was running at least as far as she. Inevitably, I passed what we now know as the MAD: The Minimal Addicting Dose. I noticed that if I finished my three-or four-mile run with a series of splints, I was rewarded with a spate of exhilaration flowing from or into my pleasure center. Whatever feels this good in the head, must be good for the rest of the body, I concluded. In those days, running just for exercise was assumed to represent a major emotional disorder, whereas today it's assumed only a minor one. I ran only at school because if I ran elsewhere, people would stare. "A strange person is loose," I could hear them thinking, "someone who needs help, or is escaping from help." The next year, my sophomore year at Bethesda-Chevy Chase High, I joined the track team. The abashment of learning that my spiked track shoes had cost Dad eight dollars left me feeling dutiful. Now I simply had to do well in track.

It was not to be. All that season a matter of utmost consternation to me was my inability to win, place or show. I trained hard by the standards and exercise physiology of the time. I tried all distances from 100 yards to cross-country and came up short across the Held. This unjust situation confounded me. Not until years later did I learn that speed is a genetic, physiologic quality --a gift. Its value can be enhanced by scientific training, but without the gift no amount of conditioning will make a match against those who have it. As a football player said to me, as if straight from the lips of Yogi Berra, "Those guys have speed." They don't just become fast, they start fast. If I had had the opportunity to leave at the gun with somebody coursing the mile at four minutes, I could have

kept up with him for, oh, 220 yards, half a lap. At the age of 15 this was another fresh reality to deal with, even though the coach was tolerant enough not to tell me take a walk. But addictions don't change just because of other actualities. And it made me feel so good. I usually ran with spikes instead of tennis shoes because I preferred grass or tracks to concrete. Some years later running shoes were invented, and occasional eccentrics could be spied

Charles in High School Senior Year

running in public. For years I ran around football, soccer and softball players at practice; I even ran the track around games in progress, provided spectators were sparse. I ran around cow pastures and an air field. My favorite turf was the golf course, and I lapped them in most of my nearly dozen home towns, always steering clear of golfers when possible. If denied time or place to run, I would swim. If there was no water I would walk, but that was never as satisfying. After singles tennis I would run or swim for real exercise. I sprained my left ankle 12 or 15 times during a quarter of a century, but the denial of the addict is stronger than the common sense of schoolboy or physician, so I ran before healing was complete. After a surgeon removed the torn meniscus (cartilage) in my knee, I ran ten more years, ten more than I should have. Finally, my legs told me in no uncertain terms that it was time to find a new fix. I shopped for swimming gear.

Fast Times at Camp Robin Hood

Early in June of the summer I would turn 15. My neighbor and classmate "Jet" (John Edgar Tipton) came to our front door with an invitation that isn't tossed over an adolescent boy's transom every day.

"Would you and Stan like to take care of horses with me at Camp Robin Hood for girls in Pennsylvania this summer?" Would an actress like a phone call from Warner Brothers? Jet's sister, an 11-year-old camper, had heard from the owner that three new stable boys were needed to fill out the staff of six. None of us had had any experience with horses, but if interest in horses is what it took to land us a slot at Camp Robin Hood, we were interested in horses. We reported to camp late June. Six boys, 300 girls, perhaps 30 college women as counsellors, and the permanent staff.

The owner, Miss Ruland, was Southern, an old maid, and the image of Miss Manners, no doubt precisely the assurance wanted by the campers' parents. Of the minority-sex six, three were camp veterans, the Johanssen brothers (Bert and Eric, whose dad was stationed at an Air Force base in West Virginia), back for their second summer, and Ben Harrington of New Jersey for his third. That was all to the good, since they knew horses, and we Bethesda boys knew nothing. Miss Ruland introduced us to the permanent staff, mostly mature, widowed women except for the maintenance man, an older gent who had been Miss Ruland's aide-de-camp, so to speak, for decades. We were issued our uniforms, which resembled Marine fatigues except that they were white cotton. Our cabin was not out away in the woods but close in, next to the end of a row of girls' dorms. All were built as you would expect for

145

summer in the woods, with pine-board and screen siding and overhanging roofs. Our cabin differed from the girls' only in that theirs were multi-decked, ours was a bungalow.

Camp Robin Hood had tennis courts, a big swimming pool, a theater with stage, a rainy-day rec hall and athletic field. But the center ring, figuratively and geographically, was the riding field. Some of the campers may have preferred tennis or swimming or ballet to riding, but the axis of Miss Ruland's world was her horses. The campers were divided into two teams, Green and White. There would be a summer-long war of the colors in sports, drama, and some particulars of behavior. The Pittsburgh girls of the Green team would win the singing contest with their rendition of the Three-Rivers classic, "Glory to Shadyside." And there would be a beauty contest, judged by a distinguished panel of widows and stable boys.

Miss Ruland seemed relieved when she met her new boys, Jet, Stan and me. Not because she saw us as something special, but because it was plain to me that she sized us up as having been raised by proper parents and therefore as having the same control over our testosterone as the Johanssen boys, those sons of an Air Force officer, and the reliable Benjamin.

The only distasteful duty at Robin Hood was the early morning rise. Up by seven to clean the stables, water the horses, feed them their hay and granola mix, then curry and dress them for the day's lessons. Then breakfast at the big screened-in dining room with the girls, except that Miss Ruland restricted us to an appointed table. We mucked out the

146

horses' beds and tended the stables until well into the morning. After riding lessons we had lunch, first with the horses, then with the girls.

Miss Ruland's staff of horsemanship instructors impressed me then, and, although I'm certainly no expert, impresses me now. Bert Johanssen could have served as a fill-in instructor, but Miss Ruland nurtured misgivings about letting her boys into that role. So, Bert had to be content with teaching his three new dudes from the suburbs of Washington. Aunt Cath, our secret name for Miss Ruland, allowed her stable boys to take the horses away from camp after training hours and on weekends. We raced them at speeds that were reckless, given our short experience, but made it through the summer without grievous consequence. A horse, protesting while I led him to his stall, fell on my leg after dragging me down, but luckily down was flat-down where there was no leverage with which to fracture anything.

There was plenty of occasion for good times with the girls. We spent most of our evenings in the counsellors' den, their cabin for after-hours relaxation. Aunt Cath knew about this but looked the other way, probably because she trusted her counsellors. Early that first summer we six had been tempted, even charged-up, by the age gap. What a prestigious mark it would be for a 16-year-old to be able to prove to his buddies that he and a college- junior girl had gone star-gazing at the barn, or even more boldly, on top of the stables or at the riding course (the tack room wasn't posh enough). But as much as they seemed to enjoy us high school boys, there was no way these young women were going to accept our invitation to an evening of dancing chez hay barn. The counsellors were "senior citizens", most having accomplished a full score years, some of them a score and two, and were above such silliness, even if they saw through it as a harmless lark.

Besides, most of them wanted Aunt Cath to invite them back for another year. We were disappointed that they didn't connect with our hay-barn, but their discretion enhanced the distance of our looking up to them.

The orchard was different because it was not far from the den and had an openness about it. It wouldn't be so much like we were sneaking. It was all-in-all a more classy locale. So, some of our favorite counsellors were willing to stroll out there with us. We worked out an inspired explanation should Aunt Cath stumble across us with a handful of her counsellors at the orchard: "Why, good evening Miss Ruland. Isn't Orion spectacular tonight!" When these moonlight trysts began to bore, the counsellors' lair became more comfortable. Their lounge-cabin was an all-purposes-met hangout. We were tickled and somewhat flattered that these big-sister types allowed us into their den for a sober high time of Coke (the beverage), evening music and cards by lamplight. Compared with that of the high-schoolers, conversation with the counsellors was on a lofty plane and rarified subjects, or so we thought at the time. They tried to teach us life basics such as the differences between men and women and a skill they felt came less naturally to males, the art of romantic behavior-for later application, not for their benefit. Their college-level lectures on these subjects were most persuasive, but I'm not sure how much of it took. Summers are short, and their course was maximum theory and minimum lab. Practical appliance would entail years of comedy and error, which rhymes with terror.

With the campers it was a different story because the ones our age were closer to our grade of maturity, allowing the acknowledged primacy of females in that crucial attribute. This was before the sexual revolution but not before hormones. Advantage of this open opportunity was begging to be taken. And then there was always the temptation for six boys to compete. We succeeded quickly in persuading some of the senior high -age campers to meet us at the orchard or hay barn after dark, sometimes one-on-one, sometimes two boys with two or three girls. This led inevitably to the establishment of contests. We six competed for these Rendezvous Oscars, to be presented end-of-summer:

The Errol Flynn Award for the most campers, summer-total, after dark at the orchard or bam; the Frank Sinatra Award to the guy who would meet the most counsellors at the orchard; the Don Juan-Henry VIII Award for the most liaisons total, campers plus counsellors; the Mickey Rooney Award for the most trysts over the summer with the same girl; the Giovanni Casanova Award for meeting more than one girl per evening the most evenings; the Black Beard Award for the oldest counsellor rendezvous, orchard; and the Aunt-Cath's Lothario Award for Distinguished Service to the boy devoting the most time in selfless dedication to the entertainment of the girls (consistency of show). We had to keep score partially on the honor system. If, say, one or two guys had rendezvous at the orchard, that would leave them in an impossible position for checking simultaneous exaggerations and cheating by those at the barn.

By mid-July our second summer, Aunt Cath still was not onto us. Quite the contrary: we were in her favor. In July, on my sixteenth birthday, after the campers had done the twixt-dinner-and-dessert

"Happy Birthday" songs and rhymes, she approached me in front of the assembled and proclaimed, "Sweet sixteen and never been kissed," and kissed me. This did not evidence any particular fondness for me. I was the only one of the six to have a camp-time birthday--the only test case. We took this as confirmation of our continued good standing.

Toward the end of our second summer at Robin Hood a jealous counsellor became a jealous informer. Upon hearing of our nocturnal barn-warmings, now toward the end of their second summer, Aunt Cath concealed her fury for a few days, probably tempering it with some deliberations beginning with "Well, on the other hand,...". She held off the conspirators' audience with her until adequate cooling-off days had passed. Probably because the summer was getting on, she decided against immediate furlough.

We doubted that she would believe the truth. Most of our high times with the girls had been open swims, tennis, judging contests, and so on, but even the covert was innocent fun, although Miss Ruland probably would not have reputed it innocent had she been aware of the fun. Whether Miss Ruland trusted her six boys or not, our only transgression with the counsellors was the forbidden journey, geographical, not sexual. Once at the destination, whether orchard or den, the only thing that rolled in the hay was our dice. There was no action in the straw beyond telling stories and card games except some necking by candle or flashlight. Miss Ruland's trust in her counsellors was sound. The counsellors were far too even-headed to get involved sexually with us, even if that had been on our docket.

As for all this barnstorming fun with the high school-age campers, the not just sexual fantasy and play part was the same reason people jump with bungee cords or parachutes: a Siren's call to win these illustrious awards and 10 percent to face up to danger. We suspected we would be sent packing if Aunt Cath found out.

Miss Ruland let us finish out the summer. She simply did not invite us back. A superfluous rejection, since life was moving on for all six of us.

Freshman Congressman

During his freshman term in Congress Dad was voted "Outstanding Freshman" by his House colleagues, notwithstanding his being a minority member. One of my life's surpassing perplexities is that such a leader could have failed more than once to take the tide at its flood. During his first term, a new census dictated a redrawing of congressional districts. The new plan combined O.K.'s with that of a Congressman who had served for decades and had spent too much time at happy hour. For reasons far too detailed for this story, O.K. put his sights on other things and decided against opposing the inebriant incumbent in the primary. In September, we moved back to our mid-west home town, a more central location for his continuing career with the *Reader's Digest*.

Looking for Heidi

The summer between my junior and senior years of high school, through an exchange sponsored by the American Field Service, I lived with a family in Basel, Switzerland. My host's father, Hans Winter, had married a British woman, and so their boy Walter had been raised bilingually. Walter's career had brought him into contact with Americans regularly enough to fashion an accent, a blend of BBC and NBC. In any case, conversation in English was too easy, so any hopes I had for practicing German were dashed. Mr. and Mrs. Winter were kind enough to take me along on their business trips, which by the end of my stay took us to all but one or two cantons. I thought the entire country should have been set aside as a national park. It was remarkable to me that a nation with four languages could be so homogeneous in culture. They seem to have pulled it off through a homogeneity of outlook. But some say Swiss homogeneity is a delusion, that they have intense language-based cultural rivalries.

My parents were in Europe doing research for an article and were able to make time to pay us a call. O.K. and Herr Winter seemed to gain genuine mutual respect during the evening's discussion of Europe's political picture. During dinner, I had the once-in-a-lifetime occasion of seeing my parents accept a glass of wine. I was startled but managed to keep my response internal. When O.K. and Marjorie welcomed a refill, I knew they and the Winters had connected resoundingly.

PART FIVE-PLAYING THE FIELD

Very Freshman

In 1958, during my senior year in high school back in Springfield, two friends home for Christmas-New Year's break gave me an account of their college, Wesleyan University in Middletown, Connecticut. I liked the ring of what they said, but I was hesitant. My friends had attended the other and better of our town's two high schools, and I had misgivings about my groundwork. A Wesleyan recruiter reassured me, so I applied. Wesleyan's name deserves some explanation. Any overtones of Methodism (or any other form of Christianity) were entirely out of keeping with its current worldview, in contrast to that of its 19th Century founding. In all of my four years there, I don't recall any of my professors giving a hint of being anything but agnostic.

Perhaps a few were atheistic, a few orthodox Christian, but they did not let on. As for Wesleyan's surname, "University" was and is somewhat justified by its post-graduate schools. But Wesleyan was at heart a close-knit men's college with a purpose: the liberal arts. I like to think these arts were "liberal" in that they were studies free of all ends other than knowledge itself-education rather than training. Overlap might occur should liberal learning be called upon during professional training and practice, but that was not its purpose.

"Derivation: Latin artes liberales, i.e. 'liberal arts,' literally, arts befitting a freeman: so named in contrast to artes serviles, lower (literally servile) arts, and because open to Study only by freemen [Liberi]; in later use understood as 'arts becoming a gentleman.' Definition (Liberal Arts): the subjects of an academic college course, including literature, philosophy, languages, history, and sundry courses of the sciences, as distinguished from professional or technical subjects. Sometimes referred to as arts, or Bachelor of Arts."

At the time (1958-1962) and place only extreme extremal events or internal turmoil could have sidetracked a student from the straight four-year program. If there were 212 boys in my freshman class, which is close, there were 211 at graduation. When one of our classmates did leave mid-term in order to think about things for a while in the Army, it was the talk of the campus. Most of us had never heard of anybody actually dropping out of college. Taking leave, dropping out-to us there was no difference.

A freshman-year slate of core courses, including Humanities, Western Civilization, English, and a science, was not optional. The program was the Western Canon, and Wesleyan was the ideal venue. There were activities and fraternities, but there were no distractions such as girls, tolerable weather, good sports teams, or a campus town offering entertainment. The scene was set for study, or, on the other hand, for driving the students to derangement by the bleak seriousness of it all.

The natural atmosphere of the campus. rigorous and dark, was a fitting characterization of Wesleyan's academic atmosphere. These natural and academic influences seemed to conspire to instill within students a heavy sense of obligation to study and perform. I had an equally weighty concern about my scholastic readiness, as did some of my classmates. During the preliminaries of fraternity pledging and dorm lodging, a few freshman friends got their ears erect upon hearing me admit that I had never read anything by E. E. Cummings: "Charlie obviously attended public schools." Well no, actually it's obvious I spent the last two years of high school in certain public schools rather than others. A sea of shining preppies meant it was catch-up time again.

This wasn't Déjà vu. I had seen this scene before. Just as eight years earlier when my foundation was inadequate, it was time to dig in and catch up-this time without help.

The Wesleyan sports climate serves to illustrate the homey size of the college and its rivals (Amherst, Williams, etc.). During football games, our cheerleaders--students who were part clown--would take the mike and beam to us and our girlfriends in the stands: "All right, can't you guys put down your drinks long enough to clap and cheer for the team?" Fancy any need for that at the stadiums of the Florida Gators, the Oklahoma Sooners or the Michigan Wolverines. Given this context, I decided I should try out for football. Why? I suppose for the same reason that some climb mountains: because they're bigger than the climber. Of course, on any trip, delusion and disorientation can ride along, as I will describe: I weighed about 146 pounds but was just over six feet tall, so maybe wide receiver would be an option. I was surprised they didn't ask me about my high school experience, which was none. What the coaches wanted most was enthusiasm, which they must have seen heaps of to keep me. I was their loose end. Two or three weeks into pre-season, I noticed that I was usually the last one up after a scrimmage. I could see the handwriting on the ground. Finally, an assistant coach, a most generous and tactful fellow, caught me in the locker room after practice, thanked me for my loyalty, and presented me with a tennis racquet. I grew to love tennis.

Several weeks into the first semester during a lecture I suddenly broke into a sweat. My heart pounded. Not abnormally fast, just hard. I couldn't hear the words coming from the lectern. "Panic attack" had not yet come into the popular lingo, or at least I had certainly never heard of such a thing. Freud was taken seriously in those days, so the word "angst" would soon enter my vocabulary. In any event, how a psychiatrist might have labeled this incident I'm not sure, but I was having an abrupt attack of anxiety serious enough to block any rational consideration of what was happening or why. The following were agents in this "attack," or joined the assault after the first wave: Beyond the windows the skies and the air were gray, a cold and forbidding gray at that. Looking around I saw an entirely isosexual audience. Contact with any of the nearby women's colleges had so far been minimal, so anyone I could call a girlfriend was two day's drive away in the heartland, a discouragement even had I owned an airplane. I owned no mode of transportation beyond my shoes. I was Christmas break away from home and everything I was used to. I felt oppressed by obligation, as I mentioned, and by academic expectations. I couldn't concentrate on the lecture. The subject was physical chemistry, which piled agitation on my distress because I knew I should be taking in, or at least taking down, every word. I wanted to leave the room, but drawing that sort of attention was out of the question. Besides, maybe this insanity would pass in time to take something from the lecture. It didn't pass; it gained on me.

Forces I couldn't identify had my back to the wall and my front toward demons. The atmosphere, or one of the atmospheres-natural, academic, or sexual-or a sense of loss, or of being lost: one, some, or all of these beasts were holding my wits at bay.

That evening I wrote a rambling, disconnected lamentation to my parents. My father responded with a telegram expressing his understanding and sympathy, although with his implied assumption that I would do nothing impetuous such as sharpen a knife or leave school. Marjorie's note was less tactile, observing the aptness of my letter for the tiles of any psychiatrist with a curious mind. I went through several weeks of the garden-variety manifestations of depression, always much worse in the morning. It was a drag. Several upperclassmen friends were helpful, especially those who had experienced that cloistered feeling that gripped so many on campus. My condition may have been a little worse than most, partly because I was unprepped, so to speak, compared with most of my peers. I wanted to cut and run, run to someplace less oppressive, warmer, lighter, someplace where males were at most 50 percent of the crowd.

Every few weekends I took a train to refuge-my sister Louise and her husband's home in Manhattan. My brother-in-law Edmond's view of reality was prudent, forethinking and practical. He pled with me to stay at Wesleyan. His position was that this emotional travail was a wisp in the wind skirting this mountain of opportunity. His reasoning was infallible, but was I willing to allow reason to intrude? Over Christmas break Dad indulged me with a look at a few friendly campuses, each in a different state. He was more subtle than Edmond. His expectation that I would persevere as my mind got back in order was unstated but, as usual, appropriate and clear enough.

To this day I don't know which, if any, of those "atmospheres" was the prime source of my first-semester discontent. Each may have had a hand, and others may have been lurking. Factors contributing to an

160

emotional lapse can be difficult enough for the objective observer to sort out, all the more so for the head fostering the infirmity. As for my worries about academic obligation, these four college years were going to be a challenge, yes. But the impositions in my fretful head were partly fanciful, as if some diabolic assessor of scholastic performance had served me notice of "Your accomplishment or your life." What I do know is that with each return to campus for a new semester this darkness joined me as sure as a shadow. Every September and January I spent another few weeks lugging weights around, seeing things darkly, and fearing that the world might end before graduation, which seemed an eternity away. Gloom haunted me, although each time with diminished force and less staying power.

I don't know whether my experience with dreams is typical: a few are pleasant or even exciting, most are emotionally neutral with an engaging plot, and a few are bad. Since college, most of my unpleasant ones have had a common theme, as follows. Late in a semester it occurs to me, or a professor informs me, that I have not attended one or more of my courses. Or I have attended but haven't done the work. Or I have done the work, but for a course in which I'm not registered and the effort is wasted. That recurring dream is contrary to reality. I have always recognized that organizing the subject matter is one key to learning, and organization takes time.

That's aside from the fact that I don't have a photographic memory. Letting things go until a late pre-exam cram was never on my list. So, these mild nightmares probably depict my back-to-college malaise, like returning to the spoiled leftovers of a heavy banquet.

161

College of Experiment

Late in May 1959, when the second semester was winding down, a group of humanities professors invited 21 of us freshmen to a meeting. Would we like to take part in an experimental program in "comparative literature" to be conducted over the next three years? The program would pioneer the concept of "interdisciplinary studies." In that, and in several other ways, it would be a radical new approach to teaching and learning. If successful, the experiment would conclude with the establishment of a permanent department with the somewhat pompous name of "College of Letters", or "COL," and a sister College of Social Studies. After the summer break, our sophomore year would start with a study of the origins of language. We would move from there to a review of some of the ancient authors we had met in freshman humanities, to a survey of medieval epics and romances, and then on into early modern European literature. For our junior year we would then break off into our choice of French, German or American Lit.

Sophomore year we would meet two or three afternoons per week for a few hours discussion of our reading. Junior year each student would select either German or French lit and spend the year at a German university or at the Sorbonne in Paris, or select American Lit and stay at alma mater. Senior year each student would write a thesis on an author of his choice (subject only to COL-faculty endorsement) and pair off with a professor, who would guide his ward through the year's work. There would be no grades, officially numbered "hours" or "credits". Our transcripts would consist of our professors' summaries and appraisals of our efforts. There would be one minor subject, student's choice, with minor time allotted. With 21 students, we would have a nice teacher-student ratio-I recall seven professors allotted and lots of guest lecturers.

There would also be no exams except for a comprehensive after the first two years. The idea was to see whether certain students would respond to the challenge of freedom from the usual goads and prods of frequent exams, grades and daily note-taking during lectures. The theory was, "Learn the material first, then let's get together and discuss it. The quality of your performance will show through discussions and papers." At the end of our second year in the program, our junior year, professors from other colleges would come in to assess the first two years of the experiment, mainly by analysis of its 21 human subjects. These examiners would be extramural, partly because the Wesleyan administration may have theorized an objectivity deficit on the part of the program's founding faculty, who by then might have developed some emotional attachment to the program. Also, some charitable foundations, watching this strange project with grant money in mind should it succeed, may have shared the college deans' intention that no involved dons had a finger on the scales.

There were several reasons I accepted the offer. After a year at Wesleyan I knew I would like the subject of the program-the Western literary heritage. Also, I was delighted to be invited, to be included, and believed a "No thanks" from me might suggest a lack of gratitude. In addition, 1 feared--accurately, I realized later-the loss of a unique one-time, one-place opportunity.

Another factor was that, although I knew I was interested in literature, I had no idea of the direction I would take after college and felt that this was as good as any.

During that first year of the COL we met Tuesday, Thursday and some Saturday afternoons in a big lounge on the ground floor of a dorm, sat in sofas and soft chairs, drank coffee and discussed our reading with the pros. One of our tutors, Professor of Classics Norman O. ("Nobby") Brown, had become something of a fixture with the in-crowd with his book "Life Against Death", a study of Western civilization from a psychoanalytic point of view. This book was one of the most rigorously structured edifices I had ever slugged my way through. Its architecture was elegant even if its foundation was mud. Actor Dennis Hopper's looks and mannerisms are a reminder of Nobby, the point of which is that the member of our COL faculty who was the most notorious was also the most unpretentious. Nobby was "funky" in the earthy, jazzy sense. One of our afternoon sessions became a verbal tussle between Brown and professor of French Norman Rudlich over supposed Freudian nuances of a French novel, an interpretation Rudlich considered perfectly silly. Soon thereafter I showed Nobby Brown's book to my father. "Dad, what do you make of this?" After reading a few pages, Dad remarked, "This is a reminder that there are slots on university faculties reserved for the mentally ill."

Sometime before that I had credited Freud for discovering nonconscious motives within the human psyche. But in freshman Humanities I had discovered that Shakespeare and Sophocles were quite aware of such things before Freud. And freshman year I had read Freud's *General Introduction to Psychoanalysis* and considered his comments on dream interpretation entirely ridiculous. I also knew that time had a pattern of proving Dad correct in intellectual disputes. With slight reluctance, I came down on Dad's side even though I liked Nobby. In any case, after that joust with Professor Rudlich, Nobby lightened things up by inviting us to his home for relaxation and then to a mindless movie. These excursions became our once or twice a month reward for the heavy push.

We had to decide on our junior-year program of German, French or American lit at the start of our sophomore year, since preparatory study of German or French would be on the menu a full year before leaving for Europe, if Europe was the choice. As I recall, the breakdown of choices was very close to seven each. I was with the seven who chose French. By the end of the first year, things were looking favorable for the "College of Letters."

Old World, Old School

The COL faculty at Wesleyan had selected, from a list of French applicants, seven families in or around Paris to take in those of us heading for junior year at the Sorbonne, the arts and letters section of the University of Paris-the college the French claim to be the world's oldest.

Therefore, that autumn found me in a home in a Paris suburb with a family chosen partly because they did not speak English. The Pelerin family lived in a townhouse one-half mile down the street from the Versailles palace built and made notorious by Kings Louis XIV and XVI. Predictably for a resident of a suburb of the nation's capital, Monsieur Georges Pelerin was a civil servant.

Madame Pelerin was entirely endearing, just what any lad would have liked in a foster mother. Twenty-five-year-old daughter Chantal, a schoolteacher, was living in with her parents. Chantal had a lot to offer any man, and I was impressed that she had been able to hold off marriage this long. The usual practice for France's graduates of lycée (high school) was, and probably still is, to head directly to the specialty graduate or trade school of choice. At the age of 20 Chantal's twin brothers, Yves and Maurice, were already students of engineering and business. Liberal arts were more for future academics or for those who had not yet seen their way. Youngest child Anique was a 16-year old lycée student.

My fellow Wesleyans and I were billeted all over town, which kept us out of ready touch, the better for concentrating on studies and the language. My social set was a Versailles-housed group of South American and British youngsters studying French, or French culture, or French literature and their young-adult, native-French tutors--a cozy company. For whatever reasons, the melancholia that met me at the door every semester at Wesleyan was absent in France. The weather was milder. even though I don't recall the days as being any longer; my classes were coed and fun. Social set was mixed; I lived with a family. Life was more normal and I certainly felt more normal.

My routine was to take the Metro into town three or four times per week for classes in French lit and French history. Evenings and days not at school I read the plays of the seventeenth century dramatists Racine and Corneille, together the French Shakespeare. Reading this literature honed my French, but there was no honing like conversation with the Pelerin family. I wrote a paper comparing the two writers. I found an appropriate Frenchman to edit and proofread, and then endured the tedium of trying to reach a fair copy by re-typing. I then returned to Wesleyan and presented it to Professor Norman Rudich. Dr. Rudich wrote out his criticism in French, detailing all his approvals and detractions. He was kind enough to finish with: "And it's obvious you have learned much."

Not surprisingly, my experience in France left indelible impressions on me. The walls of the ancient College Sorbonne quicken the visiting student's sense of veneration. I felt the presence of medieval shades poised to materialize and, given the need, herd the errant or chasten the irreverent. I was surprised that French young people seemed to hold these hallowed environs in less awe than I did. If one grows up in the Old- World, perhaps Old-World institutions don't impress as much, much less intimidate. Or maybe they esteemed their heritage as much as I did their casual regard a false read on my part. In any case, I represented the New-Worlder, impressed and ready to render what was due anything so old and enlightened. My time at the Sorbonne gave me perspective on our moment in the historical sweep.

The French had a somewhat deferential posture toward America at the time. The French were aware enough that imperialism was no longer realistic. But I sensed that the French dream was still Napoleonic: the glory of a France with worldwide power; for that reason their respect for America was grudging. This acknowledgment of America's position was probably as much European as French.

One of my Versailles "clique of foreigners" was a girl from Middlesbrough, near York, England. Her father, Cecil Crosthwaite, an heir of Edwardian perspective and wealth, as by then living frugally on interest. His father had attained knighthood most likely the way the Beatles would much later: by enhancing the purse of His Majesty's Exchequer. I had a memorable Christmas-New Year's stay in their home during our holiday break. In my presence, he remarked to a fellow Brit, partly to entertain but as much to ventilate his inner truth: "Isn't it awful living in the American Age-unless, of course, you're an American." Here was another European acknowledging America's power, influence and prestige. It reminded me immediately of what I knew my father wanted to do with that influence: establish stable constitutional government everywhere. If some societies were not yet ready, lead the way in preparing them with education, birth control and a free economy until they are capable of the responsible living requisite for constitutional democracy.

Direction

My sister Louise, older than I by seven years, was waiting for me at the wharf in New York on my return home. After regaining my land-legs

Louise and Edmond

at their apartment on 23rd Street, Louise, her husband Edmond Cattan and I went out to dinner. Now that Edmond was satisfied I would finish my undergrad work at "a good school," he turned his attention to where he thought this sensible course should lead. During dinner, Edmond turned the discussion to my plans for the future, specifically to my life's work, my career. "Career" has its Latinate roots deep into such meanings as "wagon," "vehicle," "vehicular road," and "course," evolving later into English as "a charge at full speed" or "a racing course." Finally, the meaning "careered" onto the more familiar sense of "progress along a path." I think Edmond was concerned that my career was looking less like progress along a path and more like a charge at full speed in all directions, some directions now, the rest of them later. After all, what was I doing? Studying literature. And for what use, from Edmond's perspective? From his point of view, literature could only mean teaching. Yet, by my twentieth year I had not thought of literature or any other subject as something I would spend my life "professing". I hadn't accepted the offer to study literature for three years with any thought at all of practical application. As noted above, I chose this course because by the end of my freshman year I knew I liked the subject, and because I had been invited into this groundbreaking program and loved the idea of being included. I wasn't thinking beyond college at that time. I had discovered

169

literature and the appeal of it, but I certainly had not discovered any appeal in writing.

Writing meant only dreaded freshman year term papers, that is aside from the more enjoyable project I had just completed in France. The most practical writing profession-journalism—had never crossed my mind. In fact, very little had crossed my mind about what I would "do" in life, except that I found psychology intriguing. I expected the answer to dawn on me conveniently in due time.

"Charles, you must think in practical terms about life," Edmond said in spite of my Father's and Marjorie's careers as writers. Or perhaps he said that because of their careers, since they certainly never made close to what Edmond would consider a decent living. Edmond was the tax attorney of a big corporation. That's practical. His British-American family had been obliged to hightail it out of Jerusalem in 1947, at a loss of substantial wealth, when the political landscape changed. No problem. Edmond came to the U.S. at age 22, went to school and got practical. About four years later Little Sis oriented me more clearly to his thinking. Edmond saw me as a dreamboat--and he didn't mean my looks-destined to drift from this shore to that unless provided some guidance. I have always been susceptible to others who would have me alter heading. This time I let someone command trim and helm adequate to set my course. Edmond and Louise both had strong personalities, and I respected their opinions enormously, perhaps inordinately, and responded accordingly to the case they were setting forth.

"Well, I like psychology. Maybe I'll go into counseling."

Far too vague for Edmond. "You should go into medicine," asserted brother-in-law. Before answering I let some variables spin around in my head. The idea wasn't as startling as if somebody had said, "You should be the CIA's operative in Tangier," or, "You should take up ballet." It was simply unexpected. After a few seconds, I said something like, "Why law for you but medicine for me?" The reasons are unmistakable to me now, but at the time it was a sincere question. Edmond evaded with some vagueness such as blood not being his cup of tea-he didn't want to be blunt with his opinion about personality types and differences.

Again, a few years later Louise clarified: Edmond judged me the proud owner of few if any of the personal attributes material to success as a lawyer. Showing good insight, he suspected that, for example, I would be dangerously disposed to believe what people told me. And as for clinical psychology and other such newer callings, his heritage had implanted a deep skepticism of them, including doubts about the durability of public demand for such services. All of which from Edmond's viewpoint can be translated as "security or lack thereof". Edmond's counsel that evening at dinner was that life on campus as a teacher was too risky in terms both emotional and practical. We discussed assorted vocations as illustrations of this point or that, mostly to emphasize their negative aspects as related to my needs as he saw them.

Edmond was sold on medicine. Louise agreed, especially if the choice was between that and psychology. She contended that, for me, an interest in human behavior was one thing, while dealing with troubled individuals was quite another. She acknowledged that physicians deal hour by hour with patients ranging from perturbed to disturbed. But her point was that the medical doctor-patient emphasis is on the organic, which would make for more clarity of diagnosis and greater gratification for patient and doctor than would be provided by psychology, except, of course, for those who have specifically heard its call. No doubt I was highly impressionable, and as detailed above, had charted no course beyond the horizon of graduation. By evening's end I felt their points were irrefutable. We look back at life's dramas with more awareness of the world and of ourselves than during the play. Had I gone to grad school with the aim of becoming a counseling psychologist, I have no doubt I would have felt like a Muslim at High Mass within a year or two into the program. As for teaching literature in college, I can only imagine the frightening possibilities. My sole certainty about campus life is that I don't like what I once heard on talk radio about its politics: "It's so vicious because the stakes are so low."

The next morning it entered my mind that by the time students arrive at medical school, most had probably studied some science in college. I was about to finish my junior year having studied only chemistry, a good particle in the nucleus of my freshman program. Solid science is as essential as any other study to rounding out the liberal education, and if Wesleyan was about anything, it was about rounding. Back at college, between turning in my French paper and summer vacation, I reported my plans to my COL faculty. The general response of my worthy professors was, "So, we've tried to make a thinker of you, and now you intend to become a sawbones." I wasn't alone. During our senior year our schoolmasters got a jolt from learning that only a couple of their initial brood of COLs were headed for faculty life. If preparing us to be professors was their goal all along, it was unstated until this late in our junior year when we heard their response to our postgrad plans. Only a few COL students were planning academic careers.

To my buddy Jake, whom you have met and who was begriming to look at a career as an insurance actuary, they said, "So, we've tried to make a thinker of you, and now you intend to become an Organization Man."

That same week I wrote to a few medical schools for guidance, giving them an outline of my college experience. Their messages back can be summarized with "We have studied your transcript with its description of your curriculum and comments from your professors but with no grades or hours or credits. We have your board exam results. We are intrigued by your unique college program. During this coming [my senior] academic year and the summers before and after, take a basic course in each of biology, physics and organic chemistry. If all goes well, we will admit you."

They didn't add "as an experiment," but I read it between their lines. It would mean entering medical school with 23 hours of science when the standard for pre-med students was 80 to 120 hours of science and math. Usually this consisted of 10 each of chemistry, biology, organic chemistry, physics; 8 of physical chemistry, 5 each of embryology, histology and comparative anatomy; 20 of math.

I told my father and Marjorie that I had discussed my options for the future with Louise and Edmond and that they had favored medicine. I did not emphasize that the idea was entirely Louise and Edmond's. O.K.'s response: "I've always told people I thought you should be a doctor." That was one facet of my father's personality that seemed a paradox to me. Here was a man whose exceptional strength was obvious to everyone, but who considered his sons' plans for life's work so much a matter of self-direction that he did not feel at all free to lead in that regard.

(It was a different matter to O.K. that his sons had chosen a profession. At appropriate times he was free with advice for us on how to succeed and, especially, avoid trouble.) In any case, O.K. and Marjorie were entirely pleased with my choice of medicine, and yet casual about it. I think Dad was relieved, and I would have had to choose tobacco lobbyist to have gotten an objection from Marjorie, who always felt one should choose what is naturally comfortable and emotionally rewarding for life. O.K. favored the financial picture at the University of Missouri over that of the private schools I'd written to. In any case, no more summer hod-carrier. At the end of junior year, after returning to Wesleyan from school abroad, we were subjected to a comprehensive exam by professors brought in from other schools. There was a written exam on our reading list from the two years, and then an oral by the two extra-mural interrogators-Dr. Carlos Baker of the Department of English at Princeton and Dr. Henri Peyre from Yale's Department of French. Professors Baker and Peyre wrote a report on each student for the COL faculty and a report on the venture for the administration. The visiting professors seemed favorably impressed with the COL's founding class. I believe we convinced them unequivocally that motivated students do not need conventional structure in order to learn.

The summer before my senior year I studied organic chemistry at Southwest Missouri State University. From Racine to organic chemistry is about as polar as is possible. I found organic chemistry ponderous and dry, as I suspect scientists do, at least those who are not organic chemists.

I found in it more rote than concept and therefore more tedium than interest compared with the other sciences. I chalked it up as the doldrums during passage. I satisfied the biology requirement during my senior year of college. I would fit in the physics at Washington University in St. Louis between college graduation exercises and reporting to medical school at the University of Missouri in Columbia in September.

During my senior year at Wesleyan, we "pioneers" of the College of Letters were completing our adventure in literature. The senior year plan took things beyond even the innovations of the sophomore and junior years: one subject, one paper, one professor. Call it anything you like; it was new, it was unique, and to us it was an enterprise of some daring. Each student was allotted one elective-in my case, biology-but this was the main course. Read, write about what you have read, and periodically meet with tutor to discuss.

The subject of my year-long project was the mythological in Elizabethan tragedy: some fog to sink your teeth into. There were times when I wanted to title it, "The Tragical Adventures of the Dispirited Kid," since this was a task much bigger than any before, and the scope of it intimidated me. I fought my misgivings by putting in long hours of study. What my thesis might want in quality I would try to make up for in bulk, and therefore in labor, since this was the typewriter era, and sometimes the pencil and pen era.

The results of this probe by our COL into some uncharted wilderness were impossible to arrange in a way that could be compared scientifically with traditional courses and methods.

Sophomore and senior years I didn't see anybody slacking off in spite of the absence of the traditional structure of grades, frequent exams, official hours and credits. After our junior-year study-abroad, only one of the students was released from the program and re-scheduled into a conventional major-minor curriculum. Apparently, some distractions had led him to forget why he was in France. I wondered whether the rest of us young men could be considered normal once we moved from anywhere to Paris and were able to ignore its artistic and feminine temptations enough to concentrate on academia. In any case, other than that one incident, I don't recall any members of the faculty or administration expressing any doubts. Visiting professors Baker and Peyre had given every indication of liking what they saw after the COL's second year. Its third year, with two-thirds of its members studying in Europe, had worked out as the administration hoped. Wesleyan put the College of Letters on its permanent register.

For me, senior year was the easiest emotionally of all the years there, partly because one of my fraternity mates introduced me to his sister, who attended a college not too far away. A week or two after graduation I drove to St. Louis to spend the summer toiling at the physics department at Washington University, returning each evening to good company and a comfortable bed in suburban Webster Groves at the family home of one of the other Wesleyan Midwesterners. Because I had never come under the charm of a "calling," science was as interesting as anything else. It was a good summer. Toward its end I moved into the med-school bachelors' "fraternity" house in Columbia, Missouri.

Breaking Rank

My undergraduate experience was how different? Different enough that the medical school administrative and admissions deans described this academic oddity in advance to the faculty, who therefore knew about me from day one. I learned this in anatomy lab the first week of year "M-1." The gross anatomy staff had just introduced us to our cadavers, one per four students. That first day, during the tedium of dissection, we four lapsed into a discussion of the year's curriculum. One of my fellow freshman dissectors was pointing out that our professor of neuro-anatomy, a second semester course, had a reputation not only for drawing the most beautiful diagrams in the profession, but for having what it took to keep students' hearts and minds on the subject. To which I responded, "You mean we have a separate course on the anatomy of just the brain and spine?" While my three gross-partners laughed, I felt a tap on my shoulder. I turned and discovered a mature face on which condescension seemed to be struggling with amusement. The gentleman said, "You must be Charlie Armstrong," which prolonged the laughter of the two of my lab-mates who knew I had not been a pre-med student. The white-coated man did not add, "We know about you: you're the one who doesn't know anything," but he didn't need to. After the professor turned and was far enough away I asked, "Who's that?"

One of my cut-and-probe partners replied, "That's your great artist of neuro-anatomy." Once again, as in the fifth grade and freshman year in college, I needed to gain on the pack. But this time the need to catch up was without emotional fret. There was only the normal stress of knowing there would be some heaving and hauling to do. Though I knew I faced a challenge, my outlook toward my "difference" was, on balance, positive: I was proud of our successful experiment in college. The outlook-those who taught first and second year students and knew about my college background-seemed to be objective curiosity. They seemed to share the position of one of the admissions deans who had said to me, "Charles, if you can get through the basic science [first two] years, the last two should be a breeze." My first year was underway, but the blues hadn't darkened my view. This time the atmosphere felt normal. This time I had more confidence that I could do the job.

The first two years of medical school traditionally address basic medical science: embryology, gross (visible) anatomy, histology (microscopic anatomy), neuro-anatomy, microbiology (bacteria, viruses, parasites, and other "germs"), physiology, biochemistry, biophysics, pharmacology, physical diagnosis (diagnosis through physical exam, as distinct from history, lab and procedures) and pathology. Within the time-filling routine of medical school there are little slots into which can be tucked some basic life.

Those first two years (M-1, M-2), I took 45 minutes daily between lab and dinner for a run, a circuit through the woods from and back to the marching band's practice field. The "clinical" (third and fourth) years I did the same when I could. On most Saturday nights, those of us who dormed at the bachelors' fraternity house tried to show the undergraduate "Greek" houses along the row that we were their match at throwing a party. The rest of the time, except during the life-maintenance ritual of meals and a classmate's 15-minute Broadway-standards piano recital in the ante-room before dinner, our dorm sounded like a monastery minus the chants. And if any hadn't learned it in college, they learned now that it was more efficient to get a good night's sleep. After four hours of class in the morning, three or four of lab in the afternoon, and four more of study in the evening, adding another hour of study when the brain is trying to shut down was counterproductive.

To remind us we were not yet citizens of the world, Saturday morning meant anatomy class exam at 7:30. Thereafter at 9, we attended Organ Recital, otherwise known as "Man-in-the-Pan" sessions, officially titled "Clinical Pathology Conferences" (CPC's). These sessions featured the recitation of a case history leading to an analysis of diseased tissue extracted by the pathologists at autopsy. First, a resident or junior-rank instructor would present the history, physical findings and lab results. Others, from students to the Chairman of the Department of Medicine or Surgery, would offer diagnostic hypotheses. The rest of us would watch and learn. In the old days (older than my days), a student would defend his case from "the pit," the bottom and center of an amphitheater, with the audience of students, interns, residents and expert faculty glaring down on the victim. Since my time, the scene was and is more likely a modern theater-with-stage auditorium, with the expert or student offering a differential diagnosis (a rundown of diagnostic possibilities) figuratively "in the pit," the glaring being done from any angle. If the diagnostician in the pit was a student, the errors and false starts were tallied up as learning experiences, provided he or she survived the stress. If the head of a department (medicine, surgery, infectious disease, what have you) was "it," a good time would be had by all. Watching these top-grade experts at work is always a pleasure, especially when the expert is somebody like C. Thorp Ray, M.D., our chief of the Department of Medicine. Physicians exemplified by Dr. Ray and the illustrious A. McGehee Harvey of Johns Hopkins were among the last great masters of physical diagnosis, the art of arriving at conclusions through the hands-on examination of the patient. Last masters because technology gradually rendered many of these skills less than critical to making a diagnosis, and we of a later day sensed that these veteran sages resented the trend.

Theirs was a fine art, and they hated to see it devalued. Diagnostically difficult cases were selected because of their learning value. Mature wizards like Dr. Ray would often turn their noses up at step three of the work up (the lab data), and nail the diagnosis after 10 or 20 minutes on stage with the patient. Dr. Ray always preferred these cases in which the subject case was a live inpatient rather than a "man-in-the-pan." After everyone else had been stumped despite reams of lab results, he would call the patient forward and lead him or her to enlarge on step one, the history. He, or another authority of his class, would ask questions that nobody else had thought of; examine the patient in a more virtuoso way and then offer his list of diagnoses, invariably correct, although not always complete. Only the pathologists have the tools-including a post-mortem exam-to be complete, to be perfect. The pathologists' verdicts are definitive since there is no limit to the invasiveness of their procedures. At Clinical Pathology Conferences and in day-by-day practice they pick up after everybody else's "mistakes", the pathologists' tongue-in-cheek word for the sometimes-futile efforts of those who treat live patients.

Often an expert of Dr. Ray's measure would present, in pontifical tones, a diagnosis with a mere history, not bothering with step two, the physical exam. He may or may not have wanted to flaunt his experience and acuity, but the sticking point was to emphasize that taking a good history was crucial art of physical diagnosis, including looking or listening here, palpating, probing, or-brace yourself-sniffing or tasting there. But with medical technology's geometric advances since World War II, these connoisseur physicians showcased their skills with the sensitivity of a musician holding forth with a Stradivarius. They performed with the gravity of true believers who feel their audience might become lost souls. To watch Dr. Ray was to watch a master craftsman, and the onlooking future and present physicians would never forget the masters point.

Although our generation of physicians would not have to call upon those skills to the extent the old maestros were able to, and did, I would find the skills I did learn very handy in a more primitive Asian setting one day. During the first two years of medical school, rather than the paralyzing depression of my undergraduate years, I was frustrated by methods of teaching that I found to be a log athwart the road, even if those methods were embedded in generations of convention. They were perhaps a bit more hidebound in medical education than elsewhere simply because the medical profession, an old one, holds great reverence for traditional observance, including training. I considered much of what we students did wasteful of time and designed more to test the resolve of the recruit rather than to foster learning. Personally, if my resolve needed testing I would not have been there to begin with. My experience with our revolutionary but successful program in college had conditioned me. After the basic science years, I had a few weeks' break before the start of the first "clinical" year. These breaks, each allotted to a given number of students, were dispersed throughout the year in order to cover everybody at assorted times. I stayed at the dorm and wrote a long essay, the thrust of which was that medical education, and any graduate education it might typify, should be reformed. After finishing my bill of pleadings, I proceeded to knock on the doors of department chairmen and deans, declare that I had written something that might be of interest, and present it to a hand that held my destiny.

To summarize my essay: I found a four-hour morning of taking notes while listening to my lecturers an inefficient use of time. If a professor of neuro-anatomy draws elaborate, refined diagrams and gives clear, attention-holding lectures, let him provide those in finished form as only he can. Why should the student have to rely on his or her own third-rate go at copying the expert's diagrams and words? Why not devote the program to learning instead of to gamesmanship? If a student has an advantage of say, knowing shorthand or having a recorder in hand, why not take that advantage a step further: present every student with the material in absolute form, undiminished by the student's imperfect recording technique, be it pen or tape. If a professor wants to explain something thus, print out and provide thus. Let the students study the pure, prime source and gather in class only thereafter to discuss and question. If the professor notices that some of the questions are good, he goes back to his word processor and enriches his text with the answers to those questions so that the next time around they don't have to be asked.

If Professor Probe is a better researcher than teacher he can unapologetically hand out printed or recorded lectures by his colleague Professor Lucidate, known for clarity of delivery and for getting the ideas across. Those ideas may even have originated within this same brilliant researcher, Probe, who is nevertheless inherently unable to keep the students' perspective on the whole while he expounds on its minutiae. Probe's teaching would accordingly confound the best scholar in class.

182

Leave the teaching to Professor Lucidate. Exams and grades should be used as ongoing tools. If a student is testing poorly, what's the problem? Assuming the student is capable, is he or she slacking off? Is he distracted by emotional problems? Have events caught her up within a field her mind follows but her heart does not? Or is this an instance of a professor who knows his subject but is out of his element when trying to extend that knowledge to others? Who hasn't experienced the confusion of one expert's muddled presentation, after which the smoke-clearing articulation of another who is routinely a model of transparency and organization?

That was the gist of my forty-page paper. This exercise was strictly "academic" in that I was not so far out of touch that I expected any practical change as a result. At least not soon, and especially not soon in professional training as opposed to liberal education. It was also an ill-advised-and certainly unadvised-drift toward defiance, with the appearance of arrogance not too far in the offing. I didn't have the nerve to show the paper to Dad because I knew he would consider it politically imprudent and reckless: fine to write it; quite another to show it around as if flaunting it. Toward the end of that (my third) year Dad learned about it from the deans at a conference they called to discuss my situation. Soon thereafter one of the deans said to me, "We found your father to be entirely open-minded and understanding."

But to see some of the points of my essay in practice we can look to Professor of Surgery Hugh E. Stephenson Jr., who had the gift. When he taught, the matter was hard to forget. His package had all goods and no filler. The following non-technical example in no way illustrates Dr. Stephenson's technical prowess or his refined clinical judgment but illustrates his ability to make sure that the first picture the student sees is the big one. Buerger's Disease (thromboangitis obliterans) is one cause or type of arterial constriction of the lower extremities and can lead to gangrene and amputation. On rounds with us students he asked, "What's the first thing you notice about an inpatient that suggests Buerger's Disease?" Any student might reasonably conclude that, since Buerger's disease affects primarily the arteries of the lower extremities, there would be the place to find the first signs.

First student: "Diminished pedal [foot] pulses?"

Second student: "Acral cyanosis [feet and maybe calves purple from oxygen deficiency]?"

Dr. Stephenson: "No, the first clue is the array of tobacco products on his night stand."

Dr. Stephenson was a master not only of surgery, but also of making technical matter as straightforward as that non-technical example. He had a talent for expressing the principles of medicine and surgery in aphoristic gems that were almost difficult to forget ("In cases like this of painless jaundice, always consider malignancy, especially of the head of the pancreas.") After Dr. Stephenson finished speaking, whether a lecture or a fine point, some fellow student would usually lean toward me with a remark, something like, "Why didn't Dr. Turbid or Dr. Murk explain it that way?" This talent put Dr. Stephenson on a short list. Dr. Stephenson was the good professor who provided vista first, then its details. In my paper, I emphasized that if the student is spinning his wheels or is sidetracked, the capable tutor should be able to put him back on the high, dry road heading in the right direction. He should be able to impart to the student that if his or her heart isn't in it, neither will be his or her mind.

I was up the hot water in a leaky canoe without a paddle, especially after I printed up copies of my seditious tract and dealt them out to the faculty and deans. Probably some of them were thinking that surely the admission of a non-pre-med student had been a mistake. When I put my ear to the ground and heard the distant rumble of faculty hooves heading my way, I began to think that only vertigo or a vision agog could have led me to do this. At that very moment, surely some Marine recruit stepped up unasked and advised the commanding staff on ways to improve boot camp.

One of my schoolmates read my critique and said, "Now I can't be seen with you, Charles." I had shown several professors and deans copies of my petition of grievances expecting to hear "Very interesting" all around, only to find their response mixed. Many on the faculty were quite receptive about what I had written. Otherwise I would have ended up in another line of work.

One young professor of pathology actually wrote "Right on!" and other more analytic notes throughout the margins. At a school banquet another pathologist's wife told me she had read it and offered her congratulations for being so "gutsy". The venerable Chairman of Internal Medicine, Dr. C. Thorpe Ray, came out with a hearty endorsement of my points-in my dreams.

Several of the professors who read my commentary were quite happy to sit down with me and discuss my ideas. Most remarked that my assumptions about students being motivated (that they would study Friday evenings facing no exam Saturday morning) exhibited a scarcity of exposure to the world. Well, the COL-twenty had studied Friday nights, so I figured any graduate student would do the same without any further daycare. The words of Professor FB. Engley, Chief of Microbiology, spoke for the other receptive faculty: "Your ideas are constructive, but practical only where there is student motivation and discipline."

But to many faculty members, this stunt of mine was inappropriate. To a few of them, it was out-of-line, an apprentice's presumptuousness, an insult to the traditions of rank. And the plot thickened with another issue. The most junior of the deans, who served also as instructor in physical diagnosis, called me in to point out that after watching me making rounds he had concluded I was a "ship out of water." "Why don't you take some time off this summer, sit on a beach and look inside." I certainly wasn't going to see any truth there may have been in that--»I had already been launched. My port was in sight. My bearing was, "I'll do anything the faculty orders-just so I get under way." My eyes were not open to any wisdom of the dean about looking more deeply inside.

There was still another matter. There were strange sightings, such as my body at the library researching my patients' diseases when it should have been at the OR assisting at their surgeries. My position was, "How can I assist when I don't yet know everything about the disease?" Only later did the question on that position cross my mind: "You'll never know everything about this disease anyway, so get off it and get some practical

186

experience." Toward the end of year M-3 I was summoned to the Dean's office. He informed me that during a faculty meeting several days earlier they had debated my destiny. No professor argued that I wasn't bending my back to the task: I wasn't seen at the golf course, but at the med-school library. Fortunately for me there was a faction of the faculty and at least one dean who thought such an essay was appropriate, and at least two on the faculty who thought it was overdue. The faculty's decision was to test my dedication to the program. I would have to repeat the third year-and this time their way. Willingness to do so would show I was there to do more than just cause trouble.

During a two-month break I had plenty of time to discuss things with select friends and relatives. I craved the opinion of anyone I respected and trusted. It seems paradoxical that I would seek fair winds when I considered my course fixed. Probably I wanted backup. With the exception of being convinced in one evening to go to medical school, I've often been one to take a poll when my momentarily firm step feels the merest drag of doubt. At the time, I wasn't confident whether I was Captain of my own destiny or merely watch in the crow's nest. I took advantage of the break to go over the matter with my father. I knew O.K. would empathize: He knew something about ships in drydock, having practiced law for only six months after earning his LLB. He reviewed objectively with me the ins and outs of this maze, and would not have resisted if I had announced that the dean was right about my ship being high and dry. O.K. advised ultimately that I follow my heart but obliquely suggested continuing long enough to be sure. My own view of the matter was beclouded by a shortage of the sort of self-knowledge that for some comes only with maturity.

Jonathan Winters supposedly knew he was a comedian at age 5. But even that clarity of inner-recognition would not have simplified the matter, since by this time I was able to see Edmond`s point that a calling and a good job aren't always the same thing. For some weeks I sought out the judgment of others, but my mind was never really open. If I was a ship out of water, why were the waves so rough? I never harbored the notion of not returning to med-school in September.

When I returned to school for my second third year there was news, bad and good. I would learn the bad on day one, the good a few later. Bad: Day one I drew general surgery as my first nine-week assignment, not encouraging, as I sensed the greatest suspicion of my behavior and motives in that department. During surgical orientation I felt myself going into a low. Perhaps not lower than my troughs in college, but unhappily similar, and more persistent. My outlook at Wesleyan was darkest in the morning and brighter after dark. This low was relentless, with recovery starting only after favorable developments described below and then progressing only gradually for some weeks. From its onset I could hardly eat, barely move, and could speak only in an indistinct whisper. I got out of bed only with utmost resolve, which is hard to find within a black case of the blues, as you may recall from your last trip down.

The good news wasn't forthcoming until a few days into that first week. A surgical team doing an operation generally consisted of a student or intern, sometimes one of each, and a surgical resident, all at the table under a professor's guidance. There were variations on that, such as professor and student only, resident and intern, or, on a tough one, two professors and a resident or student or both. In all cases the student was there not for his erudition but to hold and use instruments as told, and ask questions-or worse, answer them. What was predictable was that the student, intern and resident scrubbing in were those who had "drawn" that patient for workup at the patient's admission. This was his or her patient. Which instructor connected with which procedure was sometimes arbitrary, sometimes a matter of the instructor's own patient.

The combination of instructor, resident and student on a given case was also happenstance. By chance of the draw, I had never come across Hugh Stephenson Jr., M.D., full Professor of surgery during surgical rotations the previous year. Dr. Stephenson had served as Chairman of the school's Department of Surgery, and 17 years later would begin a 12-year term as Chief of Staff of the University Hospitals and Clinics. He served as Interim Dean of the Medical School from 1988 to 1989. But most important, Dr. Stephenson is a "natural", a surgeon's surgeon. I had been privileged to encounter him only through his lucid physical diagnosis of surgery, a couple of surgery lectures for us sophomores 15 or so months earlier. Two or three days into the surgical rotation, my patient and I were assigned to Dr. Stephenson, and my spirits were considerably lifted by the three or more hours in the OR with him. During the second week it dawned on my mind and morale that all but the first two or three cases had linked me with Dr. Stephenson. I had hoped that the trend would continue. It did indeed, which led me to imagine that I had been assigned to Dr. Stephenson, and I deeply hoped that he had arranged it. I certainly was not going to inquire about this coincidence.

After our first scrub together, Dr. Stephenson called me into his office. He had been such a gentleman during the operation that I didn't worry too much about what he had to say or wanted to hear. He let me know that, although we had not worked together the previous year, he knew all about me. Not surprising, so I took this to be a less than favorable opening of our conversation and felt a moment of apprehension. But his words and avuncular presence made it clear that he was intent on being helpful. "Now Charlie, let me tell you something. All you need to do is play the game and you'll do fine." Dr. Stephenson went on to explain all about "playing the game," which more or less meant, "Don't fight city hall until you're the mayor." He implied that after our nine weeks of surgery together, things should go smoothly. And for my blues, which he saw as if they were painted around my eyes, he added: "Now remember, it's darkest just before the dawn." Adages at the right place and time can be remedial eloquence. I left our meeting feeling reassured. After nine weeks with my hero, I felt as if I could sail on through, as if my heeling was now being righted.

I credit my ability to slog through the emotional morass of a second third year largely to the support afforded by Dr. Stephenson. Having since assisted dozens of surgeons in half a dozen locations of training, military and private practice, I elect Dr. Stephenson as the most gifted general surgeon I have seen in action. I recall three members of a distinguished American university's surgery faculty stepping into the OR to observe Dr. Stephenson at work after he and I had started a case requiring some meticulous dissection within the neck. The neck is a complex convergence of items-nerves, vessels, glands and such-that want to be disturbed only by someone who knows them intimately and will do them no harm. These surgeons' eyes betrayed the expressions on their masked faces. After about 15 minutes their chief said, "beautiful dissection, beautiful dissection," and after 20 more, said it again. Dr.

Stephenson tried to deflect this admiration by changing the subject to the diagnosis at hand. I knew they were figuratively shaking their heads in veneration, and I was enjoying a faint ray of reflected glory. A stronger ray was the feeling of a bond with Dr. Stephenson. Even if it was my feeling alone, it translated into one of security, the antidote of anxiety. I was beginning to believe I would survive the year emotionally and administratively.

Several weeks later a general-surgery resident tipped me off that the ship previously out of water seemed to be under way. He told me that some new faculty members had learned that I was repeating the year and were puzzled as to why. Once again, I could sight my landfall.

St. Louis, Gateway to the West Pacific

Senior year was time to start thinking about internships. We "M-4's" were allotted enough leave to look at a few teaching hospitals. After several Midwest winters, I gave a first look at hospitals in Atlanta, Georgia, and Gainesville and Jacksonville in Florida. But the warmest climate I found was St. Luke's Hospital in St. Louis. The head of the Department of Medicine was Dr. Robert Payne, a pleasure to work with and a gentleman in the finest Dr.-Hugh-E.-Stephenson tradition. Why do I repeat this point about the "gentleman"? Because the structure of medical training-with students, interns, residents, fellows, instructors, assorted ranks of professors, department chiefs and deans-resembles the military hierarchy. If somebody of higher rank wants to make an underling's life miserable, he or she as a matter of course can pull it off unscathed, at least for a while. Physicians in power were generally ladies and gentlemen to the degree of their competence. C. Thorp Ray, MD. was aloof and a little pompous, crucial to his Moses persona and not surprising in an academic patriarch. Doctors Stephenson and Payne were walking evidence that virtue can coexist with virtuosity. They were not only gentlemen--they were warmhearted and the opposite of petty.

St. Luke's attending staff physicians divided their time between teaching and private practice. Whether or not that was the reason, they were much more informal and approachable than the regulation university academic. Dr. Payne was not inappropriately chummy; he was refined and reserved. But he was amiable and entirely accessible.

The internship at St. Luke's was "rotating", defined as a cycle through specialties, as opposed to a "straight" internship in only medicine, surgery or pediatrics. The four rotations at St. Luke's included two months each of pediatrics, gynecology, and surgery, and six of medicine.

Another rotation was the on-call schedule: every third night for us interns, which meant spending on-call nights at the hospital. It meant reporting for duty six bells into the morning watch (7 a.m.) and working until 5 p.m. the next day. After midnight, things would often calm down enough to allow us a gesture or ten at sleep, such as changing into scrubs and even lying down on our bunks, but these were mocked with shrill regularity. My memories of phone calls from floor nurse to intern's quarters are vivid. What is not vivid is the intern's memory of what has just been said by a nurse who woke him 15 minutes into a slumber that started 20 hours after the previous wake up. I would grope for and grab the phone in my on-call den and for some ten or thirty seconds hear a series of words strung together with no correction or retention one word to the next, though I was distantly aware that word-by-word the language was English. Instead of struggling with the matter by phone, I routinely mumbled, "I'll come up." I would roll out of bed being startled 10 minutes after dozing off. At the end of my thirty-six-hour intern's shift Tuesday evening, l would have dinner with my friends at the hospital and then, if my eyes were open, drive to the gym for a swim. Or l would have a good run at Forest Park, two blocks from home (yes, I could run while asleep). In any case it was to bed by eight or nine. The next evening, Wednesday, was a date with a student nurse or with a few students and residents. Camaraderie every third evening--an unthinkable indulgence during college or med school. We were as good as broke, so there was nothing so fancy as dinner out.

Ordinarily, we single interns and residents whose off-duty evenings coincided on a weekend took our nursing-student friends out to someplace inexpensive or to one of our homes if a weeknight. My place, an efficiency, was typical, although a few of the foreign residents had real apartments. The student nurses' quarters was the dorm adjoining the hospital. Above-lobby was off limits to male medical residents and interns (there were no male nursing students that year at St. Luke's). Mrs. Elberta Smith, a widow, was seen as mother hen of the student-nurses' dorm, and tried to do the same for us. Mrs. Smith was free with her opinion about our choices in pairing off with her brood. Gradually we learned that she usually called these relationships right. A weeknight out was two hours of fun then call it a day. Saturday nights we could loosen up a little, provided we were not on call, since Sunday morning rounds started late.

l said we were broke. "Residents" are so called because in the old days they resided at the hospital during those years between internship and private practice or between internship and a "fellowship" if they were headed for academic careers. In return for free room and board residents were more or less always on call. That became modified somewhat over the years, as it finally occurred to the establishment that the residents might be more capable of learning and performing from med school even though we spent anywhere from 84 to 98 hours one week-and that much plus Sunday call the next week-on the job at St. Luke's. It was novel not to feel as if our every move was being scrutinized. There was a refreshing liberation in the air, regardless of a schedule fit only for the young and sturdy. Unlike medical school or Marine boot camp, if the first-year M.D. did his work everybody was grateful for it, happy with it, and showed as much by offering some respect. Most of the nurses were gracious to us,

194

and the experienced ones were helpful-even more meaningful to new doctors. Even our superiors, though they didn't have to, allowed us interns some regard, with mutual awareness of rank, of course. We had one resident who fancied himself Napoleon, but he held no throne, so it didn't matter. Otherwise St. Luke's was a cozy, family scene.

Most of the residents became our friends and treated us virtually as peers. The student nurses and foreign residents drew us interns, all single, into their social circle much more than did the American residents, whose circle was home with spouse. Nurse-students, interns and single residents dined together at the hospital cafeteria. Meals at St. Luke's were on the house for doctor and nurse trainees, a crucial benefit since the salary for interns was $330 per month. That left enough to make do. My apartment rent was $75 per month. The rest went into the usual needs of life such as car maintenance, YMCA dues, an occasional article of clothing and a little for entertainment. Admission to a movie in 1967-68 (Elvira Madigan, Wait Until Dark) for a couple cost between $2.00 and $2.50 depending on the theater.

The year was a series of triads: night on call, night to "crash", night to be social. If Monday night was on-call, duty started Monday at 7 or 8 a.m. and ended Tuesday at 5 or 6 pm, depending on the rotation. Monday night permitted occasional half-naps, if that's what you call when not in a state of disabling fatigue. Also, how would you like to live at your office, good sleep or not? Therefore, by my day, literal residency was optional. My friend Shu Sum Chuk, MD., resident in surgery, was unusual in accepting the hospital's offer and was quite happy in his St. Luke's den. But then perhaps someone who grew up sharing a two-bedroom apartment with five people could deal with the masochistic setting more benignly.

In mid-spring of that internship year an official-looking letter arrived in my mail slot at St. Luke's Hospital. The envelope's return address was: Pentagon; Department of the Army. I opened it with quickened pulse and audible breath. My year as a "MASH" doctor in Vietnam is another story.

PART SIX-REPORTING FOR DUTY

Vietnam Calling

In the spring of 1968, about two months before the end of my internship, a letter from the Army appeared in my mailbox at St. Luke's. I opened the Pentagon envelope to find a letter headed "Welcome to the Vietnam Transient Detachment." "Transient" meant I would spend only 365 days in Vietnam. "Report 7 August 68 to Fort Sam Houston, San Antonio, Texas for medical officer training." I was not being singled out, as this notice was mailed out to every male 1967-68 M.D. intern in America.

Even the lads who had signed up in advance with Navy and Air Force programs were told, "Sorry fellas, the Army needs you more than they do." My mind became a simmering cauldron of concern, with a dram of curiosity tossed in. My feelings were cross-grained about this adventure [up]on which we were about to embark.

My father, O.K. Armstrong, had been an ex-Congressman for some years and was writing full time for the *Reader's Digest*. "O.K." had given up any hope for sane leadership in the Vietnam War until after the November election. If I had had a crystal ball I would have warned him that the Nixon-Kissinger leadership would be a slight improvement, which is to say highly-disappointing.

The weeks between internship's June wrap-up and report-time at Fort Sam Houston were free. [I spent them traveling about in my Rambler, visiting relatives in Florida and doing too-young-to-know-better things such as driving alone from St. Augustine back to St. Louis without a motel break because I was broke] [previous sentence may be pointless]. The summer was a short but pleasant break. I don't recall the exact date of early August '68 that I reported to Fort Sam Houston; a clue is that while I approached the gates of Fort Sam a song entitled "Hey Jude" was introduced to the airwaves.

The purpose of the training course at Fort Sam was to make drafted doctors into some likeness of U.S. Army officers and do so in somewhat less than two months. The first few days were filled with the most basic of basics: lodging, mess assignments, hours of paper to fill out and hand in, fitting for uniforms, class orientation and so on. On day two my fellow recruits and I reported for uniform pick up. Putting on uniforms as officers of our nation's Army made us feel [that] we were donning distinction of a grade a bit inordinate for us. We felt a little self-conscious for this promotion in that we had not yet experienced the rigors of training. While my group of half a dozen were trying on our new livery, one of our buddies, Walt Gooding, said, "Now, what is it on here that says we're Captains?"

Chris ("Brooksie") Brooks, who knew a thing or two, replied with mock uncertainty, "I think it's these two bars here," pointing at Walt's shoulder. A couple of the guys laughed at Walt's ignorance, but the rest of us let go an embarrassed half-laugh at our own.

Sporting our new uniforms, Walt, Brooksie, Lamar Turner and I stepped out on a veranda over[looking] the building's curved front driveway. We looked down upon an attention-fixing sight: a soldier with shoulder-to-elbow stripes, a sergeant, a seasoned, been-there-and-seen-it sergeant.

He looked up at us with a brisk "Good morning, sirs!" embellished with a salute that was so swift and deft that it struck me as visual art. We froze. After we had stared at him, amazed, for a couple of seconds.

Walt had the presence to show some leadership with a limp return salute, which reminded the rest of us to do the same with rough ones of our own. I [hoisted] [raised] my hand so fast trying to make up for lost time that it hit just enough of my eye to make a flash. By then, my neurocircuits had connected enough to accomplish a return greeting. But since the sergeant had caught me by surprise I responded in kind with "Good morning, sir," [I said,] which Walt and Lamar mimicked almost in unison an instant later. Whereas the sergeant's intonation had been a snappy and military "GOOD MORNING SIRS," our replies were anything but that. The sergeant then swept his arm downward in a flourish of polished craftsmanship. We lamely lowered our right arms and looked at one another with assorted faces, but let's call them chagrin. After turning away from the sergeant's direction Walt asked quietly, "We don't say 'Sir' to sergeants, do we?"

"I don't think so," I replied, in unison with Brooksie's emphatic "No." The sergeant's perfectly serious, straight face through this farcical display spoke to me of the self-possession of a veteran, whether or not he was used to such behavior at a birthing depot for medical officers. Brooksie then reminded us that at check-in we were told that it was customary to reward with one dollar the first enlisted man to salute us. Instantly we turned and hustled off the veranda, down the stairs, and just out the front door where the sergeant was on his way in.

"Sergeant, we owe you a dollar apiece," we said, while rummaging our wallets. The soldier permitted himself a trace of a grin or was trying to suppress one, in which I detected embarrassment at having caught tenderfoot officers unprepared. "Thank you, sir," he repeated upon receiving each dollar bill. I wasn't sure whether small talk with sergeants was appropriate, or even acceptable ("He's a real soldier --maybe I'll say something stupid," and "I'm an officer: maybe it's forbidden."), but decided to take a chance. "Sergeant, if you have a minute, we're going to Vietnam. Have you been there?"

He probably wanted to say, "Is Vince Lombardi a football coach'?", but said, "Two tours, sir, '65 and '67; First Air Cav," with that classical, clipped enunciation of the career soldier.

Then I said, "We're on our way to orientation class," in the tone of the 4-year-old boy who says, "Hi, this is my new red wagon." "Yes, in that building right over there, sir," he said, pointing. It was clear he knew we were beginners, and that was a relief. I would learn later that the respect shown us by the sergeant during this episode was real and not just the conditioned bearing of a soldier. My close friend (Major Infantry) Andrew Messing later explained this sergeant's attitude: "The infantry does not look upon its doctors as mere REMFs ("Rear echelon moms," you might say). In Vietnam, the Medical Corps and enlisted medics were as much revered and respected by the infantry as the helicopter pilots, whose job was also in part to save the wounded. I would learn during the months to come that we Medical Corps officers were to earn that respect.

Every morning we gathered in companies in the quad before marching to breakfast. I liked the crisp early morning air even though I wasn't a morning person. We would bring manuals, study material or newspapers to read while waiting for the drill sergeants. Reading or chatting with buddies, either way, we stood and shuffled around in a rough counterfeit of order. Our drill instructors always addressed their collected officer-recruits as "Gentlemen". Several mornings, until we became familiar with timing, the sergeant [of the day] would stare a few seconds at our casual likeness of formation and begin with, "Now, gentlemen, if we can end our conferences and put our newspapers down perhaps we can shape up for drill."

The sergeants were always tactful with their gentlemen. There was no "Isn't it time you idiots knew something about rank and file?" though by the fourth day we suspected they were thinking as much. We weren't trying to be smart alecks; we were just being ourselves until we got the picture, and the sergeants were trying to break us in "nice" for a couple of reasons: We were above them in rank; also, while we were like 18-year-old recruits in knowing nothing of the military, we were not 18 and were not assumed to respond as 18-year-olds to the shock of boot camp. Actually, I enjoyed drill. Most of us did, partly, I think, because of the fun of learning something done synchronously, especially to the rhythm of martial music. By the second week we weren't all that bad. And we were invariably impressed with the aplomb and disciplined flair of the drill sergeants.

Our short course in becoming officers included most items of career Army basic training, enlisted or officer. We spent a surprising amount of time on History of the Army, considering our support role. On the other hand, most of the regular army training in combat skills was abridged for us medical officers. They didn't need us as Infantry; they needed us as doctors, and they needed us yesterday. Rifle-and-pistol training, for example, was a two-day course, comparable to law school offering a two-day course in Constitutional Law. Two days to teach physicians how to handle M-16's and Colt-45's. Day one of the two began with the Sergeant saying, "Now gentlemen, today if we will listen and watch before doing, perhaps we will refrain from shooting each other in the head."

The exercise culminated in a crawl through the dirt-trench cradling our rifles, barbed wire just above our necks and live horizontal machine-gun fire just above that --in the dark to accustom trainees to every disadvantage. We could feel the concussions of grenade-simulator explosions, all part of helping the recruit [to] feel at home in real combat. With the crack of machine-gun fire came the smell of cordite. In the ranking of scents, on a rung not too far below the top --where we find the enticing aromas associated with the female sex-- I would place cordite, whose smell has a possessing [power] [authority] the match of hydrocarbon anesthetics and glues (which I know, of course, only as a dental patient). Most of us discreetly enjoyed these heady hours under the gun.

Toward the end of the program the command offered a certain number of flight-surgeon slots. For centuries, there have been two categories of medical doctors: physicians and surgeons. Since the time of the Revolution, American military personnel have referred to their assigned physician as "the surgeon", undoubtedly because in the old Army surgeons were it --no need for a physician without a knife. The doctor in *Gone with the Wind* and "Doc" in *Gun Smoke* had quite useful surgical skills, primitive as they were next to today's operating room and emergency department. The military or the wild-west surgeon also played his physician role, but it was minor since his medical nostrums were often worse than nothing. That is, a wounded Civil War soldier didn't need a physician, he needed a surgeon. Physicians came into greater military demand when they had more to offer, scientific medicine being a child of the 20th century. Today the U.S. Army doctor is still "the surgeon" because the military loves tradition, and rightly so. Thus, our modem Surgeon General may not have brandished a scalpel since his or her internship. A flight surgeon is a physician who attends specifically to the medical, and a few surgical, needs of pilots.

Those of us who considered the alternative of becoming flight surgeons couldn't marshal any distinct pros and cons except for the slightly higher pay for flight time. Would the flight-surgeon path mean we would know more of what we were getting into? (go for flight surgeon: you'll be a flight surgeon; pass it up: no telling what you'll get). On the other hand, would knowing our specific assignment in advance be any better? The answers were "can't say" on both counts since both flight and non-flight offerings, we would learn, were loaded with possibilities. Flight-surgeon would rule out an evacuation-hospital assignment in the Mobile Army Surgical Hospital (MASH) tradition, but that still left little basis in our ignorance for choosing "search-and-destroy". I spent October in flight- surgeon training at Fort Rucker, Alabama. My Medical Corps buddies and I gathered in San Francisco for departure. I recall we were cautiously optimistic, as this was one week after the November election.

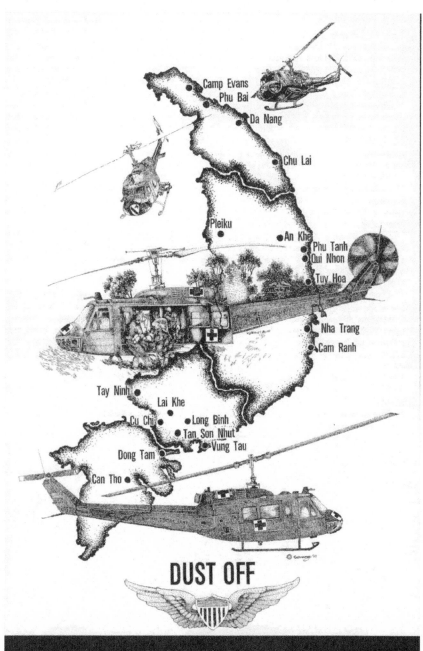

DUST OFF

Dust Off by Luis P. Carranza

In Theater

Our DC-8 flight from Travis A.F.B. to Vietnam gave us about three hours in Hawaii and two in Guam. We touched down at the Ton Son Nhut ("tahn sun oot") U.S. Air Force Base at Bien Hoa ("b'yen wah") about 0200 hours. We boarded deuce-and-a-half (2 1/2-ton) trucks, armored personnel carriers (APC's) and jeeps for the drive to Long Binh. Therefore, our introduction was an open-air convoy on a moonless, tropical night. As soon as we moved past the gate our young escorts locked and loaded their M- 16's and their M-60 and 50-caliber machine guns on the rails (one of each for APC's, two each on trucks).

About every two minutes they aimed four-deuce 81-mm mortars skyward and shot flares, which exploded at their crest far above the top of the surrounding foliage, gray in the distant light. Forest shadows swayed in phase las the flares danced below their parachutes. The growth, gray in the exploding light, became green as the Hares fell toward and through the jungle canopy. At Long Binh we dropped off several troops, including a couple or three doctors, to billet for a day or two and receive assignments. Then we drove on to Bearcat Army Installation to do the same.

I noticed what I would soon learn was standard form among American forces, a custom I, too, would adopt. Dead of night and with flares flying, from the driver's portable radio came American pop music –up-to-the-minute pop music. American radio from station AF VN (Armed Forces Vietnam) broadcast from Saigon, from 0600 hours ("Good Morning Vietnam") to the next morning. Most of the soldiers had little radios strapped to their helmets or their hats. Operating rooms had radios. Unless combat maneuvers were underway, the troops usually had AF VN as a backdrop to the action of the moment. Infantry would tune their PRC-25 radios to AF VN. This was our umbilical cord to the mother country, carrying red-blooded American culture, including music, news, and special programs. Our daily personal reinforcement was the fix of letters and voice tapes exchanged with home and AF VN.

The next day the Medical Corps command handed out orders.

Charles on a real "Wakeful Watch"

Colonel O'Shannahan informed me that flight-surgeons were not needed at the time, but field-hospital surgeons were. I was to report to the 91st Evacuation Hospital on the central coast. I didn't know what to make of this turn of the wheel. My feeling wasn't so much disappointment as suspense. I collected my gear and boarded a Chinook (CH 47 transport) helicopter. More than an hour later, we touched down in a wilderness encampment of buildings on the beach. By "buildings" I mean tropical, army-style canvas and screen over 2 by 4's, with white crosses painted on the roof. While touching down and stepping out under the moving blades, I liked what I saw--a tidy, looking medical outpost up against an emerald ocean. But I still wasn't sure what this was all about.

"Where's the nearest town?" I asked the pilot as soon as the engine had wound down enough to allow conversation. "Down the beach about 20 miles, sir. You'll like it here. Besides, there's a big South Korean base camp next door, and Charlie (Viet Cong) doesn't want to mess with them." South Koreans were ferocious fighters, not known for giving quarter or for taking prisoners.

"You'll be getting enough wounded here to make for a good day's work. And you'll get total respect from the infantry, sir, wounded or not. They see themselves and you as being at the two ends of the damage. Here, sir, I'll carry your gear to the quartermaster's hooch. He'll take you to yours." "My own hooch?" He must mean quarters," I thought.

The 91st Evac Hospital was commanded by a "regular" army Lt. Colonel who was good at getting along with irregular, cram-course officers. The hospital staff included regular army nurses, eight or so physicians drafted from their surgical residencies, and one or two young regular army surgeons. The drafted physicians were all majors, the rank awarded to doctors at the residency level of training. Those who entered post-residency began as Lt. Colonel. I was the only Captain, at least of the Medical Corps (as opposed to Nursing Corps) who was at the 91st Evac since I was the only one who was between internship and residency. Several of the doctors at the 91st were amid orthopedic residencies, most appropriate for an Evac hospital's needs. Two, Keith Whittaker and Ted Schultz, had been training in general surgery and one, Jerry McPherson, in urology. The quartermaster sergeant told me I would be sharing a hooch with the chaplain. Although quite comfortable for tropical war zone living, this wasn't Pine Lodge at Yellowstone. The home the chaplain and I shared was one room (12' by 12') in a "dorm" of four to six hooches built like almost all other quarters constructed by the Engineer Corps in Vietnam, the variation being only in size. The operating rooms, the mess hall, the officer's "club" and sleeping hooches were boards or canvas from ground to waist high, and from there screen to the sloping roof, all braced by 2 by 4's. Our rooms were separated by screen and canvas. Our beds were sleeping mats laid over boards--far superior to mere cots.

The next morning at the mess hall while most of the 91st Evac team were having breakfast, one of the surgeons, Major Mike Devereux, delegated by our commanding Lieutenant Colonel (Lt.C.) to be his "Lieutenant Lt.C.", stood up to make announcements. He led off with, "Well, I found a new surgeon," which was greeted immediately by laughter, hoots, cat calls and applause by the company. I didn't yet know why the bantering grief for the Major, but my instant impression was that nobody seemed to be pulling rank here.

Surgeons, corpsmen ("medics"), and nurses from lieutenants on up were joining in to give the major some familiar treatment. He then casually reviewed with the 91st personnel the distribution of duties for the day, asking as much as directing, always with the awareness that any plan could be disrupted by wounded medevacked in by helicopter. Such talk as the following made me realize this was something different from Camp Lejeune Marine Corps protocol: "Jerry, you and Keith are still working on Jablonski, right, and Ted says he can debride that Chu Lai case with Cathie and Sarah (nurses). So Rob, how about you scrub with the Durango Kid for the morning? Now, as you all know, we were promised a replacement for Wells. He has finally arrived." More laughter and applause amid mock congratulations to toastmaster Devereux, especially from the nurses, a joke pertaining to, I would later learn, who would be credited for finding Wells' replacement. The breakfast crowd was giving Major Devereux such a hard time because he had been bragging on how quickly he would land another surgeon and was now trying to tease them by taking credit when they knew he had nothing to do with it. As I learned later, the credit belonged to the sergeant who had spoken by radio to Col. O'Shannahan's staff-sergeant, who presumably pointed out to O'Shannahan that he could spare a flight surgeon for the 91st to use as they saw fit. The hospital troops knew about the sergeant's good work. The 91st Evac needed at least one good hoax every day.

Continued Devereux: "Now, our new member of the team is a flight surgeon. Captain Armstrong, please stand up." Devereux's feigned efforts to replace Wells had landed a Captain, a flight surgeon at that.

They all knew that meant surgical training time for the captain, even if he had done a straight (one specialty) surgical internship, and mine had been a "rotating". "All right, now, by the way," Devereux's hand on my shoulder, "Charlie here prefers to be called Charles." This lame allusion to "Victor Charlie" brought forth groans, guffaws and banging of tin cups by the assembled worthies. I managed a sheepish grin. I was gaining confidence that this was going to be a lot better than flight-surgeon.

"Quiet! Now who's going to start the Captain out this morning?" Translation: "Who's going to volunteer to start his training?" I knew the answer to that: the team with the toughest case, to grab an extra hand. Keith Whittaker and Jerry McPherson jumped at it: "Here!" Whittaker shouted as if bidding.

Our job was to treat wounds of the extremities and of the torso, provided there were no complications such as peritonitis (intra-abdominal infection), in which case the soldier would be sent to a larger hospital.

211

About 90 percent of our cases were extremity wounds involving shattered bone and torn soft tissue. Our aim was to restore function as close as possible to normal. Probably two-thirds of our patients were American soldiers. The rest were Vietnamese, many of them injured prisoners, divided about evenly between ARVN (Army of the Republic of Vietnam) and Viet Cong troops. Invariably after these communist guerillas got a look at things from the horizontal perspective of an American recovery ward, their stand was "You name it and I'll do it; just don't send me back."

Jerry and Keith kept me for about two weeks and then declared me ready for any cases. Not solo, mind you: I was always the assistant to a Lt. Colonel or Major. We usually did two cases per morning per team, one to three during the afternoon. The work was tedious debridement of necrotic (dead or dying) tissue, reconstruction of vessels, setting of fractures after debridement of bone. The next day we debrided again whatever tissue didn't survive the night, re-dressed the wound, and re-entered daily until healing was far enough along to send the patient back to the doctors at his home base at Chu Lai, Da Lat, Pleiku, or wherever.

During my first day being broken-in at the 91st, while we were closing a wound the radio called for all available to report to the "launch pad" to bring in a Huey that had been hit while picking up wounded.

McPherson told me to run--he would finish the wound. Along with Devereux, several nurses and medics, I raced out to find a Huey descending with its tail boom slithering side to side from loss of some of its tail rotor control! It hit the pad hard and askew, and while it may not have been at a dangerous angle, it was enough to stir up a bigger than usual cloud of dust. I could feel the hot breeze of those rotors, and I could smell the fumes of the JP4 (fuel). The pilot seemed to be having trouble getting the engine to slow down. We were able to triage the three wounded soldiers while we pulled them out of the helicopter and placed them on legless cots for the run into surgery, props still rotoring and stirring up dust. Two had wounds of the leg (calf) and were less urgent than the third, who had thigh wounds and already had an IV, placed by the field medic. While trotting to keep up with the medics carrying the cots, a nurse and I held dressings on the calf wounds while another nurse bound the thigh wounds.

I would learn soon that these wounded soldiers, especially the one who took rounds in the thigh, were typical of the 9th Infantry Division troops medevacked up from the Mekong rice-paddy Delta. All over his body were scars in various stages of healing and a few of them slightly infected. These could have represented abrasions, or leeches, or both. His face was spotted with blackhead pimples. He needed dental care. His fatigues looked like they had been slept in for several weeks on a riverbank bed. They were stiff and smelled of "bug-juice" (insect repellent), urine, sweat, stale smoke and water-buffalo waste matter. His pants were ripped in the crotch. Each of the ten pockets of his jungle-fatigue jacket and pants held something, and several of them bulged. His hair, almost Marine-short for hygiene reasons, was nevertheless matted by blood and grease. A long gap in the lateral pant leg revealed the dressings of his thigh wound. He was groggy with narcotics. A morphine syringe was fixed to his lapel, standard procedure by field corpsmen and the OR anesthesiologist as a narcotic count to prevent overdosing. The nurses had cut everything off him except his dog tags and mud-soaked boots, which they would soon attend to. The top of one boot was peeled back from a bullet round. When I re-entered the triage room after scrubbing, I saw in the comer his compass, his .45 pistol, plastic canteen, poncho liner and boonie hat. His pocket accouterments were piled on top of his fatigues: letters and photos, acetate maps, C-4 explosive, demo knife, snap link, code lists, small notebooks and 45-caliber rounds. Also on the stack were his Chieu Hoi slips, propaganda to be disseminated to enemy soldiers promising them good money to come over to our side. Still in his breast pockets (until one of the nurses removed them to his collection) were iodine tablets, a shaving razer, and what looked like the remains of C-ration condiments. Affixed to his fatigue shirt just above the left breast pocket (theoretically over his heart) was his CIB (Combat Infantryman Badge). The equipment brought in with wounded men varied somewhat with specialty. One wounded soldier had his M-72 grenade launcher medevacked in with him.

The CIB was awarded to Infantry officers and 11 (11-Bravo: Enlisted Men), or Artillery Forward Observers, assigned temporarily to Infantry, who meet all of the following criteria: wounded, or having been in close combat for over thirty days, or artillery FO's in close combat along with their assigned infantry for over thirty days. The nurses couldn't shower him because of the wound, so they covered him with a sheet. We injected Valium into his IV, which had him carefree within a minute; then Innovar, an oblivion-inducer general anesthetic. While the anesthesiologist and nurses were placing the endotracheal tube, we scrubbed. We put on masks and gloves --and gowns, which we didn't always have. As soon as we loosened his dressings red blood spurted from his Peroneal artery. Jerry clamped it on the spot.

The nurses got his boots off, and although he had evidently not spent the last few weeks at a spa, at least he had no signs of immersion foot. We debrided foreign matter and necrotic tissue for an hour and a half. We pulled a bullet from his thigh bone: my first look at a bullet flat from impact. We re-debrided every other day and sometimes daily until the only remaining tissue was viable. When there was no more necrotic tissue to debride, we closed. If there wasn't enough skin for closure, we shipped him off to the plastic surgeons at Ton Son Nhut.

During procedures our conversation was much the same as the old days in med school and internship. OR can get serious, and the needs of the operation have interruption rights, of course. But politics, sports and man-woman topics were favored. Most nurses would join in readily if they had been "in country" long enough to know the surgeons. Shy ones sometimes had to be led in ("Jane, help us out: Why does Clark Gabel get more sighs than Robert Redford?"). Meanwhile, the chaplain seemed to be everywhere, covering the OR, recovery area, chapel, NCO's or officers' shack to socialize and be available when counsel was needed. Although Protestant, he was authorized to administer Last Rites to Roman Catholics.

Now, I won't say that "MASH" the movie or TV sitcom are a copy of this script, but these dramatizations are true to the essence except for the missing sensory elements such as touch and smell. The movie and television serial are in some ways an exaggeration of life among medical troops whether the setting is Korea or the 91st Evac of Vietnam. But even if it sometimes takes things a bit further than reality, the TV sitcom captures the spirit of the medical corps at an Evac hospital in Vietnam. Young adults acting like kids to make the time go by when unaccustomed

215

to certain challenging conditions: That's the scene the sitcom accurately, and rather slyly, portrays. We were not only unaccustomed to the war environment, we were restless due to the flagging morale of an army with leadership vacuum at the top. On the positive side for us non-regulars, and probably for regulars too, in the theater of war the rituals, regs and polish of the peacetime army are traditionally relaxed. Even more so for the medical corps, especially in Korea and Vietnam. "MASH" the sitcom perhaps somewhat overcolors the picture (we didn't have any mincing Bostonians at the 91st), but its general focus is authentic.

After work there ordinarily was time for a good lounge on the beach. And occasionally "after work" could be pretty early in the day. Of course, any beach-lounging could be, and regularly was, precipitately cut short. We spent at least a part of most evenings at the officers' club, the "Chez When", another tropical shack decked out with reel-to-reel tape music, makeshift wooden tables and chairs, and a bar. On the walls were college banners, duplicates of Green Bay Packers and Chicago Bears numbered shirts, pro-baseball caps, 1st Air Cav insignia (the Horse Blanket), and World War II pictorial adds for Coke and R.C. Cola.

Those of us new in-country were made to understand that all the nurses were already paired off with guys returning to the States before we were and that it was looked upon as poor form to make a move until after the nurse we liked had bid goodbye to her Dr. Feelgood, and that our time would come, so cool it. But even that rule was relaxed by many a combination of friendly nurse and her "short" (soon to leave), indifferent doctor. The nurses presented the expected scale of attractiveness. And yet there was something about jungle fatigues that seemed to enhance their enticement. It was as if clothing designed to conceal curves only intensified their allure through suggestion: If she's captivating in combat fatigues, what will she be in something else? Much of the evening time not passed at the Chez we devoted to connecting that umbilical to home by way of letters and voice tapes or a reel-to-reel tape concert at someone's hooch.

Vietnamese women took care of our hooches for a fee that was probably a lot to them and not much to us. Our living expenses came to less than a dollar per day and ordinarily less than fifty cents, which allowed me to pay off my med school debts during my 12 months in

Mama-san at Charles' "hooch"

Nam. The general procedure throughout South Vietnam during the war was to hire women from neighboring towns or villages in a carefully controlled, formal manner. There was no "I like you, will you come work for me?" Whoever cleaned our hooch and fed us samples of her own cooking was hired through proper military channels. It was easy to get attached to most of these young women, but there was no acting on it since, by regulation, they left the post at dusk. Once we got to know one, she was "Mama-san" if over a certain age, "Baby-san" if under. Most of them learned enough English to communicate with no misunderstanding. "You number one G.I." meant I like you; "You number ten G.I." meant I don't like you, at least for the moment. And if a number ten GI made her mad, it was, "Dee dee mau," her way of saying "Get lost." On the other hand, "Lai Dae" meant "Come here."

These women were remarkable caretakers. They would polish and then line up our boots according to her particular ideas of boot age, or wear, or beauty, or attention earned, or rank (boot rank, not soldier rank). They deployed their sense of order over most of our affairs. Each mama-san would arrange a GI's papers, letters, tapes and clothing in order of her judgment of their importance. Each ironed combat fatigues as nicely as your best dry cleaner. And they put together hot and cold snacks that tried to make us forget where we were.

Before long I began to hope that the army would forget this flight-surgeon business. If I was forgetting it, then they should too. By now I was downright connected with my comrades of the 91st. I liked scrubbing in with any and all of my surgeon buddies, and besides, early on they and the nurses had begun to treat Captain-me as an equal outside the O.R. I wasn't just getting into the whole big-91st Evac-family mode, I had become a part of it. I was a needed assist at surgery, which had become as routine to me as to a resident.

I attended church services and listened to my roommate's short sermons. I joined the Christmas choir. I was the 91st's token Captain. I belonged. Days were hot, Bre'r Rabbit in the briars for an insulation-deprived G.I. like me. Nights here on the shore were cool, and an aromatic breeze blew through those screens. We could hear the waves on the beach. I was ready to settle in for the year. I was settled in for the year.

About 16 weeks after I was introduced to the 91st Evac-family at breakfast, I received new orders: "Report to the 307th Combat Aviation Battalion, 121st Aviation Group near Can Tho in the Mekong Delta." What? Wasn't the Army interested in continuity and efficiency? Weren't unit cohesion and loyalty high on the list of Army priorities? Wouldn't things go a lot better if a guy stayed where he was needed most, where his training was just now really paying off, where he had bonded with his buddies (of both sexes)? I had found my home, and now they want to send me abroad, down to the Delta! I had even become one with the natural setting, a crucial point of morale. Surely, they would see the incontrovertible reasoning behind this if only the sergeant-major had a chance to point it out to the order-issuers.

Later that week I was aboard a C-130 turboprop cargo plane headed for my new assignment. We landed at the Air Force Base 12 miles outside the city of Can Tho. A staff sergeant and his jeep met me at the air base and drove me a few more miles beyond Can Tho to the U.S. Army Airfield Dispensary of the 307th CAB, adjacent to the sergeant's engineer battalion. Differences from my coastal 91st Evac home were already conspicuous. It was hotter and more humid down here in the Delta. Everything was bigger. The terrain was different. Up at the 91st it was lush jungle green; down here it was red Georgia clay, with sparser green above the clay.

Our layout up at the 91st Evac was a bivouac compared with this army airfield, a classic firebase area. Here, in addition to the aviation battalion, there were an artillery battalion, probably a regiment of combat engineers, logistical and signal support companies, and Medical Corps and Medical, Service Corps personnel. The airfield accommodated O-2

Birddog and Mohawk reconnaissance fixed wing aircraft as well as Huey, Cobra and Chinook helicopters. Latrines were 55-gallon drums sawed in half and loaded with used diesel oil. As soon as the drum contents reached a certain level we burned them. There was a big mess hall, a PX, and --for crying out loud- a movie theater. It was as if the geniuses running this war had sent word down that "You're going to be there a decade or two, so you may as well build fort communities." This was Our Town.

The TO&E (Table of Organization and Equipment) was more detailed down here, more sophisticated than up at the 91st. The operating tables were more, shall we say, hospitable; even though we did less surgery here; the x-ray machine was permanent, not portable; the generators were larger -100 instead of 5 KW. Our dispensary was wood-walled and roofed, in contrast to the screened wall, tin-roofed pooches I loved up at the 91st. All dispensaries, headquarters, and notches in Vietnam—even my homey hospital community known as the 91st Evac-were protected by sandbag revetments to at least waist high. Chest high and above was open or screen for breath and breeze, crucial design differences for the tropics. From there the differences so outweigh the similarities that it was as if my 91st Evac and my Mekong Delta experiences were of a different war.

Here at our firebase in the Delta, one latrine burner or another smoked constantly because of the population size of the compound. The mess hall was always busy with cleaning up. Some of the more vulnerable units or valuable equipment were afforded the luxury of revetments reinforced with PSP (pierced-steel plank). Up at the 91st we had merited no such thing. At this base camp compound in the Delta the energy sources and communication center rated PSP. The engineers give the control tower and perimeter guard tower revetments a wrap or three of concertina wire, to which they attached tin cans containing noise-making pebbles. At the wire they spaced machine-gun bunkers and dug trenches between bunkers and towers. Peripheral to the wire they laid mines, both fixed and claymore (surface mines that are convex and explode horizontally). There were bunkers every 25 or 30 meters. At night the perimeter was manned by guards vigilant against attack. Everybody except the doctors and medics carried sidearms or M-16's or both. At the forward position, the perimeter, the guards had M-72 grenade launchers and everybody carried grenades. Just beyond the bunkers were mortar pits. 105 mm artillery guns were offset from the compound just enough to serve as a sleep-sound lullaby machine, as soporific as rhythmic thunder from afar.

There was continuous patrolling by serial nights of fixed-wing aircraft, as well as Huey and Cobra helicopters. I had to wait only two days for my first mortar attack, which immediately set off sirens, the starting gun to grab your LBE (Light Basic Equipment: first aid packet and combat pack, which held four ammo pouches with several 30-round magazines and grenades and grenade snap, pistol belt and suspenders and web gear), and race to the bunkers and getting positions if not already there. Generally, we Medical Corps officers were already inside the dispensary, which was centrally located in a big compound. Most of this was new to me. Up at the 91st we had for defense sand-bag revetments and the ocean. That's for a couple of reasons. One was that we had a garrison of South Korean next door. The other was that a hospital does not the greatest military temptation make. That some of their communist comrades were undergoing capitalist-dog surgery at that very hospital may or may not have weighed onto the Viet Cong's predilection for heeding the "Do Not Disturb" sign at the 91st Evac. Up time we had no airmen patrols, no mortar attacks (although we had a bunker or two just in case), and diesel smoke front the latrine was as rare as holidays. Also, the 91st Evac was a little outpost of Americana here in the Delta. We had Aussies (Australian Army troops), a few ARVN officers and entertainers from all over the Pacific. At the 91st there was no dropping by the battery of 155 and 105 artillery to smell the cordite and feel the concussion distort our faces and hair, as we did here. Unlike the 91st Evac, at the 307th we had a ham radio operation, which provided phone service to the U.S. We would call around midnight. since home was 11 to 13 hours away. There are no interruptions when conversing by ham. When the talker decides it's time to listen, he says, "over," signaling the operator to reverse direction. Phone calls were rationed, and I recall making two of them during my year. They were as thrilling as a first ride in an aircraft.

We medical officers were billeted at the dispensary, consisting of several treatment rooms, two operating rooms, an administration and records area, and private 9'x12' rooms for each doctor. Our medical facilities were by home standards, but far more finished than we had expected. The dispensary was staffed by four physicians, two dentists (Captains Dick Gardner and Frank Meyer), a dozen or so medics (enlisted Medical Service Corps specialists), and other support personnel in records and supply. Each medic had specialized duty, in-patient care, pharmacy, surgery and treatment room, x-ray, or lab. After Fort Sam and the 91st Evac, this was my third arena of exposure to the skills of U.S. Army medics. Their training had them beyond ready for war-theater conditions.

The 307th Combat Aviation Battalion was attached to the 9th Infantry Division, the division assigned to southern South Vietnam, which includes the Mekong Delta in the IV Corps Tactical Zone (CTZ) of Vietnam.

The 307th CAB, our flight unit, carried out reconnaissance and combat missions in the Delta and was allotted two flight-surgeons. My arrival filled an open slot, the other one having been rounded off nicely for some three months by Captain Larry Freeman. Major Robnett and Capt. Bill Rice were not flight-surgeons. The care of pilots was left to Larry and me, but that was the lesser part of our work. The greater part was care of the other troops, the combat engineers, flight support, signal corps, and so on. Cpt. Freeman and I shared those duties and the dispensary with Major Robnett and Cpt. Rice.

Captain Freeman and I observed that medical problems of the pilots were among the most urgent and that they responded the most gratifyingly because the pilots were the most conscientious and diligent patients. But our responsibility was prevention, procedures and training. In war or peace prevention is futile without doctor-patient teamwork. My experience was that aviators and most other officers were highly motivated by the principles of disease prevention. The enlisted men seemed less so, probably somewhat because of a lower level of education, but more so because of lower morale. In any case, we gave them all periodic physical exams, routinely checked the pilots' flight gear for safety, and reminded them about habits of health.

But our banner job was to provide sick call and preventive maintenance to the 3,000 men within the perimeter of the air Held. Combat injuries could arrive at any time. They could originate at any distance away from our compound, especially as a result of helicopter search-and-destroy (S & D) missions; or within the compound, such as mortar raids, "incoming" rockets, or sapper attacks. In a high proportion of these we would deal with the wounds surgically and the soldier came

Dust Off Operation

with us. If we couldn't, we started treatment and transferred him to an evacuation hospital such as my old home up on the beach. If he required exceptional procedures such as for extremity wounds involving a big artery or sucking chest wounds, we medevacked him to a field hospital in Saigon, Cam Ranh Bay, or Japan. The flavor of war at the 307th Combat Battalion, dealing with the freshly wounded or killed, was more pungent than that at an Evac hospital like the 91st, where the soldier is almost certain to survive and knows so.

There were also routine medical (non-surgical) disorders. Routine often meant tropical, including some skin disorders we had not seen outside a book before arrival at the outpost. Hepatitis and systemic tropical diseases such as malaria are examples of disorders we could only diagnose and evacuate, most often to the 29th Field Hospital, a big inpatient facility near Saigon. Supply tended to meet demand. For our gin we had ample quinine, but for our regional lack of malaria we scarcely had quinine tablets. Venereal disease was a headache, since the idea of off-duty relaxation for many soldiers was to pack a 45-caliber pistol and head into the city for some fun. To free ourselves for other diseases and duties, we taught the medics a synopsis of venereal diagnosis and treatment. In the old days, these Mars and Venus problems were punishable in the U.S. Army, but that policy invited its own complications when troops hesitated to lay the facts bare for the surgeon. Punitive measures were replaced by preventative efforts such as one-minute spots on AF VN. But venereal casualties continued to take a big part of our clinic day notwithstanding our efforts to air the risks of sexual action.

Another task was that of psychosomatic disorders and malingering. The two are alike in having emotional sources. They differ in that the emotional basis of psychosomatic (also called "psychophysiologic" or "functional" disorders) is more or less unconscious, while the physical symptoms are real. Often anxiety, with or without depression, is implicated in causing the symptoms and thereby takes part in the diagnosis.

Psychiatrists refer to the ulterior motive --largely unconscious, as pointed out, in the psychosomatic case—as "secondary gain". The malingerer, on the other hand, is aware of his inner conflict, if one exists. He is faking the symptoms he recites to the doctor. Conventionally the malingerer is apparent by his bearing and his fabricated complaints, which are inconsistent with any diagnosis. We occasionally had to evacuate these cases to a psychiatrist.

Drinking was a lesser problem at the 307th CAB, but enough to justify a 24-hour bottle-to-throttle rule.

Marijuana was just budding during my tour but grew during the last years of the war, especially among infantry. One earlier reason for this problem is that in 1967, most army units declared alcohol, including beer, out of bounds for ranks E4 and below, thereby enhancing the temptations of pot, which was easier to get and use. There was a later reason. By 1969 morale was beginning to slide; Conduct hostile to health was its reflection. The ferment that prevailed within our troops issued naturally from their feelings of resignation and frustration. If circumstances were more comfortable, as with some officers and NCOs, this sense of futility was revealed as much by words as by mood. Lower rank enlisted men were not so free with speech around "Doc", whom they didn't know well enough to entrust confidence. But mid-rank officers after an evening drink or two at the club, and multi-striped sergeants (even when Mormon-sober), were increasingly expressive of their disgust with the management of the war before I arrived to witness in '68. Not surprising when the commander-in-chief brushes off this "acceptable level of casualties." Olympian hopes when Nixon took command were quickly "Kissingered". As American troops increasingly sensed that the war was without heading, they correspondingly recognized themselves as political chess pieces and answered with proportionate hostility toward the civilians in charge.

These attitudes varied somewhat depending on the soldier's position. Disillusionment was the prevailing mindset of the career soldier, who looked upon our war policy with a newly opened and inflamed eye. Dejection and defiance better described the drafted men's apparent purposelessness of the effort.

226

In "Nam" the number of days until wake-up-and-go-home were always in your mind. These thoughts became more pronounced with every year the war wore on. Some of us thought, "Let's see if I can get through today without a reminder of my countdown," preferring not to obsess over the number of days lest that increase drag. But I think most troops, of whatever unit or rank, felt that there was a demon on them, with exorcism beyond a miracle until it had haunted for 365 nights. Admittedly, there were those, of any rank, who saw Vietnam as the straightest road to promotion and would re-up without concern for duration. But for most of us, disgust, alienation (despite unit loyalty), and malaise became so blended that who knows which caused or aggravated which. Thus, the ever present radios. Life at home, regardless of any struggle or pain, was more "normal". Voice-tape letters, pictures, news-clippings of special interest and care-packages from home all were sweets with a squeeze of lemon since any reminder of this more normal life teased out just a little unwelcome recognition that some of us would not return, and some would return damaged. Tinge of bitter or not, we craved care packages from home.

Having reached the down slide, the second half of the year's tour, many troops concentrated on the countdown until "wake up and go home." I did not; I was among those who concentrated on getting through today certain of the day's routine as customary.

"Okay, I'm used to taking care of patients. These war casualties are patients. Meals at home were plentiful and good. Meals here are plentiful and, other wars considered, very good. At home I loved crunchy peanut butter; Lots of people I love are sending me crunchy peanut butter, as well as pictures and letters. I worked out every day at home; I do the same here on a ready-made flight line. I despise cold weather; It's hot here."

There were many times when I thought of buddies at home who that evening would be out with their "babes" to hear the St. Louis Symphony or George Jones and Conway Twitty in concert while we were here trying to plug the blood dam with our fingers. Less frequent, but harder to forget, were the instances when I grabbed something and held on while thinking, "Get a hold of yourself, hang on; Don't go mad." These sweaty episodes most often transpired after pronouncing dead or after a surgical procedure on a hitherto fit, intact, like-factory-new body. These mental squeezes could relax within a few minutes; but they could just as well leave the blues in some canister of the brain where they would fester a day or two, come to a head, and then spill over and out. They were an unwelcome reminder of those times in my freshman year in college when my mind, sick for a day, despaired that some personal or global occurrence would block escape forever.

Speaking for myself, then, there were moments of borderline mental illness. My buddies related similar episodes, with the common sub-theme of imagining their friends in the relatively sane world of Missoula, Natchitoches, or Chicago, or serving their country in Europe or at Fort Bliss, and doing just fine, thank you, despite the fatigue of too many hours of work or school. And at the 307th there were occasional cases of panic. I had to pronounce dead our compound's one suicide during my tour. He had fixed his M-16 in a way that much of his magazine unloaded on him, and it was a bad scene. But, I think my own staying attitude was one of simply holding on, trying to use the day's routine as the best mind-preserver.

O.K.'s Post War Analysis

Reasonable people debated America's role in Vietnam. President Kennedy promoted "counterinsurgency" as the answer to Communist expansion. After a 1961 meeting with Soviet Premier Nikita Khrushchev in Vienna, Kennedy said, "In the 1940s and early '50s, the greatest danger was from Communist armies marching across free borders, which we saw in Korea. Now we face a new and different threat. The local conflicts they support can turn in their favor through guerrillas or insurgents or subversion." Vietnam, Kennedy said, would be a test case of our resolve to combat that subversion, and he set out to redesign the military for that purpose; The CIA's Douglas Blaufarb, in his 1977 history of the counterinsurgency era, noted that President Kennedy "took the lead in formulating the programs, pushing his own staff and the government establishment to give the matter priority attention." Kennedy fired Army Chief of Staff George Decker for insufficient commitment to counterinsurgency. Kennedy championed the Army Special Forces ("Green Berets") and increased the number of U.S. military advisers in Vietnam from 900 when he took office to 16,300 at the time of his death. Communist insurgents disappeared from battle in Vietnam following their disastrous 1968 Tet Offensive. (South Vietnam was not defeated by guerrilla insurgents but by a massive cross-border World War-II style blitzkrieg of 20 divisions of North Vietnamese regulars in 1975.)

As for the management of the war, for several years O.K. had been tearing out his hair over the Johnson administration's galactic, invincible incompetence. In 1981, he looked back: "Just as Dean Acheson felt that the best policy was to avoid winning and just hold them enough that they'll get discouraged, so Johnson and MacNamara in Vietnam. We mustn't win the war, but we must keep throwing men in there, and that will discourage them.

To O.K. Armstrong civilian control of the military was imperative. On the other hand, any military commander reticent in the face of civilian defeatist policy lethal to American troops and sailors was a servile coward.

O.K.'s contempt for waxen soldiers was in direct proportion to their rank. In 1966, in a letter to Richard Nixon, whom he suspected would be the next GOP presidential nominee, O.K. set forth his six-part outline for bringing the war to an end favorable to the Vietnamese people. On the part of the (U.S.) government: 1. Announce a clear, easily understood statement of policy... and our determination to restore peace and stability in the area. 2. Stop all weakening statements about negotiations. On the part of the military: 1. Give free rein to the U.S. and Vietnam military forces, working together, to carry out the policy of winning the war quickly. 2. Mine the Harbor of Haiphong and other coastal import centers, notifying all foreign shippers...no more military material...to come to North Vietnam. 3. Bomb the military targets of North Vietnam until all have been systematically destroyed. 4. Permit commanders in the field and on the sea to co-ordinate their strategic and tactical activities. Not included here but a point I heard repeatable from O.K.: If the U.S. Navy and Air Force were allowed a sane military strategy, only minimal, if any, American ground troops would be needed.

Nixon wrote back: Dear O.K., (preliminaries; then): "I agree with those who contend that repeated statements of our desire to negotiate weaken our position and only serve to convince the enemy that we desperately want 'out.' An increasing number of Americans have come around to the view that if we are going to fight this war, then let's not fight it by communist rules."

General John K. Singlaub offers the following history: "Communist supplies from China, Russia and East Europe destined for North Vietnamese and Viet Cong forces were being offloaded at the Port of Haiphong and moved through Hanoi to the logistics system which brought them through a network of trails. There was one major railroad that came down from the Quijing area through a gorge. The more significant movement of supplies from China were on a single railroad down from Nanjing connecting to Lang Son (at NE border of North VN and China) and then into Hanoi. We interdicted that, after which they found it easier to move supply ships into the Port of Hai Phong where they had sanctuary, 'they' being the Chinese, the Russians, and the East Europeans. Russia, Poland and Czechoslovakia were much greater sources of supply than China. MACSOG, the Military Assistance Command Studies Operations Group, was a joint Army-Navy unit specializing in clandestine-missions such as assassination and infiltration. For example, MACSCG troops placed ARVN guerrilla forces, customarily 120 indigenous led by 16 Americans, at a key road junction in the north on the Ho Chi Minh Trail up toward the northern border of South Vietnam, just inland. For three days at a time one company would locate and destroy ammo dumps and direct bombing offensives to cut the trail. A company would bivouac at a critical road junction or on land overlooking such a junction where they could call in air strikes day and night. But what we damaged or destroyed the Communists would repair within 24 hours. Operation Tailwind, by infiltrating major North Vietnamese transportation unit headquarters, captured some of the cardinal documents of the war. With this information we could have done much more damage to the Trail, if allowed. Even at that, if we had taken out Hai Phuong we could have ignored the Trail. A competent plan would have included the elimination of the enemy's supply routes and sources, including his ports, and elimination of his command and control centers and of Chinese rail lines and sanctuaries. MacNamara and Johnson just didn't get it." [end Singlaub].

As for any Chinese troop threat: They were not suited up for the game. The Chinese were in the midst of their Cultural Revolution at the time and had to pull their troops out of Vietnam. They did occupy the northernmost province, Phongsali, of Laos, and they kept advisers with key North Vietnamese units. (Many of these advisers were removed by U.S. Army special-operations troops during the Son Tay raid led by Col. Bull Simon.) The Chinese Communists also had air defense units around and north of Hanoi. There were restrictions against attacking those and against going up to the border of China or across the border of Laos.

Marjorie Armstrong's brother, Lt. Gen. Joseph Harold Moore, commanded the U.S. Air Force Pacific-Vietnam theater at the time [under the general Pacific command of Admiral Sharp or McCain or, perhaps, Gen. William C. Westmoreland. During leave to visit his ailing mother who lived in our home (after O.K. Armstrong had written his letter to Nixon), the Air Force General very clearly outlined measures needed to bring the war to a speedy end, after which a toddler Vietnamese democracy could begin its first steps. In 1981, O.K. remembered: "Now, Marjorie's brother sat on our settee there (pointing), having come all the way from Vietnam to see his ill mother before she died. I said, 'Well General, tell me how we should win that war.' And he said, 'There are three things. In the first place, we should close the passageways open to the Communists coming into South Vietnam. In the next place, we should take out the port of Haiphong. Bear in mind, Russian ships were coming in constantly, and American fliers were not allowed to put a stop to that atrocity--one of the most craven policies ever followed in war. And he said, 'We know where their depots are. We should blast those out. Finally, eliminate all military communication and supply infrastructure, such as rail lines, roads, bridges and ports. The war would be ended in 90 days' time if not before.' Well he was right. These measures would have required few, if any, U.S. ground forces but Vietnamese troops in cooperation with the U.S. Air Force and U.S. Navy. There was no excuse for Johnson's sending half a million men to Vietnam. They were utterly needless; fighting in the jungle on the enemy's terms."

A win strategy in Vietnam would have pertained in either major phase of the war: during the guerrilla-counterinsurgency phase that ended with the disastrous failure of the enemy's 1968 Tet Offensive, or during the post-Tet North Vietnamese Army phase when the NVA invaded South Vietnam with tanks and artillery. Except that if this win strategy had been operative during the first phase, there would not have been a second phase. By reason of that, my opinion at the time was that we should decide whether or not we belonged in Vietnam. If we did belong, then we should turn the war over to professionals who knew what they were doing. If we had no legitimate role, then pack up and go home.

Meanwhile there was something about the U.S. military leadership that disturbed all of us allied in Vietnam, and we of junior-officer rank felt free to discuss the matter amongst ourselves. That "something" was

233

the military chiefs' moral deficiency in failing to stand up and inform the American people that a political syphilis had invaded and corrupted the head of the American body politic, and that President Johnson and his band of the best and brightest blockheads and whiskies were conducting one of history's most eminent military, political and moral disasters. From the time I was transferred to the Delta I began to hear, mainly through off-the-cuff remarks, about how the real soldiers of all ranks felt. Infantry soldiers from sergeants to majors related to me their frustration: "While our huge resources at the depots and stations such as Cam Ran Bay and Ton Son Nhut sprawl unused, we watch a dozen helicopters take off simultaneously to wage another search-and-destroy mission on the enemy's terms."

As 1969 aged, Nixon and Kissinger were giving the impression of having learned nothing and having forgotten nothing. By 1973, all the main combat divisions had pulled out, the South Vietnamese marines and special forces were calling the shots against, and defeating, the North Vietnamese. President Thu requested from President Nixon permission to take the war up Highway 1 north against North Vietnam (In 1974, Kissinger vetoed this). Now things were coming unhinged. The Kennedy-Tunney Amendment to the 1975 D.O.D. appropriations bill curtailed ammunition to the Cambodian campaign and was followed hard by Congressional restrictions of assistance to Vietnam's anti-Communists. The Communists knew American resolve was gone and made their plans accordingly.

Again, from O.K.'s 1981 reminiscences: "Let me go back to that Tet Offensive. In the Tet Offensive, the Communists went all out to attack the cities and towns, forty some of them. They thought that the people of Vietnam would rise up and join them. They were mistaken. While they demolished the towns in some areas, none rose up to join the Communists, which should not have surprised anybody. "The Tet Offensive should have been followed by the President of the United States saying, 'Now you are defeated, now you must surrender, and if you don't we'll continue until there is no North Vietnam Army left.'" If he had said that they would have surrendered, and we would have brought that war to an end. But he didn't have the nerve, he didn't have the guts, he didn't have the manhood. Furthermore, if MacArthur had been allowed to win the Korean war, the Vietnam war never would have happened because the Communists would have been broken in the East. In neither war did we do anything we should have done. In Korea we missed a great chance to stamp out Communism in the Far East. Now, some weak-minded people say, "Well, it's a good thing because now (1981) the Chinese are opposing the Soviet Union." There are two faults there: Communist China looks upon us as their enemy, not the Soviet Union, and such people underestimate and misread Communist Chinese intentions.

Charles' Own Post-War Analysis

About half way through my year in Vietnam I felt the need to ventilate. The worst of my duty at the army airfield was something I never had to do at the 91st Evac: pronounce dead. The bodies of any helicopter pilots killed in action, and some infantry as well, were flown to our perimeter. After pronouncing one of the pilots I had treated, I decided to release some steam by making a statement to the press.

The steam burned only me. In the spring of 1969, I sent to my home town newspaper my impression of the situation. Before submission to the press, my dad deleted the more inflammatory parts, which he knew would be an embarrassment to the Army. He did that, even though I also knew he was tempted to print it uncensored to provoke a Pentagon response, which would give him an excuse to "raise some Ned" (his words) with his friend and former colleague Secretary of Defense Melvin Laird. Dad knew that Laird thought that this Kissinger strategy was a catastrophe of McNamara dimensions, but knew also that Laird was being "a good soldier." Nevertheless, even if the brass agreed with everything I had to say, they just might not like a drafted Medical Corps officer stirring the cauldron. Dad submitted my report with his modifications to the Springfield News-Leader. No more than three days later the colonel commanding then 307th called me into his office. He greeted me with "Doc (to a soldier, the surgeon is always "Doc"), didn't they teach you fellows anything about the army at Fort Sam?" I tried to manage a "What-are-you-talking about?" face.

"You're in the army now, Doc. You don't want to do anything that might harm the enlisted man's morale." The irony of that comment left me trying to sort out various responses, none of which I liked. The enlisted man's morale was being destroyed by lunacy from the seats of authority, and the colonel knew it. I kept silent. He was not being hostile. His demeanor was a lot kinder than his words, and I decided that he was looking for a way out of this and that all it would take was a go-along, a "No problem, sir, I was just trying to help." Actually, I began to like the colonel during our talk. The more in tune I seemed to him, the more harmonious the conversation became. Later, at the officers' club, the aviation group's Lt. Colonel discreetly told me that the colonel had been ordered, "Call in the surgeon and scan his compass," or something of that persuasion. These officers not only agreed with what I had written but most likely had been grinding their teeth over its message since long before my broadcast of it. But they knew the rules. I staged no more crusades in Vietnam.

There was always more to learn about Army ways. The duty-province of a little cadre of sergeants at the dispensary included keeping the medical officers informed ahead of time of regs, customs, and the special ways of this war, this airfield, this dispensary, this colonel, and so on. In short, their job was to deny us entry into trouble. This mission was more consequential at the army airfield, with its mix of units, duties and ranks, than at the 91st Evac Hospital, which was as isolated as the gang on TV's "MASH", and where un-army-like activities could thereby be swept under the cot. At the Aviation Group Dispensary, our chief of non-coms was Sergeant "Laz". At the end of sick-call one morning soon after my transfer from the 91st Evac to the 307th Combat Aviation Battalion, we officers were into some light talk with the sergeants. Major Robnet observed casually that, boy, it sure would be nice to have more 4-0 nylon suture, more cat gut of any size, more of the new IV antibiotic cephalothen and less pen-G. And nothing could be finer than to have some fresher coffee in the morning, with more of a certain kind of doughnuts and less of the other, and two more small radios. Within two days 4-0 nylon and cat gut suture were mysteriously bountiful. Within three days sweeter smelling coffee and more of the preferred doughnuts arrived. And within four days, a radio in every OR. With the exception of the IV cephalothen, all the goodies, without a word, much less fanfare, came from Laz. A day or two later Doctors Robnet, Freeman, Rice and I were standing just inside the short-wave radio room conferring with Sergeant Lazick and Spec-4s Carlos and Woodgie. In the midst of our review, or preview, of the day I blurted out, "Holy Santa Claus, Laz, what a fantastic job! Where did you get all that stuff?" Major Robnet coughed and quickly changed the subject. After the sergeants had left, Robnet said, "Dammit, Charlie, after you let your sergeant know you need something, you don't ask him where he got it."

And with that, at least two indelible lessons for me: Wars cannot be won without sergeants. And, at least in the war-time army, don't bump into something that goes, nor into those who made it go, and certainly not a sergeant who has valiantly liberated something for the company. A President and Secretary of Defense wanting to win that war quickly need not have consulted their admirals and generals. Their sergeants and chiefs would have directed them to swift victory.

Flight hours, about four to six per month as I recall, were mandatory for flight-surgeons. This was a sort of third life for me in Nam. First life, surgeon at 91st Evac; second, "Doc" at dispensary in the Mekong; third, side-seat airman in the Mekong. On with the survival vest (always for Mohawk reconnaissance sorties; only sometimes for Huey missions since ballistic armor protected the Huey, or at least its pilot), flight suit, and ballistic flight helmet with its intercom plug. Off with the jungle boots and on with the full leather flight boots --more flame retardant than jungle canvas. Most of my hours were tallied in Hueys. I'm confident I will recognize the sound of a Huey's engine in the distance even if the next time is well into the next millennium. The same recognition for its other sensory particulars: the smell of its JP-4 (kerosene) and its exhaust; the sight of the pilot scanning his gauges to catch their tilt into green; his shotgun or CAR-15 (an M-16 configuration rifle with a telescoping stock) slung over the back of his armored seat; the crew chief's inspection of the aircraft, checking for JP-4 or hydraulic (transmission) leaks, looking for smoke from someplace it shouldn't be, and examining tail rotor balance; the door-gunner--his .45 strapped to his thigh--going through his check list: putting on his titanium-steel vest, then loading the helicopter's M-60 machine gun and pulling back the charging handle to inject a bullet into the chamber, and looking around to make sure the pilot wasn't navigating the tail rotor into another helicopter while jockeying to take off; the feel of that characteristic jerk and vibration of lift-off; the split second of hover on a horizontal plane and change of the engine's noise while the helicopter cants forward; the diminuendo swish of the rotors as they shut down, the only constant being the whine and whir of the turbine. This sequence was always the same, at Fort Rucker or in Vietnam. The Huey was exhilarating to the senses. Recall in the movie "Patton", it's the sensuousness of the finished battle, with the fog and smoke and the dew making dusk of day, that moves General Patton to inhale through his nostrils deeply and say to himself, "So help me God! I do love it so."

Vietnam heightened the Army air combat sensations I had become accustomed to at Fort Rucker. Here in the war arena there was OD (olive drab) tape over bullet holes in the frame or bullet abrasions of the fuel cells. There were dried blood stains mixed in with the mud and spent casings on the platform. On the pilots' helmets and on the plastic-lined maps covering the insides of the helicopter were graffiti slogans, "This is for Sarah," "Oakland Raiders," "Baby San from Vung Tau," "50 and a wake up," the "50" crossed out and replaced with "49", and so on. As at Fort Rucker, the machine gun was outside and astride the helicopter and pointed downwards during takeoff. But we were on an air assault mission, so, while ascending, the gunners, one each side, would pull the guns in, lock and load, and then test-fire. The idea was to be ready for anything a hundred meters beyond your compound's concertina wire. In this war there was no flying off to the front. The front was just beyond the wire. The command pilot would search out a test place, and the squadron's gunners would "hose it down" for a few seconds to make sure they were in order. There was a pleasant metallic taste to the gun smoke.

I was also a frequent assistant riding shotgun in fixed-wing, twin-prop Mohawk reconnaissance planes. The pilot and I would put on our chicken-plate survival-vests and our ballistic helmets; get into our flight suits; load our .45-caliber pistols, put them on "safe" and put them in our shoulder holsters. I don't recall these rituals of survival as being terribly reassuring. We would fly in parallel rows, plowing-a-head style, memorizing the area with a camera that clicked off frames machine-gun speed, somewhat slower than standard movie frames. The pilot would say, "Now", and I would squeeze. Somewhat too often for my taste the pilot liked to see how closely he could buzz something on the ground without hitting it. There was none of that sort of worry in the Hueys, even if I didn't like the idea of a wing having to rotate to provide lift. Helicopter pilots' descriptions of their "auto-rotation capability" upon taking a hit were less than comforting. The seductive sleekness and power of the two-tandem-seated Cobra attack helicopter helped me rise above my fear. But any such longing for thrills was a safe one --the Cobra was off limits for all but its pilots.

There was diversion at the Aviation Group and the larger perimeter of the Combat Battalion. Late every afternoon my buddy Frank and I would go out to the airfield and run. The first day we tried this we asked a perimeter guard, "What are the chances of getting shot out here? We want to run along the runway." We meant alongside, parallel to it. Frank and I were dressed in army-issue green boxer undershorts and running shoes, but the guard recognized Frank as his dental officer.

"Usually not much action, sir, till after dark. Besides, they're more likely to come after us first." After our daily run Frank and I usually had enough left to join in on the daily game of jungle ball, sometimes officers vs. enlisted men, sometimes dispensary vs. engineers. Jungle ball was volleyball modified to provide no limit to how far fists could reach over the net into enemy territory. After a few minor injuries the colonel reinstated Olympic rules. On-tour entertainers visited our officers' club two or three nights per week. They would do the circuit of a camp's "clubs" (Officers, non-commissioned officers and enlisted men's) and then move on to the next outpost. This was seen as a morale boost by the Army, and we agreed with their focus on that. Most of the entertainment was music, but there were comedy and dance routines featuring Philippine, Hawaiian, South Pacific or other oriental women.

On nights when there was no show, most of us split the evening between the club and home-reach with letters and tapes. And, of course, there were evening and night emergencies.

One night in January a few of the troops from Maryland were planning to stay up and listen on short wave to Super Bowl III, in which the Baltimore Colts with quarterback Johnny Unitas were certain to run and pass over Joe Namath and the New York Jets. The troops from Maryland had already placed a big sign over the roof of the Officers' Club: "Baltimore Colts: Super Bowl Champs". The live broadcast would start at 0100. I didn't have the right stuff for an all-nighter, so to bed. Perhaps half an hour after falling to sleep I was aware of sirens. For a few seconds, the characters in a provocative dream seemed to have pitched camp in my head, but that notion gave way against the onslaught of reality. I opened my eyes, literally and figuratively, but could see nothing physical, not the form of my own room. This was darkness as close to absolute as I had experienced outside. I sat upright in my bunk groping for my mental coordinates. I heard explosions coming from the direction of the airfield. My inner voice may have said something like, "God, this isn't going according to our agreement." But my exchange with the Lord was interrupted within seconds by the voice of Sergeant Laz. I knew he was in my room, though I couldn't see so much as his silhouette. "Captain Armstrong, we are under sapper attack, sir. We're having incoming and hit-and-runs at the airfield. They're hitting the Hueys and Chinooks. Most of the Cobras got away. They may be coming at us. Sir, if you will stand up, please, I'll put on your flak-jacket and helmet. I have your rifle if you need it later."

My flak-jacket? My rifle? That I owned a flack-jacket and helmet was an unexpected intelligence and certainly that I owned a rifle. I said nothing except, "I'm here, Laz," which seemed silly as soon as I got my head enough to realize he already knew that. I had been awaken from a non-rem (deep) sleep. My body was Adrenalin-soaked, a novel condition. Now, perhaps thirty seconds after waking, I was trying to get my bearings. I didn't want to say anything stupid to our favorite sergeant. In total darkness --no flashlights during incoming-- Laz's experience was evident as he put my helmet and vest on me. The zipper of the jacket snagged, and I let Laz jiggle it free, which he did patiently and without an oath since, as I learned, it habitually snagged [-s.o.p]. The helmet's sweat band dug uncomfortably into my head. "Now, sir, if you'll grab the back of my jacket I'll lead you to the control room." The sergeants of the dispensary had trained to cold rote how to handle the doctors during "incoming". One part of the procedure was to keep our rifles away from us until extremis.

We went to the radio room where specialists were monitoring transmissions between the control tower and Cobra pilots, who were searching -for the enemy. Some of the VC liked to hit at night and hit they did. The VC had thrown sapper charges at a guard post, killing two guards --enough to make entry. Then they had destroyed a line of Hueys and Chinook transports by running and throwing explosives! I don't know why they failed to hit the Cobras first, except that they probably didn't know where they were and took what they came to first. The scene reminded me of a medic's account of a shot-up helicopter's crash at his compound near Play Cu before he joined us: claxons screaming, everybody running out to pull men off the gyrating machine and put out the fire in the fuselage while trying to dodge the flying rotors. In our case, the bedlam was caused by a supper attack rather than a crash. We treated the wounded and pronounced the dead, and then listened to the Cobra-control tower exchanges until dawn. By then the VC would have disappeared even if the pilots had not finished their "search-and-destroy".

During my eleventh month in Vietnam orders came for my second year of duty. I was to report to Redstone Arsenal in Huntsville, Alabama. "What's Redstone Arsenal?" I wondered. I soon learned it was the headquarters of the space program. Cape Canaveral was just a launching pad while Houston was merely where things were tracked. Redstone Arsenal was where the action had been all along--where Dr. Werner von Braun did his work.

In late November 1969, I left the 307th compound for my flight to Tokyo and on to San Francisco. For me and a few others, the curtain was coming down on this exceptional year. I surveyed the stage of this drama one more time while driving in our jeep to the flight line and while the Huey lifted off for the airport near Saigon. My feeling was not so much elation as relief. There was none of the wistfulness or sentiment of attachment that I felt upon leaving the 91st Evac several months before. But I wondered what this "home" for a time, the dispensary, the landing zone which was our volleyball court, the mess hall, the O-Club: what all this would look like ten, twenty, forty years later. And I felt sorry for the troops who had to stay two or 365 more days. What tremendous and mixed feelings I had about the year. There was the sense of privilege for helping care for these brave young troops and the realization that, after all the carnage was added up, the sum might be futility. I had no thought of ever wanting to return, but now I'm not so sure.

PART SEVEN-REVIVAL

Strange Looking Glass

The sea serves as an image for the passage of life's brief voyage. Each gaze upon it from a vessel with unique variables of seaworthiness and bearing. Below the horizon is the unknown. Through the fog we see, and sometimes find, fulfillment, as in beauty and in love. Illness itself is sometimes an annealing heat that enhances love. Part of that heat is the diminished ability of the infirm to return love in kind, or at least to express it. Ill health and its miseries inflict a self-absorption best escaped by recovery. Full realization of life's affirmative moments presupposes riddance of self-preoccupation and self-absorption. It presupposes wellness. There are countless illnesses, but there is only one health.

When I was a resident in medicine, it occurred to me that I was distracted by other things that seemed just as interesting. Given that, I allowed myself a spree of speculation: "What if I were to leave medicine and pursue one of these distractions as a calling? But what if I then changed my mind: back to medicine or off to another interest? I can't leave medicine-I'm not going to make a living following my whim of the month. But what if I learn one of those whims well enough to teach it? And then what if the demands of teaching restrict my whim of the month just as much as a residency does?" The matter was teeming with unknowns. Even if full realization had come to me during medical training that this was not my true calling, I probably would have proceeded anyway for lack of conviction about a true calling. "I'll stick with medicine," I decided. Soon I discovered the rewards of the emotional give-and-take with a gratified patient and the reassurance afforded by a growing practice, which presumably signifies patient satisfaction. Then I felt safe in concluding that I had probably done the

246

right thing. But I'm not given to drawing firm conclusions. I began to feel a gnawing, irrepressible resentment for having to work for a living, unless, of course, paid work meant doing my interest of the moment. I was taught, both explicitly and by example, that behavior and consequences are wed. But we are also served reminders that there are unforeseeable consequences, some unrelated to behavior and some the unexpected upshot of behavior. For example, when I opened my first medical practice my office manager, trying to be helpful and motherly, asked me about my health insurance. "I don't have any; I don't get sick." Even though I had rarely gotten sick, I meant it somewhat tongue in cheek. Her look read "Smart aleck!"

Well into my second decade of private practice, stress was nullifying the rewards. I was in Alexandria, Virginia, working solo in a very busy practice and therefore always on call. I was a fitful sleeper. I was increasingly frustrated with patients who showed no interest in healthful living. I was bothered by the insane politics of medical care. I began to resent the time constraints, which allowed little for my personal interests. I was sick with flu more often than ever before. For eleven days I was an inpatient with pleuritis ("pleurisy" or inflammation of the pleura, the lining of the lung), which features a jabbing pain neutralized by refraining from breathing. The antibiotics I took made food look so repulsive that I kept cereal boxes in the bathroom where I wouldn't see them. So, I lost 12 pounds, not healthy in someone genetically unable to produce reserve fat. Even after recovering, my brain must have been thoroughly in a fog not to have seen the Semaphore flags that read "Change heading!" Meanwhile, I was divorced and dissatisfied with single life.

Early the summer of 1989, about three years after the pleurisy, I noticed by way of the bathroom mirror a subcutaneous lymph node below the curve of my jaw on the left. Subcutaneous means just below the skin, for the most part where nodes belong, but in the healthy person they behave: they are neither seen nor heard. Symptoms are complaints by the patient. Signs are objective findings detected by the eyes, ears, nose or fingers of the physician. When confronted with symptoms or signs pertaining to themselves, doctors, probably more than lay people, are prone to the extremes of "Who, me? This is nothing." Or, on the other hand, "This is going to kill me unless something quickly proves otherwise." I managed to convince myself-and it didn't take much coaxing-that this node was draining some minor infection and was accordingly trivial. The absence of symptoms (an enlarged node being a sign), reinforced this frame of mind, so I watched the node grow for several weeks.

There was another sign but apparent to me only later. Snap shots taken that summer weren't from my camera, and I didn't see them until well into the fall. I wasn't happy with what I saw, and it wasn't just a matter of the cruel tick of time's metronome. I looked sick. But that was after the fact. During that summer, I didn't get the picture looking in the mirror. "Cancer Suspect" was not on my self-diagnosis list.

Medical jargon is mostly pilfered Latin and early Greek. "Tumor" is Latin for a swollen something. By mid-August I had to face myself and admit that this tumor was too big to ignore. I showed it to my plastic surgeon friend Khosrow Matini, M.D. He scheduled a surgical resection of the probable node, which would then be sent down the hall to be read and translated by the pathologist.

Dear Diary

August 22. I was lying on a gurney, torso inclined, in the OR, pre-op section, of Alexandria's Mount Vernon Hospital. Joe King, M.D., head of the Department of Anesthesia, walked up and said, "Hi, Charlie." He wanted to shake my hand, but both of his were full of paraphernalia. He inserted an intracath line into a vein of my forearm and told me that what he was injecting would make me feel relaxed, and then slightly "dizzy." This was a good example of a physician's judgment on proportioning the mix of technical-professional and lay jargon with another doctor who is now patient. "Dizziness" is a nonspecific term—vertigo is one type, lightheadedness another, gait instability another, and so on. Dr. King meant a dizziness different from the three or four types every physician is used to dealing with. Within seconds the ceiling and upper portions of the wall in front of me started waving and billowing in a pleasant sort of way.

Instantly, it seemed, I awoke in recovery. I had no time awareness between pre-op and post. Within a few hours I was delivered by wheelchair to Marilyn (my first and always office manager) and Lou (Lourdes, our senior nurse and dean of my employees), who drove me home and helped me to bed.

Two afternoons later my head was clear enough that I could ring up Marilyn at the office to ask if she had received the report on just what kind of infection this had been, or, at the worst, still was. Marilyn, after a halting and brief introduction, replied, "It appears to be a neoplasm."

There are several possibilities why Marilyn used the word "neoplasm" instead of "cancer" or "a malignancy". The least likely is that this was Dr. Matini's wording to her-doubtful since preferred doctor-to-layman would be something on the order of "The biopsy was positive for a malignancy." Most likely, Marilyn was familiar with "neoplasm" but used it as an equivocal term for "tumor", the better to be easy on me. Sorry, but a verdict of neoplasm is not equivocal. Her matter-of-fact delivery may have been an attempt to keep me or herself calm. My summer vacation from reality was over.

After some seconds of hearing only silence from me, Marilyn began to cry and left the phone. Judy Cummings, who had joined our team as junior nurse only two months earlier, quickly picked it up and spoke some words that I recall only as being the natural, warm Judy. Whatever we said, our exchange was brief because I was suddenly incapable of conversation. I could summon only, "Come over as soon as you can," in a hoarse whisper. She left me a vague awareness that someone would soon come be with me. Cheryl Keane was a close friend, especially so during times of stress. She and I had dated a few years earlier. She had since married and was now an employee of mine. Judy may have said that she would call Cheryl, this being one of Cheryl's days to manage her dress shop instead of my patients.

Words are imperfect descriptions of human emotion because any word selected most likely carries its own spread of overtones beyond the meaning intended. Perhaps the arts convey emotion more accurately, but the medium for my account will have to be words. As soon as Marilyn's words got to my brain, I could feel my heart begin to race. At the time there was no thought, "My heart is racing." My awareness was of cancer and its connotations, of its onslaught against my mother and my sister, its hold on them and its eventual victory over them. I became slightly nauseated and unmistakably weak even though I was sitting down. My body responded with these physical symptoms, even as my mind's eye was dazzled by a blinding flash of doom.

I had no rational thoughts, such as, "I need to get rid of this nausea." If there were any thoughts at all, they must have been the primitive, garbled "no" of a two-year old whose language is spare but whose head is top-heavy with the concepts of refusal and rejection when a favorite toy is snatched away. My toddler naysaying clashed with a more adult awareness of the end, my end, coming soon. These mental impressions were not articulated, such intelligible thoughts being unnecessary or even impossible. My breathing changed: long expirations, strangely audible, as if forced, no more under my control than the other physical changes cascading over me. I felt a generalized constriction; It was closer, I would guess, to what it must feel like being chained to a wall than to the sensation of the chest being squeezed by a vise as described by coronary patients.

Fancy yourself caught in an arctic blizzard unprovided: no coat, no shelter, no dog, no sled. I found myself in the totalitarian element: the abrupt arrest of all self-determination. Its sinister companion was helplessness that I would never know the reason why. This particular strait between seas that are the human condition might be compared with the following scene, which I will sketch without any presumption of describing the helplessness of totalitarian entrapment in just a few sentences. Consider yourself leading your normal life in the company of family or friends in a room that is tastefully provided to represent everything "positive" about your life. Suddenly the "authorities" arrive with their enforcers and announce that irregularities in your file have been noticed. You will not be permitted to leave the room until the Committee makes further decisions about your case. Your friends and relatives can come and go as they wish-having cancer does not confine one to Solitary, except emotionally at times-but you must stay. Your warm room is now an elegant brig that fills its prisoner with spirit-strangling frustration and fear. You feel mentally incarcerated by a dreaded but still unknown outcome. To further understand your sudden loss of control, suppose yourself arrested for a capital crime in a case of mistaken identity. You hear the jury read a faulty verdict: "guilty", There is no appeal, no rationale. You are helpless, anxious, dreading the sentence: "Death". This incapacitation, this defenselessness, is the cancerous mind.

My gloom was darker than all-lights-out in Vietnam because that night in Nam I thought I would survive. I groped for some reason why I developed cancer. I, who had tried diligently to be Mr. Prevention since adolescence, what had I done to cause this? Was I that innocent Mr. Health whose life is arrested by the Secret Police, then confined and immobilized without any clue as to why? Were my assumptions about prevention just hot air contributing to the whirlwind? Within several weeks my mind would clear enough to wonder whether years earlier I should have traded in bad stresses for good ones or merely avoided chlorine in swimming pools or the chemicals in decaf coffee? But back then, searching out a clue on my own would have required thought, not my mind's frame at that moment. So, I brooded.

The mental-emotional state of defenseless dread, close upon staring death in the face, can most easily be portrayed by its physical attributes. One's emotional condition brings along its physical attendants; or if the condition is physical, the attendants will be emotional. Physical and emotional are not so much a mortise joint as they are a servomechanism, which keeps a level or a heading by correcting any deviation downward or left with a sufficient upward or right. But if human mechanisms of self-correction are wrenched by illness, they may become self-aggravating, bad making for worse. Although physical and emotional are integrated, for purposes of clarity they should be dealt with separately. Physically, it was weakness that felt like paralysis for some moments. I had trouble calling up enough resolve to get out of the chair and go someplace to lie down after dropping the phone receiver. If the phone had needed to be put up instead of down, the up-putting would have been a task. The normally reserved autonomic nervous system reminded me, with nausea, palpitations, and dry mouth, that it was there and in working order. But this reminder was a matter of later recall. The fixation of the moment was on feeling, on emotion capable of being penetrated by nothing conceptual except oblivion. Any assurance is clung to like flotsam floating by one overboard.

As I mentioned, having just heard Marilyn's words, I couldn't manage more than a hoarse "Somebody come." I stared at the wall until Cheryl arrived. I heard her open the door and search my townhouse until she found me. Cheryl's a veteran of this war, herself now several years in remission from Hodgkin's disease, so she could empathize-she met me with understanding and sympathy. As soon as she hugged me I started crying. She began a speech that was partly pep talk and partly a gentle reprimand for showing signs of weakness, a disposition she judged inappropriate for the fight ahead. Her sermon included such counsel as, "It's time you started doing more of the things you want to do," and "I'm not going to let you get down."

Lou and Marilyn followed Cheryl's arrival at my house by about 15 minutes. After some quiet conversation, Cheryl said, "Now we have to go to lunch, and you're going with us."

There was a distinctly macabre atmosphere inside that restaurant, and I was puzzled and resentful that the diners at other tables didn't seem to notice the weird gloom. M' Ladies put on their best cheer and made sure I forced down a bowl of soup.

The news of having cancer turns on the switch labeled "Mental Impotence", and that mode prevails until someone or something comes along to turn on another. Cheryl knew the benefit of generating a change of mental atmosphere, of attitude, and to do this she early on exercised the leadership that goes beyond passive friendship. The immune system is eternally grateful if anxiety of this order is countered quickly so as to fortify the mind and body for repair.

Morale has a direct line to immunity. The patient must realize, the-sooner-the-better, that he or she must stand and fight despite being haunted by unknowable's such as the eventual outcome or the amount of meaningful human contact to be received along the way. I would imagine myself alone, locked Admiral Byrd style in my ice-bound lair for several months with no telegraph line. The absence of healing human contact might parch the healing humors and kill me before the cancer had its chance. For myself, solace from others and the thought that there might be a "greater power" with like concern for my wellbeing were comforting enough that I now regard it as having been therapeutic. As a medical doctor, and as one who has never heard the Greater Power speak clearly, I find that having a human medium for spiritual solace and consolation is in one way advantageous: It is received by the human senses and is at least in that regard more persuasive.

One reason even the spiritually most fortified would have a hard go as a cancer patient in seclusion is that many manifestations and conveyances of spirituality are human in expression. All spiritual realization is human, or at least what contains that awareness is a human being. It's partly through the works of nature and art that the mighty resonances of the eons and of universal creation make their way to our souls. Music that moves us spiritually was composed by humans, inspired as they were. And even the spiritual components of our appreciation of nature, whose arrangement speaks of a more skilled composer, are realized on human terms. Nature is not expressed "humanly", it's expressed naturally. But our perception of it, our enrichment by it, our sharing of it and gratitude for it happen only on the best human terms we can come up with. One of the most beautiful scenes in my memory, a sunset on a beach in southern Washington, I had the misfortune of experiencing alone. I can tell you that sharing it with another human would have enriched its meaning to me far beyond my having shared it only with its Artisan.

If an experience a person finds spiritual brings more satisfaction when shared with another person, it also brings more strength. When we reach out with our utterances to the infinite Almighty, don't we do so with feelings of inadequacy, in human terms and with the hope that our mortal effort is noticeable? Along with that stark, hoarse cry to the Healer we hope is sitting on the edge of our sick-bed, to include others in the struggle with illness and to have communion with them during recovery is to foster and abet the recovery I speak as a crossover study, because I've been the subject of the experiment both ways, sick with and sick without. My sickness of mood freshman year in college when my best support was miles away was "without". Given an illness, I recommend "with".

Recall that this is still day one, if you'll forgive these heavy-fingered digressions. After that tasteless lunch with my office family, work was beyond thinking. So off to home for the afternoon with my company-Cheryl, our receptionist Marlene, and Lou-who that afternoon watched over me in shifts. My Alexandria brother Stanley's pastor dropped by. His young Olympic decathlon athlete appearance and wholesome outlook were helpful like sunshine after weeks of sullen clouds.

Marilyn was on the phone in search of a physician to fill in during my absence. Within hours she found an internist, Rosario Ignacio, M.D., who became more than a fill in: she eventually joined our team. My girlfriend Jay Malkie and I had parted ways some two weeks earlier. It was the highest relief to hear her voice at my door and have her presence that evening. Although she was not able to intervene in the practical matters of my illness as others would do-she was a divorcee working full time and raising a teenage son-she continued to provide the most comfort imaginable under the circumstances. Later that evening my two oldest brothers, Milton and Kay, arrived from Florida thanks to Marilyn's notification. Marilyn and Cheryl spent much of the afternoon arranging visits for me to various specialists for the work up. My office family, clan-family, and friends were rallying around, bringing with them an inkling to my mind that I might survive.

Role Reversal: Getting Worked Up

August 25. Since the node was metastatic, the search for the primary cancer site begins. First is bronchoscopy, an exploration of the throat and trachea with a flexible tube-shaped scope and its light-source and biopsy tool, to be done by Felix DiPinto, M.D. The relatively new drug, Merced, was a significant advance, bringing on "sleep" less deep and leaving the brain more intact hours after the operation than the usual general anesthetics. The surgeon, or bronchoscopist, does his or her work, the patient remaining as passive as with any anesthesia but destined to come out of it with amnesia for all but a snapshot memory of the procedure. Except my snapshot wasn't visual but an instant of Felix's voice over an impression of something foreign inside me somewhere. The verdict on Felix's work was negative, meaning all findings normal. That brought on opposing thoughts. I was glad all findings were normal because it increased the chances that the primary site was small and early. On the other hand, I had reason for concern if the primary was too small to find: That would mean chemotherapy--a shot in the dark for this cancer. So, it was not to celebrate the report that Lou called together a little party for dinner that evening at her home. Dinner by Lou or my girlfriend Jay was to become a regular gift to me for the next few months.

Another visit to the operating room had already been scheduled for the next day. One day Merced, the next day the real McCoy: general anesthesia. Dr. Miguel Acevedo scheduled me on his OR roster for a series of biopsies, a series meaning anywhere in my mouth, pharynx, Eustachian tube or larynx that he, the otolaryngologist, deemed appropriate while wandering around therein. That night I was restless with chills and muscle cramps, which I now attribute to worrying about surviving the next day's anesthesia. I hadn't worried about surviving my first anesthesia with Dr. King just a few days ago, maybe because no such concern could penetrate my cancer fear, and Dr. DiPinto's that very morning had seemed quite worry free. But this night the anxiety over the sleep of general anesthesia kept me awake. Any sleep deep enough that there is no sense of time is cause for anxiety in a normal human, even for doctors, who know better than most that it's no more dangerous than travel by train.

August 26. When I awoke in Recovery my two visiting brothers greeted me with "all negative," to which I responded, they later reminded me, with a thumb-up. Thumb and up each had a reason. Maybe because the sleeper newly awake from anesthesia is not your first-class conversationalist and because my throat would be unable to make language sounds for the next day or two. This was the first of several invasions that would keep me hoarse or speechless until the end of the year. Thumb up because, again, with the primary (cancer) too small to find readily, maybe it was not too advanced to deal with. The other thumb should have been up in gratitude for waking after the feared anesthesia, but I'm sure I was too much under the influence to recognize the minor point of still being alive. As I pointed out, problems with anesthesia are rare: The only people who worry about it are those being put to sleep-physicians being notoriously the worst. I was about to become very familiar with hand cramp, the reward for communicating minute after minute with pen and paper. I think it was when I was being wheeled from Recovery to my room that Cheryl, increasingly impatient with the proceedings, ambushed my moving gurney. She announced that she had scheduled me to see an oncologist at Georgetown University.

August 28. CAT (computerized axial tomographic or "CT" for short) scan morning at Mount Vernon Hospital. The required motionlessness drove me crazy. I made a very unprofessional shimmy after about thirty minutes on that hard table, and they had to repeat a section. For purposes of professional orientation, we physicians should submit ourselves once, and in advance, to all procedures we order. My entourage and I met at otolaryngologist Dr. Miguel Acevedo's office to discuss options. So far, the work-up was negative. Dr. Acevedo advised me to see the head-and-neck surgeon Haskins K. Kashima at Johns Hopkins University (Hopkins School of Medicine and "distinguished" being redundant). This we scheduled for a week ahead, the earliest date possible.

August 31. Cheryl and Marilyn took me to Georgetown University. The pivotal outcome of this appointment with an oncologist was to be scheduled soon thereafter with someone else, Dr. William Harter, head of Georgetown's Department of Radiation Medicine. But what was seared into my memory about this meeting with the oncologist was some want of diplomacy on the part of Dr. Harter's colleague. Marilyn, Cheryl and I were sitting side by side, Cheryl between Marilyn and me. Some minutes into our discussion, the oncologist remarked that if no primary were found, my five-year survival chances were "so-and-so." This inarticulate filler stands in for the figure offered by the good doctor, for within seconds my mind had rejected it, or I should say had deleted the memory of it. This left me no less sagging with the emotional weight of his message, a weight greater than the mind's capacity for losing with computer speed whatever knowledge it finds intolerable. After some later reconstruction, without the sick mind's need to suppress discouraging words, I can allow that the aforementioned so-and-so equaled somewhat less than 50 percent In other words, "If we don't find the primary, get used to the idea of closing things down before Earth does five more around the sun. He was reminding me of medical knowledge I had shifted to my brain's oblivion-hold to lighten its burden.

But let's go back to the moment the doctor spoke this malignant number. Instantly I became short of breath, not in the form of hyperventilation but of an attenuated breathing, the immediate loss of either the urge or the ability to breathe regardless of the nervous system's call for more oxygen. I slumped but didn't collapse. The inner ear's labyrinthine balance mechanism that contributes to keeping us humans upright on only two legs is able to compensate somewhat for an unexpected collapse of muscular strength. Thus, I stayed in my chair despite the sudden failure of my posture and with no possibility of effort to regain it. My visual field constricted to a small tunnel-end at some part of the floor in front of me, and that was blurred. My body was overcome with these physical reactions to the doctor's percentage, even if my mind was not. My mouth became dry. I remember most of the symptoms, and they were a variation of the syndrome I had experienced when this saga began seven days before.

My only awareness at that instant was dread, not its physical sensations. All thought but one was obliterated. I didn't think, "My mouth is dry, my chest is constricting, I'm nauseated." I was consumed with a thought that blocks out all other thoughts or awareness: I might or probably would soon die. I was a dazed, speechless mass of invasive physical responses with a mind that now could take in or process nothing involving deliberation, a mind aware only of fear. Within a second or two of the doctor's announcement of my chances, Marilyn, separated from me by Cheryl, said to her with a tone of urgency and slight reproach, "Cheryl, hold his hand." I didn't have the energy or inclination to look up to Cheryl's face. The feel of her hand around mine I confirmed what her body language had already told me. Our responses to his statement were instantaneous reflexes, but mine was distress, while hers was anger. She was trembling with fury at the oncologist and was struggling to contain it. He had undermined the foundation of hope she had taken a lead in building for me. I had never seen Cheryl constrain herself under such a challenge as this doctor's insult to her sensibility, although that didn't occur to me then. Nothing occurred to me at the moment except general impressions of Cheryl's disgust and my tormented forebodings. Marilyn was positioned so that in the periphery of my vision I caught her flushed face, which probably registered concern or embarrassment rather than anger. As we were leaving the hospital and the doctor was no longer lending us his ears, Cheryl expressed some feelings by word but more by expression. On the way home, she and Marilyn were quiet. They made no reference to the doctor's statistic and didn't review what he had said about my illness. They did repeat to me the schedule he had outlined, because after the doctor's remark they had noticed I was incapable of taking part in the discussion that followed and knew I had retained nothing of it. Cheryl again reviewed the plan for me later, and Marilyn had to remind me after that.

September 1. More CT scan views of the pharynx were taken. They taped my head to the table for the 90 minutes. My reputation was spreading.

September 5. Marilyn, Cheryl and I met at Georgetown U. Hospital with Dr. Harter, who recommended radiation to the neck, a nine-week course, five days per week; no surgery.

September 6. The three of us drove up to Baltimore to meet Dr. Kashima at Hopkins. I knew very quickly I was in the room with a master, that is, one in love with his work, in that rarefied stratum far beyond competence. It wouldn't take two rounds of my fingers to count those I have known during my career, a majority of them at universities, where there is more of what they love than in private practice. Some of them, such as Dr. Thomas Troost, now of Washington D.C., leave academic for private practice for personal or "political" reasons. These are the C. Thorp Rays of medicine, the Hugh E. Stephenson's of surgery, representative of those whose place in the scheme of life is so natural that to watch them work is to watch an eagle in flight. To find a Jascha Heifetz of violin, a George Patton of battle, a Vermeer of painting or a doctors' doctor is one of life's rare privileges. Such maestros' interests in life are restricted, but their method is focus; In other words, their furrow on the earth may be narrow, but it's deep. After giving Marilyn and Cheryl a grand tour by scope and video of the inside of my neck, Dr. Kashima was undecided about surgery. When a surgeon, especially one presiding at the summit, is a straggler about surgery, one tends to jump down on the "no" side of the fence, especially if one is the patient. I trusted his analysis.

We then drove directly from Baltimore to Georgetown University for a meeting with Thomas Troost, M.D., head of their department of otolaryngology. Dr. Troost, as I mentioned, has the qualities that evoke complete confidence from fellow professionals, and, in my case, early on.

Like Dr. Kashima, Dr. Troost had mixed feelings about surgery and was leaning toward radiation alone. But first he wanted to have his own go at my throat with the biopsy pincers. That evening I called Jim Kerry, M.D., my trusted surgeon friend of not too old days in Santa Barbara.

Jim advised that I listen to my own inner voice. My inner voice counseled against surgery. Maybe Casey Stengel would have said, "If in doubt about a 'Y' in the road, don't take it." Then I called up my friend Khosrow Matini, M.D., the surgeon who removed the node two weeks earlier. Khosrow was even stronger against surgery.

September 8. Marilyn and Judy drove me to Georgetown for Dr. Troost's biopsies. This time I was awake while they wired me up for monitoring during anesthesia. I don't know how many hundreds of times I've scrubbed in for surgery, but this was my first time to enter an operating room both supine and awake. The walls were lined with masked knife-people. My gaze shifted to the anesthesiologist who had my life and my mind in her hands. Not only could I feel my heart pounding, I could hear it on the monitor, which was Morse-coding back to me "Your anxiety is now increasing geometrically with every beep you hear." They put me out of my panic within a couple of minutes, although I can tell you it seemed longer. May this pre-op method be put permanently to sleep.

September 8-10. My worst anesthesia hangover so far, the most frustrating symptom for me being its interference with sleep.

September 11. Speech was difficult even with the voice enhancer my brother Kay bought for me. Dr. Harter called Marilyn to say he wanted to see me. Cheryl drove me to Georgetown. I spent most of the afternoon on the X-ray table in the Simulation room, where Dr. Harter and the radio- therapy technicians prepare the patient for radiation, which is administered in another room. The technicians gave me a few moments warning that I was about to be tattooed, amounting to a few tiny colored spots on my chest and neck to guide the placement of radiation. My imagination took this business much further than needed. This invasion of my body! This permanent reminder! This tacky insult when my dignity is already escaping my grasp! I was about to learn I could choose between dignity and therapy.

September 13. Marilyn tells me that Dr. Harter called to say Dr. Troost's biopsies indicate the left tonsil as the site of origin. "Origin" carried the unhappy implication that it had migrated. Well, it had, to the node that starred early in this chapter. The next day Dr. Troost called me with the same information. The day's delay was perhaps for time for a visit to Pathology.

Some of My Own Medicine

September 18. A Monday. Radiation therapy begins. The mechanics of this were to lie supine on a standard hard radiology table, passively allow the technicians to arrange my body in a precise position, take a holding-rod between my front teeth, listen to the technicians escape from the room, and lie motionless for two minutes and accept what I couldn't see or hear, and for a while, couldn't feel. As the weeks went on I could feel cumulative effects, first on and inside my neck, and then systemically (within the rest of my body). Being treated for cancer was a semester with many lessons, and here I wish to deal with a few. First, I emphasize the knowledge and experience gained as a doctor can easily aggravate, rather than alleviate, his mental turmoil as a patient. His tendency is to dwell not on the rosiest scenario but on the scenario with no rose at all, in tandem with creating imaginary ones, all bad, that may not exist. And a corollary to that-true for any patient but perhaps enhanced by medical training--is that every occurrence takes on meanings bounded only by the possibilities inside the patient's morbid head. Consider the blue and red tattoo points marked on my neck to guide the technicians while aiming the big machine. "So you're hoping to get this behind you, are you? Well, these marks will stay with you even if you survive." The technicians didn't say this, of course, but I said it for them, loading each point of the dye-needle with punctilious and overwrought symbolism. If you saw the movie *The Doctor*, recall that doctor's patient was distraught because some phantom in his brain had the rays, aimed at his throat, missing by the span from there to his gonads. The technician had to keep repeating, "You don't need the lead apron, doc, you really don't." Now as I said, physicians-at least I'll speak for myself-tend to revert further than just to a layman's point of view when the tables are turned. I was doubtlessly worse than most people, lay or medical, since I'm one of those with the disposition to turn to old worries long laid aside, to revive dormant ones, and to create new ones where none existed, all at the slightest pretext. I let these barely visible color spots on my skin assume a gravity far beyond their literal significance.

The mind can become quite creative in designing implication, which adds weight to the already heavy burden of anxiety that started the malicious cycle. My desire to forget everything I had ever learned about squamous cell cancer, or any cancer at all for now, thank you, was a part of wanting to have all this ugliness and soil wiped clean: the cancer, the knowledge, the fear, the side-effects and any unwanted mementos, forever gone and forgotten. And these thoughts were taking lull wing while therapy was still a fledgling.

Another lesson is that radiation therapy to the neck is not designed to feed self-esteem or to nourish pride. My tattoos were another little cut into anything favorable remaining of my self-image, about to be trimmed daily by the ritual of treatment. After my descent into the bowels of the Georgetown University medical complex I would lie on a hard table underneath an intimidating Star Wars contrivance. I had become familiar with the friendly hardware of radiology a quarter century earlier, but now it was a weird, menacing, alien machine. To keep my head still and for purposes of guidance, I was directed to bite down on a wooden stick attached at the other end to a robot staring down at me, and to remain for a time utterly motionless, kissie-face with the robot. After weeks of biting this ridiculous object, I began to believe that the primary function of this ritual was to further ravage that arbitrarily defined emotional core known as the ego.

The indignity of therapy was compounded by a feeling of vulnerability unmatched since the opening day of kindergarten. Following the shock of unwelcome news, there is a reintegration process that tries to bring back the capability of valid thought. The power of reason returns pretty much arm-in-arm with morale, although which one supports and which leans probably varies with the personality of the patient. But in at least one respect, the sense of helplessness still prevails. I don't mean helplessness about the outcome but about altering the circumstances of day in and day out to one's liking. I was not about to be hanged, but the silent assault of radiation for only two minutes daily and the uncertainty of its outcome amounted to something of a "concentration of the mind," which may be why I felt lightheaded after each session for no adequate physiological reason. The concentrated mind is liable to be tugged between ideas of how best to spend the remainder of life and the less invigorating question of just how much this remainder amounts to.

My quiet sessions with the robot under the Star Wars apparatus were an ideal setting for the creation of sick, loathsome broodings of someone aware that his or her body has been invaded.

Incidentally, during the two-minute stretch I often wondered whether the right kind of piped-in music could have lightened the influence of radiation-room gloom on the fancies of a darkened mind. I also further contemplated how medical students and residents might become better doctors by being more at the receiving end. A few workups on the doctor, complete with lab and several procedures of his or her specialty might help. Add enough sessions in the art of bringing-along with unwelcome news-hope and other things positive to make the physician a therapist of encouragement as well as of science. These sessions are especially needed for those doctors to whom this doesn't come naturally. I recalled that Dr. Payne had earned an "A" for making sure his faculty at St. Luke's was strong on the upbeat for the patient.

The worst of the nine-week course was both early and late. During the first or second week, I began to feel as if the creatures who brought us that Star Wars engine were holding their guns on me. There was some nausea I think, and it paralyzed me, from terror rather than weakness. Its affect on me was from a fear that if I moved, my body would become undone, in the ruinous sense as well as through unraveling. I felt light, not in a pleasant sense, but in an expectation of disintegrating and rising away in a charged vapor or an invisible smoke. The feeling was electrical to the effect of being slowly, gingerly electrocuted or of a tissue-destroying electrocautery, except that I didn't hear the expected buzz. It didn't change, but my conception of it began to clear. Soon I was in a state I could imagine a futuristic beam-weapon might cause, as its subject begins to feel as if every electron in his body is captive to a foreign, malignant vibration trying to destroy the cells that contain them. It was as if the aliens had used a weapon to permeate me with their equivalent of pain. Their equivalent was capable of capturing the Earthling's entire attention, leaving him unable to think about or deal with anything else, leaving him willing to say or do anything to get the invader to put down the gun. This was a strange way of becoming despondent, in that neither depression nor pain was the cause.

The low point came one day while Cheryl was driving me home from therapy. I was unable to say anything, and after several minutes "hearing" more than just my silence she looked at me and said, "I feel so sorry for you." I had never before known her, faced with someone in need, to say anything not designed to shore up and strengthen and never in that comparatively helpless manner, her characteristic emphasis always being to keep the eyes up. Paradoxically, within a few more days of piled-on therapy this weird feeling passed, which was fortunate because if it had not I would have.

As this sinister current faded, however, new challenges loomed. Fatigue set in so that by the third week I had to rally resolve just to climb stairs, a humiliation for someone addicted to running. My weight decreased to about 140 pounds, significant for someone just over 6 feet tall.

How did I lose weight? Let me count the ways. Chewing was soon an ineffectual drudge, first because it became impossible to open my jaw more than just enough to admit a few peas on a spoon (a fork wouldn't hold them securely enough to pass), and also because of the near absence of moisture as the radiation guns sent my salivary forces into retreat. Within two or three weeks of starting therapy, even those silkier fishes such as salmon became too rough to swallow. By then my throat couldn't tolerate any substance rougher than overcooked vegetables. My taste buds were damaged, or at least singed, so the best case was to find foods that were wallpaper-paste flavored instead of repulsive-tasting things such as desserts, one of my normal favorites. I grudgingly concluded I could survive a while without a health food, another favorite: fruit, which felt like slag in my mouth. That meant a diet of cooked veggies, oatmeal, unseasoned cheese omelets and Ensure Plus, the drink for people who can't eat. Into the second week of radiation my need to eat was no longer signaled by hunger but by nausea, a strange marker I learned by accident and I fortunately learned early on. Another hindrance to my weight and nutrition program was that 30 minutes into a meal found me having eaten only about half of what I needed (I didn't want any of it, except to relieve nausea), by which time the rest was cold. It was no great source of suffering but significant since cold food took several seconds' work to swallow. I ate most meals at our community hospital because that's where I could get overcooked veggies, tasteless to a healthy palate and therefore not repulsive to me. After a few bites were down the fare was cold. But I couldn't re-warm it, so I would toss the towel in and the food out. Between a tired jaw and cold fare, it's better to just try again later. I became nauseated (the signal of hunger) again quickly, so multiple small feedings became the order of the day.

The absence of saliva was a relatively minor nuisance, but I dreaded the possibility of its allowing tooth decay. So, I was scrupulous with bedtime care, a four-part ritual: floss, regular brush, and machine brush topped off with a coat of liquid fluoride. The chore here was to tough out the toothpaste, which was acid in my mouth. But I was determined to save my teeth despite the sting of the paste. The radiation dispatched the hair follicles of my beard, permanently shaving some of my face (sparing mustache and chin) and thus further pruning my macho image.

Try to go a day without using your voice. I venture it will be harder than a day without chocolate. Mine was effectively lost for a period of a few weeks, followed by recovery at glacial pace. Communicating with only pen and paper was a new experience. It was an emotional and mental constriction at a time when give-and-take was crucial for morale. A Radio Shack power megaphone was helpful when I became able to whisper. On the phone I kept sentences to two or three words and became one of your better listeners fortunately learned early on.

The other bookend to the aforementioned worst part came close to the end of therapy. Weeks eight and nine featured a new alien, the cyclotron. This invader sent radiation to the tonsil "bed" (the tonsil's underlying structural tissue), with aim so true it left the surrounding tissue unscathed. I could feel its havoc precisely where it was aimed. It burned an ulcer on the adjacent surface of my tongue so that the slightest motion provoked a need to scream, quickly stifled when I discovered that screaming is a prime mover of the tongue. Getting food beyond my charred gorge was almost impossible for a day or two and for a few more a matter of self-command. The pain was also costing me sleep, for which every loss means a gain in anxiety, especially for anyone who recognizes the immune system's dependency upon rest. Physical misery augments itself as the symptoms interfere with sleep, nature's prime restorative. Sleep deprivation intensifies frustration and slows time, which wears on until the cycle is broken. When with friends during this interval I tried to counter with humor, but it quickly became clear that comedy was not my strong suit. The worst of this lasted maybe five or six days but seemed as many weeks.

Friday, November 17, 1989. My last day of therapy. After being congratulated by the radiotherapists for "graduating," I drove to Chi Chi's to meet Dr. DiPinto and my staff members for lunch. I left Georgetown that day with no sense of exultation, and hardly any of celebration, but with distinct mental relief and hope. Being dismissed from therapy might be likened to being discharged from a dungeon after having your wrists and ankles clad to the walls for several weeks. The relief and gratitude are palpable, but to be released from shackles is to face the temptation to push this newfound freedom by using parts of the body that aren't ready. As if to toast this milestone, I recklessly plopped a big glob of red-speckled guacamole into my radiated mouth, all too eager to think that if it's 30 minutes now since the end of therapy, it's time to be well. I let out a guttural scream, muffled by my mouth clasped around the guacamole. For the afternoon I could pass nothing more through my burnt chops except water. Here I was, a would-be celebrant for having just received my degree as Radiation Graduate, and now I was pouting because I couldn't enjoy this little event with my office-family and the amusing Dr. DiPinto. I resisted the temptation to take this mishap in symbolic terms-that my hopes were being scorched along with my mouth. But the slight misadventure reminded me that one struggle was over and another was beginning.

That evening I was a guest at a seafood banquet. Food was still paste-mush, and my oral cavity was still very touchy, but the point was to be out among friends rather than to feast.

Another reminder of my condition came two days later when I caught a cold while walking in the cool evening air and had to cancel a much-anticipated trip to visit relatives and friends in Atlanta, for four years my home town. Then it occurred to me that even without the head cold I would have been too tired to pack my bags. I had booked the trip in the frame of mind "Finish therapy on Friday, life back to normal on Saturday"-only slightly lengthened from the 30-minute timeframe I'd expected at Chi Chi's.

Within three weeks there was improvement in my ability to open my mouth and say "ahh," some healing of my tongue, increased toleration of food besides overcooked veggies, and some replacement of nausea by hunger as the signal to eat. By the end of November, I was able to eat my first normal-sized meal. Swallowing was still uncomfortable, but my voice was making a comeback, at least after each midday. A daily ritual was: "Sorry I didn't answer your message when I got up, but I can't talk before noon." By early December I was able to get some grapefruit down. There was still no taste, but the sting had damped considerably. I ate my first peanut butter sandwich too (crunchy at that), although it felt utterly dry. By early December the pain of chewing and swallowing was gone, a sign of good healing of my tongue ulcer and some improvement in the generalized inflammation of the rest of my throat. Sweets were no longer repulsive, merely tasteless. I was off the ground, so on December 7, I staged a surprise attack on a piece of cake, my first dessert since summer. I thought I was making splendid progress until my lunch friends told me the cake was rather blah and certainly not sweet. If it had been properly sweet, it would have tasted strange, not just tolerable. I wouldn't try another dessert for several weeks. By mid-December I was able to identify some foods by taste. On the other hand, along with these hints of progress I also noticed throughout December that it still took the same mustering of resolve to climb from the living room to the bedroom. By early January I was able to see a few patients per day.

By mid-January I was ready to brave the 82-degree chill of a Fairfax County Park Authority indoor pool for some laps. But the energy shortage was to drag on for months. By mid-March, chocolate was beginning to taste a little like itself, an eminent landmark. By high summer of 1990, about a year after Dr. Matini's biopsy, my energy was normal, and by that fall I could bound the stairs like your standard sap-on-the-rise teenager.

Invasive Therapy

In late March 1992, I noticed an enlarged node just under my jaw on the left, the same side as the bad node two-plus years before. My response may be summarized with, "No". "No" kept reverberating in my brain as if I had stepped into a studio in which engineers were testing whether they could prompt every variation of volume, rhythm, crescendo, tone, and echo and were doing this with only the resounding two sounds of the word NO. I weighed possibilities, and the scales in my head were lower on the side of ominous. I wanted to notify Dr. Troost of this ill omen at once; but I discovered this invasion at the bedtime bathroom mirror, so a call now was pointless. I realized the futility of trying to sleep, but I went to bed and tried to even up those foreboding scales by conjuring up benign lightness. Lightness and sleep were the night's slighted wallflower.

There was as much reward as trying to sleep through a hard rock concert. Cindy Hinson, Cheryl's friend since college and mine since meeting Cheryl, had recently moved to Georgia and was back for a visit. Just days earlier Cheryl had remarked to Cindy, "Doesn't Charles look great?" Whether this meant great for his age or great in comparison to his ghastly appearance during the fall (a better word than "autumn" at that stage of events) of '89, I was afraid to ask. But now, staring in the mirror, I tried to take Cheryl's comment for all I could by imagining that, if I had cancer, shouldn't I look as bad as I had before? With such musings my tormented mind tried to escape.

But to no avail, and the same for the absence of symptoms, since in '89 I had had no complaints, only an enlarging lymph node. I never take, and rarely prescribe, soporifics (sleeping pills, of which barbiturates are the long-gone ancestors, and Valium, the semi-retired gray eminence).

Until the release of the short-acting sleep aid of the late 1990s, I would occasionally prescribe small doses of the anti-depressants that have relaxing side effects or take one myself if prospects for sleep seemed hopeless. Prospects did seem so, and I took one of these anti-depressants, 1/3 of a tab. I may have slept a couple of hours, after which no more until about dawn. Then came some of what I'll call anti-REM sleep, or anti-sleep, with disturbed ragged-edge dreams, which I recognized as such while they were unfolding. Sleep can't be deep if you are aware that you're dreaming.

When my watch said two minutes after 9 a.m. I hurried downstairs and called Dr. Troost's office. Since therapy began-and to this day-I've had a radiation-induced shortage of saliva, leaving my voice an impression of Marlon Brando's Padrone Corleone, especially upon getting up mornings or after talking with too many patients at a stretch. This was even more so in March 1992, considering the tortoise-paced improvement of my hoarseness from the day they laid their ray gun down in November 1989 until this dark morning. Now, with renewed dread piling on the fumbled ball in my throat, my breathless voice sounded full of sand and dirt. Dr. Troost's experienced receptionist understood my words and my state, a kindness I'll ever appreciate. She would make time for me at 11. I couldn't express the indebtedness I felt, the first of many such favors in this chapter of my story, so I didn't try beyond thanking her. A benevolent emotion, such as gratitude, endures being torn by the talons of fear. I won't forget.

While waiting for the good surgeon Troost to examine me, I called our receptionist Marlene and told her I would be late because I had found a new node and was at Georgetown. Her voice betrayed more apprehension than I expected, and for this I knew she was with me in spirit. But I was also afraid the concern I felt from Marlene might be grounded on justifiable pessimism. A few minutes later I was being examined by Dr. Troost, who quickly concluded that a biopsy was needed, and needed now. After he phoned his friends at Pathology, I walked the halls to out-patient surgery and waited about 45 minutes. The Belgian lady who did the fine-needle biopsies was intriguing to me and something of a diversion from self-preoccupation.

Some pleasantries between us in the French I could retrieve from a 25-year-old trench gave me an excuse to shift my mind, or at least pretend to. She seemed somewhat entertained having a cancer patient who wanted to talk about something a universe away from the subject at hand. My hopes were having to brace themselves against a gust of hind-sight self-sniping (I should have returned every month for an exam) that would become a storm-driven front of bad news. For some reason I wanted her to know something of my sentiments, as if this sharing would influence the outcome of her work. The biopsies involved her passing a fine needle into my big bad node, the needle being at the end of a suction gun. Three jolts with three passes, but the pain vanished with the needle.

While driving alone back to my office I began to feel that hoping for a benign report was hoping for too much. A node was there in '89: it meant something. A node is here now: it means something. Upon reaching the office, any notion of attending to patients was ridiculously farfetched. So, I sat at my desk trying to do paper things, such as "charting" (dashing off written instructions to the staff on what to advise patients by phone depending on results of tests), reading mail, or triaging journals, each for several seconds until I rejected it as inadequate diversion. The staff was busy up front, and I kept wanting any one of them to come down the hall to my office room and be with me. Dr. Troost phoned sooner than expected, about 4 p.m., and said something close to, "This is the worst of possibilities, a recurrence of squamous cancer."

Except for a vague idea of his follow-up instructions, "worst" is all I took from the phone call. I wanted to tell my staff people immediately but couldn't because I didn't have the strength to stand up. We had an intercom, but this latest news shattered my capacity to think or to switch my hands or my voice on. There is an interplay between the thoughts and sensory manifestations of stress.

Both can, to some extent, be characterized in words. This time my immediate thought was that very soon I might die. One prominent sensation was again profound weakness. I didn't have the palpitations of the first time, but I felt too weak to move. Immediately my voice became so pale that if Dr. Troost had had some background noise in his office, he wouldn't have heard me respond. After he told me to schedule an MRI and an office visit, the only response I could manage was not much more than "I will." We both seemed to realize that any discussion of how I felt was useless.

When the ability to reason returns and the mind again comes together enough to consider life versus death, one of its first thoughts is of goals not yet achieved. At that stage, the question "Will I have time?"

is a faithful consort of anxiety. Possibly someone who has reached all his life's goals and then learns he has cancer could insist that any shock he might feel, any concern he might have, is based solely on the instinct for survival. For the rest of us, I believe much of the preciousness of life has to do with "to do", not just "to be". "To do" includes adventures and accomplishments only encountered in dreams. It includes being with those one loves. While sitting there having just concluded my phone talk with Dr. Troost, I wondered how much time remained for doing, for accomplishing things started, for reaching things looked at but not yet touched, for opportunities over the horizon and hopes that had not yet occurred to me. At this instant, I was certainly robbed of any capability of thinking. Gee, I wonder whether I'll live to try anything new.

A realization of things not yet done, hopes and plans that had been put off by circumstances-such as having to work for a living-came to me in a terrifying instant. But I don't recall whether I even tried to think about the possibility or unlikelihood of setting them in motion. Further thought for the moment was out of the question. Hope for time to do things still undone had to be a heavy part of the weight I felt. Hopes may be generally expressed in thought, in mental language, but any "thought" that could make its way through my dread-filled head was concentrated into a desperate "Please!" aimed at the firmament. All mental process here was compressed into feeling: at this moment any elaboration of ideas was unnecessary and probably impossible. Anglican Father Eldon A. Bayard, his wife and grown children were my closest friends.

In church as a family during my years in Santa Barbara, I tried to hear Father Bayard's words. He would say, "Put yourself in the hands of the Lord," but I wasn't sure where the Lord was at the moment, or whether He might be occupied with more pressing matters, or whether or not He wanted to interfere with fate's impartiality.

Furthermore, the highest satisfactions, the sources of genuine happiness-affection, nature, friendship, intimacy, and other more individual pleasures such as goals-are not the entirety of what we crave from life. I believe most of us mortals want to be aware of the world and its goings-on. There may be those who dismiss as pointless any curiosity about the year 2250, but to me it seems natural to project forward life's interests and involvements into the future with a yearning to be aware of what each of us particularly cares about, from the destiny of a child to the exploration of the universe or the survival of planet Earth. It's the awareness I'm trying to emphasize, that desire to be aware even of those events in which we cannot participate to the extent we wish, or to any extent at all. A reminder of this is the oblivion of anesthesia, after recovery. There is no suffering, but there is no awareness. Some days after waking in my hospital room the first time around, and after my hangover had faded enough so that some thought could compete with the discomfort of drains and IV lines and the Foley catheter, I wondered what everyone in my room, from Dr. Troost to relatives and friends, had been doing and thinking while I was "asleep". It was not only curiosity, it was a desire to have been in on it, to know. Please indulge one more way of saying it: Remembering this short experience with oblivion reminded me that the foreboding I felt a few days earlier with Dr. Troost's phone call was only partly a disquieting fear of not having time "to do." It was also the expectation of not being witness to the unfolding of life about me. We surely feel shortchanged being participants in only a brief scene on the human stage. If after finishing our parts, we could simply attend as audience, it's a pageant most of us would like to watch to the end.

That little trip back two years into my hospital room, be reminded, was a digression. Let's return now to my office room with the phone receiver finding its way to its nest. Helping a receiver into its cradle entails no contemplation, being a ritual, and like the previous bad news day, its trajectory was downward and so required no expenditure of energy. It's not that I was convinced that I was going to die soon; it was that after a semblance of orientation returned, and with it some adequacy to think, I knew that at best I was in for another long and unpleasant struggle. I sat still for what seemed like an hour and was probably three minutes. I was unable to stand up, walk 20 feet down the hall and tell my loving office-family the news from Dr. Troost. And as bad luck would have it none found reason to traipse into my room for the next few minutes. Their absence was noticeable because I needed company, especially if company brought a hug.

Finally, I found enough resolve to phone Cheryl, my need for supportive company overcoming weakness of spirit and flesh. "Thank goodness, she's home," I thought when she answered. I said to her, in a voice barely audible over the phone, "Cheryl, I have cancer again."

Cheryl paused several seconds while she sorted out just how to take this. She knew that, when inspired, I could do a pretty good deadpan. But Cheryl heard the truth in my faded voice. "I'll be right there," she said. Her home was a three-minute drive to my office. On the way back to her house, Cheryl said lots of helpful things, including, "This is not a death sentence." That may not sound very heartening, but this was the second crisis for me in which Cheryl knew what to say. This statement was the preamble to the re-reading of her charter-of-war against despair. It's easy for someone trying to sound upbeat to harm the morale of one who is grasping for assurance with a remark that implies pessimism. "Regardless of the outcome of this, think of the wonderful life you've had" comes to mind. The patient needs to be offered a handle upon the lug to reach for and grasp. Luckily, I never experienced such an indiscretion. I did experience the therapeutic influence of so many friends with the right words, sometimes thought out, sometimes more spontaneous. Helpful words always voice a positive attitude. Healing is fostered by the conviction such favorable words convey. This is especially so coming from someone like Cheryl-the-persuader, herself a living conqueror of cancer. By the time we arrived at her house I had gained enough strength to walk inside unassisted.

Vince Keane, Cheryl's husband, moved to the U.S. from Ireland during his 20's and was a Catholic priest until the late 1980s. Vince's school friend Father Jerry Creeden was visiting Vince and Cheryl from his parish in Central America. This trio of inspiration understood. They could see through my face the discouragement inside. They persisted in offering words of ease. After nearly an hour of their ministry of encouragement, Jerry suggested that he drive me back to my office, his excuse being to pick up my car, but his purpose being privacy. Under his guidance our conversation led us inside, into my own office room, where Jerry put his hand on my head and asked Providence to heal me. It was short, direct and personal. To me it was personal in two ways. Jerry seemed to know that Providence was listening to his appeal for his non-Catholic acquaintance. Not a conversation exactly, but Jerry seemed to have this awareness that his Friend was close by. In the past I had had that feeling in the presence of someone praying aloud only if the mortal praying seemed to be speaking to God instead of to the other mortals present. It was personal also in that Jerry seemed to be doing this more from care than from professional skill. Since he didn't yet know me well, it isn't likely that his care reflected friendship so much as humanity: for Jerry the priest or Jerry the man, my being human was all. Jerry's words were personal because they seemed heartfelt and personal in regard to Whom they were addressed because of his assured manner and in the positive sense of revealing what I interpreted as Jerry's conviction of mutual trust between himself and God.

I felt better during and for a while after this benediction, but my longing ruminations that "surely this must be receiving a hearing; please God, let this be receiving a hearing". That feeling wanted to be reinforced by some supernatural response. Telepathy or sky-writing would do, I wasn't picky, just so the response was to the effect of "Message received," followed by, "... and all due consideration will be given". However, I wasn't sure just how much consideration was due.

But I still hoped. And meanwhile, the concern and ministering of Jerry, who knew me only as an acquaintance, touched me figuratively too and gave me strength.

Jerry and I returned to Cheryl and Vince, and fortunately both were home. My life had begun to collapse for the second time only an hour or so ago, and already I was amid an aura of confidence and reassurance, an aura which if not exactly lifting my dejected spirit was at least arresting its fall. They were ready with words of strength and care, words not of false promise, but of hope, and with a persuasive tone. I would experience much more of this from many others, locally and from afar, while this event was unfolding. I wondered how Jerry and Vince could relate so clearly to my state of mind when, unlike Cheryl, they had not experienced this firsthand. I concluded that it's possible to tune into the sound of another's emotional bedlam and understand what's heard even with its fidelity distorted by crisis. In any case, Jerry and Vince seemed to be getting my message and certainly Cheryl was.

Others were already offering messages of assurance back to me. Their theme was that the outcome would be to leave me alive and with my faculties intact. They telegraphed this as intuition strong enough to be called conviction. Whatever it was, it heartened me. A cynic might say that's simply the imagination of someone who wants to get well. But I came to the opinion that most people who transmit that sort of message, whether from intuition or firm belief, are of a character that gives the message therapeutic effect. Such character prevents its coming across as a superstition or as an arbitrary psychological mind-set. I wanted to believe their conviction was like the universe: real, even if only a minute portion could be grasped.

A few months later I tried to put myself in the place of my brother Stanley and his family when their 19-year-old son Paul suddenly died. To the parent of a deceased child, one matter that looms is how, or in what measure, life can now be defined, since it can no longer be fulfilled. It's unlikely that such a parent would expect to complete life emotionally accomplished or rounded out, not that all others do. To the cancer patient, the question is whether or not there will be life to define. This matter will occur to anyone who has "miles to go" before being able to see himself in a satisfyingly completed sense and ready to sleep. Can many of us say our lives are satisfactorily realized as of today?

Only two days after the bad news, my brother Stanley (who still lived nearby) drove me to my MRI at Georgetown. Despite possibilities that could be contemplated, my spirits were not bad.

March 31 or April 1. An appointment with Dr. Troost, who told me the MRI was normal. That sounded good but had to be interpreted as "not helpful" after a biopsy read "malignant". Dr. Troost recommended neck dissection, meaning cutting out most of the lymphatic chains and the jugular vein of the "left neck," in doctors' jargon. Cheryl informed me of a new and highly considered oncologist at Alexandria Hospital, Daniel H. Clark, M.D., who was able to fit me in the next day.

Thursday, April 2: On the way to my morning appointment with Dr. Clark, driving alone, I felt heavy and sluggish. The day was bright, clear, breezy, 70 degrees, and yet repressive and offensive to me. It's not that I'm convinced that a gray day would have been any less so. It was probably the irony, the incongruity that struck me. I could sense the atmosphere about me clashing with that within. When I was called to come forth from the waiting room to an exam room I could hardly stand up. I felt as if I were walking through oil up to my neck. Voices and other sounds arrived muffled at my awareness, and any that presented themselves cheerfully would have seemed foreign. After Dr. Clark examined me we had a discussion; five minutes later I could remember only that he would confer with Drs. Troost and Halter and either get back to me or relay his conclusions through them. Cheryl later reminded me that Dr. Clark had requested that I bring the slides from Georgetown so he could have his own look-see. I had to tell Cheryl I could recall nothing about it. On these grounds I strongly advise all cancer patients, when visiting the doctor, to bring a listener.

That afternoon Marilyn took me to see Dr. Hatter at Georgetown University's Department of Radiotherapy. Why were people so often driving me places? Because experts recommend that, when driving, at least 33 percent of one's harkening should be to the road. Harter and Clark agreed it was "go" for surgery. Both also explained that if more, or extensive, involvement of the lymphatics (node chains) were found, I would be facing radium H implants, which can threaten the carotid artery and can also undermine the surgical site. That was unwelcome news, since the carotid feeds the organ that savors, worries and dreams, and is therefore my favorite artery. And a broken down surgical site would mean a struggle of undetermined consequences and with unpleasantness I did not want to consider. While Marilyn drove me home I silently mulled all this over.

How can the words of others affect the outcome of an organic process? Through their influence on the mind, of course, and in turn the mind's influence on organic processes, such as the immune, nervous and endocrine (hormone) systems. I can't refer you to proof of this hypothesis, but I'm a believer. Between March 26 (getting the news) and April 6 (surgery), I phoned as many friends and relatives as time would allow, hoping that words of credible assurance and optimism, or the faith they might have in a favorable outcome, would be a source of strength and sustenance. From certain ones I received an especially emboldening inspiration that derives, it seems to me, from their religious faith. I don't know whether it's more the type of spiritual conviction, or the personality of the one conveying it, that gives some persons the power to temper the beleaguered patient's susceptibility to resigning himself to the throw of fate's dice. That's provided the infirm is at least open-minded about any spiritual content the reassurance may have.

There were as many variations as there were offerings of aid and comfort. The effectiveness of the offerings depended upon the nature of both the gift and the giver. I was spared all but one or two counterproductive remarks from well-wishers who perhaps hadn't thought things out. "Que sera sera" is not exactly your top-of-the-line encouragement for the cancer patient.

As I mentioned earlier, from some the uplifting message came this way: there is a scheme of things, and for you, death is not yet part of that scheme. This is arrogant folderol to the skeptic and Pablum to the agnostic. But to the fearful patient who has not lost all credence in some pattern to the cosmos, such a theme comes across forcefully when offered with convincing sincerity. Of course, what's convincing to one is not at all to another, since what one person sees as plausible is another's phantom or blind spot. From certain others who held out optimism, it came with the texture of intuition: "Something tells me this will come out well for you." Intuitive, but with conviction. Some others expressed a belief rooted in religious faith.

From others came the perspective that God can be moved by our needs, longings and entreaties; we need only communicate. That's a bit too human for some who don't accept the evidence presented by the believer. I beg ignorance on the issue. A few expressed something like, "Charles, my faith speaks: have peace-of-heart." The skeptic might dismiss such assurance as fancy. A few others offered an alliance of their own individual intuition and spiritual vision.

A more specific variation on that was from Father Bayard. His emphasis was different: "I have spoken to the Lord, Who is your friend. I not only listen to the Lord, but He listens to me, since He listens to all of us, and we have just had words." I tried to look upon Father Bayard's dialogue with the Almighty as reality. His stance is perhaps less firm to those who question the ability of humans to contact the Lord's throne-room as easily as a White House usher rings up the Chief of Staff. I don't think Father Bayard ever meant that he receives clearly stated messages from his Boss. On the other hand, his theological perspective was not exactly eccentric. His frame of reference was not peculiar to himself when he said, "Put yourself in the hands of the Lord..." He regularly signed off our conversations with "God keep you." The cynic might ask, "Keep you where?" Father Bayard's answer: "The verb 'to keep' means to protect, guard and preserve." As for the mind that believes reason should reign over faith, if it abruptly finds itself manacled to the wall by the irons of fear, that mind may find itself more receptive to Father Bayard's creed. Faith seems to be forceful for those who have it. On the deepest parts of the "psyche" that can resonate spiritually when influenced spiritually, I believe their words-Father Bayard's and others'-were palliating. After they spoke, I felt a little more secure.

From most I sensed an effort to put themselves in my place, which calls up the word "empathy". To get the feel for that, perhaps those who once faced death have the upper hand. A commercial pilot cousin reminds me that anyone who has done stick and rudder for 20,000 hours qualifies, except that staring at death is over within seconds or minutes, whatever the upshot.

From whatever perspective, the effort by those of faith to bring me peace of soul and mind was effective in proportion to the personal love undergirding this intended gift. A stranger or mere acquaintance trying as a human mediator to extend spiritual assurance to someone in need could have no reliable intuitive grasp of the needful one's connection with his or her world, cosmic or earthly. Our grip on things spiritual is human and tenuous. Probably we can agree that nobody "knows" the cosmic scheme, and I would say that any awareness of it is arrived at through observation of natural and physical behavior and of moral structure, observations that may lead in turn to faith or to intuitive or even rational conclusions. Or if anyone thinks he has secure purchase on spiritual finality, I doubt that his reach will find you or me, and it certainly won't the skeptic. Given our weak hold on universal order, not knowing the soul-in-need makes for an even greater disadvantage in trying to be helpful, since there the human-to -human connection is the weakest link.

During the workup and radiation-therapy chapter in this cancer story, and during the surgery phase more than two years later, I was puzzled by the distance-from near-absence to silence-of two close friends whom I generally hear from regularly. Later each took the initiative to raise the subject with me. During my illness, each had felt at a loss as to what to say. One explained that since she had no wisdom of healing or insight to offer, any exchange would be pointless and therefore too awkward to try. She missed the point, which is that with or without wisdom, contact is what the patient needs. Another's insight came later when he discovered a need to minimize the situation. He found "Not a big deal" the best position for viewing what he wanted to see, namely an un-marred prospect. Both friends realized long after the fact that phoning me up only to hear the voiceprints of dread would have twisted their frame of reference, thereby threatening their optimism. Carrying that further, some may try to prevent altogether the bad-news carrier pigeon from nesting in the mind. One of my closest cousins later told me that she would collect "get well" cards to send me but couldn't bring herself to write a message or send them because she couldn't acknowledge to herself that I was seriously ill. Trying to do so would raise her anxiety level beyond coping. Also, she felt that acknowledging that I was ill might aggravate the illness. Some people take denial to the point of superstition.

Deep Sleep

Monday, April 6, early morning. Vince dropped me off at Georgetown University Hospital, where I arrived on the old ward section well before my 8 a.m. check-in time. Before and after the familiar pre-op rituals of history-taking, vital signs, blood-drawing and so on, I sat alone, somewhat uncomfortable on my hard chair and looked through the two big Washington newspapers. But I found myself turning the pages without reading. I wanted/needed something to distract me from my reflections, and found it around me. I felt the presence of Dr. C. Thorpe Ray and an intern or resident: my room obviously dated from the 1920s or 1930s.

Undoubtedly it had been modified somewhat since then, so I'll describe it as a more classic rendition of these hospitals' older days. The room was square with sterile-looking white plaster walls, the girth of which held rub rails or chair rails to prevent gouging by moving furniture. The continuation of a metal rod passed through two opposite walls nine or ten feet above the floor.

Before steel was widely used, walls tended to fall outward due to pressure from the roof; so, the supporting rod traversed at least two rooms and the corridor between, serving the same purpose as the flying buttress of medieval cathedrals.

The floor was dark brown linoleum. There was a hard chair and a nightstand next to the bed, which was of stamped metal, except for the angle iron that supported the wooden slats. The vertical bars of its headboard and foot were hollow steel pieces snapped together front-to-back. Human power and a hand crank at the foot lifted the head of the bed. The mattress, of course, was designed to flex.

Privacy screens were built on frames with trucks attached to the lower corners so they could be wheeled about the room. The screens were made of bleached muslin gathered like a curtain on a rod to provide opacity and thereby privacy. The casement windows of float-glass opened and closed by sliding frames of sash and counter-weights that would rise or fall in balance with the window. There were pull-down shades.

The wall over the head of the bed held a crucifix, and another wall held a painting, often of the Madonna, to break the monotony. The picture frame and the crucifix were suspended by steeples of stranded picture wire in plain view. There were no expander bolts then, but even if there had been, trying to penetrate the wall with nail or screw would have chipped the plaster and exposed the underlying lathe, or if the wall was concrete, simply bent the nail, so the picture wire was wound round a conduit or steam pipe above.

Along one wall was a steam radiator. The bathroom had a wide porcelain basin, wide-body tub, pull-chain commode, and walls and floor of tile for easy cleaning. A light hung from the center of the ceiling. Light fixtures over the door were powered by surface conduits-One-inch wide, one-half-inch thick metal tunnels that ran around the walls to the plug receptacles and light switches.

The hall had a high arched ceiling-a series of vaults, each top corner of which was the junction of four curved surfaces. The wall surfaces curved down, like a tent, to vertical posts that served as supporting members. At the end of the hall was the nurses' station, tended by nuns in full habit. On the other side of the hall from the station was a desk for check-in. Hanging over the desk from the apex of the vaults was a swinging lantern with metal frames and glass. At the station clouds of steam rose from autoclaves used to sterilize instruments.

Autoclaves on the first floor tapped into the steam pipe that ran just above the hall ceiling, and autoclaves on floor two tapped into the same pipe underfoot. The pipes extended on to their main purpose-radiators for heat and for steam disinfection of its tile walls and floor. Part of the hospital complex was a central heating plant fed by coal.

In the room and hall and throughout the hospital was the pervasive smell of ether, which was used as a disinfectant as well as for anesthesia. This afforded the interior of hospitals a distinguishing aroma that patients associated with care, assurance and authority: You are now in good hands, those of the priesthood of medicine. Nurses and doctors had shaker bottles of ether with which they would adorn their uniforms and white coats so as to take on a clinical air-good psychology for the patient.

In this room I could sense the breaths and shadows of young past-century interns and residents reciting histories and physical findings to their attending professors. These exalted teachers were the old masters of physical diagnosis. Around me in this old infirmary section was the ambiance of their first-half-of-the-century prime before the advent of high tech left their art less an essential discipline and more a nostalgically worshipped luxury. For all I knew, while doing time in solitary waiting for the gurney ride to anesthesia and the OR, my waking would be back in this 1926 ward. A day or two later I would look back and feel it was fitting in some strange way to prep for surgery surrounded by ghosts of the booming 20s and Great Depression and then to wake up in the brighter new section, the better for looking ahead.

Back to my pre-surgery 1920s room. I felt my life and well-being were as secure under the knife of Dr. Troost, from the neck up, as they would have been under that of Dr. Hugh Stephenson from the neck down. In my opinion, Dr. Troost would inspire as much confidence from any colleague. Still, some worry is inevitable before surgery, provided one's head is oriented. Looking back, I'm surprised I was able to read my newspapers with some concentration, even if interrupted by stares at the walls. I was troubled by my knowledge that the neck is a concourse of things that don't want to be cut, by memories of hundreds of experiences assisting at the table, and by my awareness that even the high-placed Dr. Troost is human. I was also apprehensive about what bulletin might be awaiting me upon waking, assuming I did.

I had already told Dr. Troost that I hoped the anesthesiologist would give something to relax me before they wheeled me into the OR, where all the troops would be standing ready to lay siege, the heart monitor beeping its relentless reminder to me that my pulse was racing, in turn inevitably increasing my output of Adrenaline with its multiplier effect on my anxiety and around we go, as at Georgetown in '89. About 10 a.m., I was wheeled supine to the OR, the pre-op section, that is.

A genial anesthesiologist greeted me and started an IV. This was about 10:15 a.m. Whether Dr. Troost had prompted her or whether this was her standard plan of attack I still don't know, but she was about to sneak up on me the good old Dr. King-1989 way. A few seconds later I mumbled to her some silliness resembling, "I think I feel relaxed." Then- and I mean then, there was no apparent passage of time since my remark- I awoke in my new room in one of the surgical wards.

After being sewn up in the OR, patients don't customarily wake in a room "on the floor" having graduated from Recovery as I did. I forgot to tell them in advance what a quick drunk I was, and after three hours in Recovery they got tired of waiting for me to regain consciousness and wheeled me to my room. Happenstance I'm sure, but when I came to my eyes were pointed at the wall clock, which read 7:30 (p.m.), some four hours later than Stan, Marilyn, and her friends, the Pattavinas, had been led to expect. Not a problem for them, as that allowed time for a poker game not far from the nurses' station. Upon waking I looked down from the clock to see Dr. Troost at the foot of my bed, with the poker players and others on either side. I was told later the look on my face was hard to interpret. Interpretation: surprise that the operation had been done with no elapsed time, mixed with gratitude and relief that I was with the living. Hard to read because the face newly awake from surgery is written in Anesthesia. Something was tight around my neck. My arms felt too heavy to reach up to check it out, but anyway the bondage of all the lines and tape left me realizing the futility of trying. Surgeon Troost made a speech to me in a very upbeat mood, the only portion of it I can remember being that I would not need radium implants.

The implication of that was the lymph chains looked too clean to be thinking radium. A matter of speculation at that moment-the pathologist being the Supreme Court, yet to weigh the evidence. But on the other hand, Dr. Troost has an experienced eye. I recall Marilyn then saying to me, "Everyone is ecstatic," a message that watered my eyes.

After most of a day having nothing but an anesthesiologist's gas tubes in my mouth, it was drier than its ordinary dry, and swallowing took several seconds of concentrated effort. For a while, post-anesthesia memory can be likened unto the newborn's: a clean slate, with no trace of recent events, in my case pre- or early post-op. Marilyn later reminded me that my first waking words were: "May I please have some ice chips?" Soon I was with it enough to realize the obvious, that the immediately noticeable discomfort below my chin was a dressing designed to keep my neck in place. It seemed an encumbrance to my breathing but probably wasn't. And, speaking of bafflements, another was being too weak to sit up.

I wanted to sleep. The anesthesia hangover would no doubt have ruined any dreams of getting some sleep even if I had been comfortable, but events conspired to ensure no sleep. The IV ran into an intracath into my right forearm. If this line became so much as threatened by a kink it set off a pulsatile alarm, a technological advance of recent years. Oh my, when I think of old days in training! We knew the IV line was obstructed only when the nurse had time to check the drip or when we found it on rounds. We knew the receiving vein had become incompetent only by a swollen arm, and if the patient had rendered up his last vein, Murphy's Law dictated that it was now 3 a.m. and time for a cutdown. Until I gained considerably more strength and mobility, there was no way I could reach this alarm off-switch from my bed. Since I was uncomfortable and restless and couldn't lie still, the nurse had to trip in and silence it every few minutes. But since I couldn't fall asleep for several other obnoxious reasons, the alarm never woke me. I kept wanting to turn over but knew that the alarm would scream if I moved. Also, still under the influence of the anesthesiologist, and with lines connecting my body's passageways to at least three mechanical givers and takers, any decision to move, much less turn over, entailed a call up of forces and resolve. Tied and bound so, the weak and encumbered can forget rolling in such a rack anyway since the slightest maneuver was a transfer requiring two hands. The Foley catheter running from my bladder was taped to my body, but I didn't trust this precaution to save my reproductive paraphernalia from being ripped if I moved. Concerned that all dreams of fatherhood might become this evening's nightmare, I grabbed the line and hugged it to my body, thus committing an entire arm to ancillary employment when all hands were needed for the main campaign, which was to turn over in bed. Drains connected my neck's surgical wounds to suction vessels that looked like some sort of tropical fruit dangling mid chest. They were pinned to my gown, but pulling them from beneath me was another on the list of chores to be done before there was any thought of trying once again to sleep.

Trying to relax enough to use the bedside urinal was utterly futile. By 1 a.m. I had staggered to the bathroom several times and had failed to void, even after hosing down (with water) the workers on strike. The anesthesia was not being sympathetic with my parasympathetic nervous system. Translation: the anesthesia had disabled the circuits that let one pee. Beginning to sense a lost cause, I surrendered my pride to the nurse. There was delay readying the gear, so by the time she began applying Betadine to the organ receiving the catheter I was trembling. It was a bed-shaking chill from the pain of a day's IV fluid distending my bladder. And when the catheter tried to pass my sphincter at the bladder neck, there was a new pain. She tried twice and failed. Now it was on toward 2 am, and I could feel the little beads of blood on my forehead that are the vanguard of panic. Finally, she called Dr. Aronstien. His arrival was a reminder of old times, since he looked like the twenty-eighth hour of a standard 36- hour on-call shift. He brought a larger tube and inserted it promptly. This time, instead of the prolonged agony of the nurse's probing, the pain lasted only about two seconds because it was the pain of passage on into the bladder, of success. Despite the relief of a now empty bladder, the imitation of having the catheter in a tunnel that wasn't used to holding it made me feel a perpetual urinary urgency ("I've got to go now"). I was back to holding on to that catheter every time I turned. Petty grievances-they kept my mind busy, which may sound positive, but what I wanted was no-anesthesia-hangover sleep.

The next morning, Tuesday, April 7. Nurses and a restricted number of visitors were in and out until early afternoon, when I was at last able to nap on and off. I was becoming skilled at maneuvering the drains and the Foley tube, but an obligatory prelude to getting some sleep was learning some tricky moves to keep the alarm quiet. By late afternoon the Foley was again removed, and by then my bladder was able to do what it needed to do. Early evening, I got out of my room and shuffled a couple of laps around the nurses' station.

But back to 10 a.m., when Dr. Troost zipped into my room appearing bright and bushy, quite in contrast to Dr. Aronstien, who during his night visit had seemed in the early neurotic phase of fatigue psychosis. To me and my imagination, Dr. Troost's words contrasted with his cheerful air when he said, "I don't know whether it would have been better to find a primary or not." This caught me off guard. My frame of mind during that two-week trudge before surgery must have been something like, "If a primary is there, Dr. Troost will find it and deal with it. If there is none, I don't need to think about it."

Facing up to the primary, that evil ancestor of a malignant node, presumes the patient has a store of mental and emotional energy to call upon. This first morning after surgery I had no store and no disposition for any facing. I hadn't asked my doctors any questions about a primary, since one isn't apt to ask about something one prefers to ban from one's mind. But I took this morning's comment from Dr. Troost's head and fed it into mine, and out from my sick imaginings came several possibilities, all having in common his uncertainty. I could conclude that he was concerned about a still-unfound primary, being that every metastasis has a primary. And likely this node still had one from a two-and-a-half-year-old job not completed. The effect on me would have been one thing if he had said, "We not only cleaned out your lymphatics, we found this little primary and sliced it away and put it on a dish for the pathologist: Have a drink." The effect was quite another given that the message was, "Where in the devil is that thing? If we could have found it we could have had a chance at a cure. On the other hand, maybe it's better we didn't find it because if it's that small and hard to find maybe it's packing up and leaving, and besides, if we had found it, maybe we couldn't have completed the job with the scalpel." In any case, I didn't ask Dr. Troost for his explicit thoughts because I wasn't ready to hear the answer.

Now the broodings and imaginings took over and overwhelmed Dr. Troost's earlier wake-up message, which had been something with the ring of "those node-chains sure looked clean to me." I pictured my new primary, yet unfound, growing and trying to suffocate me or rendering me mute, causing me to waste away from my lean frame to something much worse. My morale was doing a little free-fall. I imagined the most appropriate ways to arrange a Kavorkian before allowing all this to happen.

By early afternoon a few more visitors were allowed, one of whom was Cheryl. Without giving her the lurid imagery, I told her I was having "negative thoughts," which she answered with a gentle reprimand for back-sliding and a lecture on her awareness that this scourge had been eliminated. Her inspiration lifted me again. It was her gift of promise. Though I couldn't reach her plane of "knowledge" or belief; her words brought relief; and a small step toward peace. I didn't acknowledge her comforting words, but I'm confident she noticed the change in me with my more settled silence. With that I was able to lay my musings and weightings aside for the night at least enough to get some sleep.

My "some sleep" that night was between sessions of tussling with drains more than with misgivings and forebodings. Struggling with drains and a new preoccupation. I was discovering that, added to these reasonably routine post-op irritations, was an urge so unexpected that its incongruity with my temporary incapacity compounded the distraction of it all. There I was with my lines and tubes with nothing deeper than my skin working properly. Newly liberated from a foreign tube, my sexual implements felt like the victim of a karate accident. Lying there with all that for company my overriding desire was that a woman would join me in that bed. Pain, immobility and anxiety were with me most generously but were submerged by the paradoxical flood of sexual urging. This absorption of mine under such ironic circumstances was so surprising

301

and forceful that I have tried to look back at it objectively enough to find the origin of its craving for closeness in its true colors. I see it as a dance featuring that lust-god Pan as partner with whichever goddess you choose to embody emotional intimacy. In that setting a craving for emotional nearness is quite understandable, whereas the lust is to this day a phantom to my mind's grasp. Carnal passion has a penchant for lurking in the hearts of men and is supposed to be appropriately trained and tethered, but for it to raise its hot head in that inner-sanctum of illness and incapacity was a mystery to me. Some might attribute it to the catheter, but I know I wanted to be held.

Dr. Aronstien and the other residents came in first thing the next morning but without Professor Troost. I had my statement ready. "Fellows, please tell Dr. Troost I prefer not to hear anything more about the pathology readings until I have more strength." They stared speechless a few seconds as if slightly taken aback. Maybe they were more optimistic about the yet unseen report than I was, but startled by my comment, were undecided as to what to say. Or maybe they were thinking how nice it was, having seen the report, that I was offering them an out from their sordid duty. I lay there thinking sick, self-destructive thoughts. "They probably know the awful truth, and now it will be Dr. Troost's job to break it to me." Dr. Aronstien collected himself and said, "Oh, sure, no problem." Then they finished tending to my neck.

I began thinking how wonderful it would be to have a victory in life. It seemed so long since the last one. Some of my life's goals, especially the moment's most significant and unrealized ones, passed through my head in review, causing me to wonder whether they would all remain dreams. This from too many hours-maybe 12 or 14 alone, without someone able to get my mind and spirit back on track. Many were able, but they weren't allowed; visitor quotas were still in force.

Wednesday, April 8. The anesthesia hangover would last a while, that was clear, and the only thing that was clear. For the next two weeks I would be weak and drowsy, but sleep still wouldn't come, even after an hour or two lying in bed and inviting it. It wasn't that I had to face getting up in the morning to head for work: that was covered for the foreseeable future. But even if the rosy fingers of dawn are to bring no demands for a day of doing, sleeplessness can be one of life's surpassing irritations. The irritation isn't just that it takes its victim for a ride into the Land of Crazy. It's also the wheel upon which it racks his or her body while the mind is incapacitated with fatigue. And so, the hours pass, written off as forever wasted. The anesthesia hangover made me worry that its defining ingredient, intellectual stupor, might linger forever, even if I tried to reassure myself that at least I was sharp enough to sense the dullness.

View from the Stairs

Wednesday, April 8, continued. Dr. Troost came in about 9 a.m. and, while looking me over, told me we would have to wait several days before the pathologist's report would be ready.

Then the 7 a.m.-3 p.m. shift nurse removed my IV. Nanda Piwowar, a patient who had become a close friend, dropped in mid-morning and talked me into taking my first walk down the hall, away from the nurses' station. We went about 20 yards too far. I made it back on my own feet, but it was a close call. I reached my bed just in time for the collapse. More visitors were allowed during the afternoon. For most patients, that's progress. That night I didn't have enough energy to read, which didn't matter since I couldn't focus my eyes more than a few seconds at a time anyway. But I was able to look in the direction of the TV set. Dolly Parton was Johnny Carson's guest, singing her song "It's the Dawn of a New Day." This took me back to my junior high teacher and idol Mrs. Hurd, who, digressing from English into philosophy, said, "There are no coincidences," which expressed her opinion that coincidences are not happenstance. I hoped she was right.

Thursday morning, April 9. Dr. Aronstien removed the drains, and then Dr. Troost came in about 10 a.m. to ask if I would like to go home, with the suggestion in his tone that that's what I should do if I could muster the will. I was startled, but after a few seconds of staring, said "Sure." I still did not know-or want to know-the pathology results. Frank and Betty Gene DenOuter, who had been my patients and became my friends, drove me home. Within minutes Cheryl dropped by and lured me out into the beautiful April day for a walk of nearly a mile. I can't believe I did it. I can't believe I tried it or finished it because I wouldn't find that kind of strength again for at least another seven days.

Sunday morning, April 12, 2 a.m. I woke and looked in the mirror. My neck was swollen, and this was a sudden occurrence. It was nothing like this when I had gone to bed. Just below my jaw there was so much edema that I knew it had to be cellulitis, a serious infection spreading from the wound. Now the wound would dehisce, presenting an assortment of ways to die. I sat down on the stairs near my bedroom, the closest to despair I think I have ever known, and managed to utter, "God, what's going to become of me?" This may have been partly an interjection, but it was mostly a question. Fear was an arrow through me, with a head of inevitability. I felt empty, yet full of terror, as if I were falling out of the hands in which Father Bayard had reminded me that I should let myself stay. Desperation on this order, I think, makes a human into a laboratory for those investigating the relationship of theology to human emotion, and maybe to reason, provided the subject survives this plunge into apparent hopelessness. I think these issues pertain to my state of mind at that moment, that of someone lost in a frozen wilderness with the sun going down.

I went to the phone like an invalid and dialed the hospital. Dr. Aronstien was back on call again. As soon as he said, "Hello," it was obvious that I had interrupted one of those nocturnal naps so precious to residents-in-training. With a voice suddenly more hoarse than the day before, I muttered my disaster to him. Dr. Aronstien tried to assure me that this was not rare, saying, "I've seen that before." I think he remembered that during general training, med students, interns and residents, other than "Head and Neck" surgeons, don't scrub in on a lot of neck surgery apart from thyroid and carotid and that I might justifiably be a little rusty on this possible complication of node chain dissections. And he was probably far enough along in his residency to have noticed the degree to which professional knowledge can become distorted beyond recognition by anguished presentiments on the part of the doctor-patient. He told me to come see him on the floor at 9 a.m.

After some weird limbo dreams, dawn came, so I decided it would be better to be out of bed if I couldn't put my mind to rest until the time to call for a ride to the hospital. I ate something because I knew if I didn't I would have a new problem by the time I got to the hospital. I decided my brother Stanley would be the one I would call upon, and besides, his home was nearby. There was no point in waking him earlier than necessary, but on the other hand I had been merely surviving every second since 2 a.m. At 7:45 I couldn't hold off any longer and called him. I felt that if I were alive the next morning I would be in for a lengthy stay, so I struggled to put some clothing and shave-kit essentials into a tote bag.

As Stan was driving me away from the house I began dwelling on whether I would ever come back. "Maybe a fifth-generation cephalosporin (antibiotic) will save my life, but maybe the infection will be resistant, or maybe I'll have a serious allergic reaction to the antibiotic, or maybe my wound will come apart before I get to the hospital," followed by every other possibility my tormented imagination could find to brood over. I began to feel nauseated and within seconds of leaving home I doubted I could make the half-hour drive to Georgetown. I came close to asking Stan to turn into Emergency at Mount Vernon Hospital,

306

but didn't, or couldn't. He said some things in a gallant effort to get my mind off myself but couldn't shake my fixation.

He dropped me off at the front door so that, while he parked, I could get on up to the floor and let them know I was on time. Now, I've always been "dizzy", as Stan used to describe me in high school, but not spatially disoriented provided I keep my eyes, and the organ to which the optic nerve connects them, on the space I'm crossing. But I lost my way, a nice garnish on the morning's banquet: "All is lost, and now I'm lost." Stan was there to greet me when I finally found the nurses' station, but read the moment as inappropriate for teasing, and refrained from saying, "Where have you been?" Soon Dr. Aronstein called for me. He invited me to relax, examined me, and affirmed this was standard swelling after a semi-radical neck dissection.

He then said, "Now I want to be honest with you ..." I cut him off short with "Dr. Aronstien, I don't think I have the strength to listen to what you have to tell me. Please, can we wait?" He said, "No, you don't understand. [Pause.] Well, I'll let Dr. Troost explain." Sometimes I wonder what my feeling would have been if he had gone ahead and told me for sure. Something about his manner was reassuring. After Dr. Aronstein's words, I began to notice a weight lifting and darkness yielding to a lighter world, even if I had no certainty of what he meant to say. I, more or less, worked at not analyzing this, lest I talk myself out of this better feeling. Seeing Dr. Aronstein before seeing Dr. Troost would provide a nicely graduated transition to a new frame of mind and heart provided I kept the faith. This transition, if it held, would cover about 30 hours, from 9 a.m. Sunday to noon Monday. As Stan drove me home I was feeling a new swelling, that of peace. It was coming slowly, but it was persuasive. The good senior resident had allowed me a renewal of spirit, even if my mind still felt considerably on trial. The verdict would come the next day. I returned to the Georgetown University Medical Center late the next morning. Dr. Troost bounded into the treatment room and said, "Great news, no cancer." His positive words may have voiced a hope to keep my mind on these tidings and away from the surgery and all that went with it. Had there been an error in the reading of the "frozen-sections," the tumor tissue slides? Were benign cells so distorted by radiation that they appeared malignant? Certainly, these proceedings had cut heavily into my emotions. But Dr. Troost need not have concerned himself over whether I would focus on the events culminating in surgery or on continued life.

Instant and indescribable gratitude for knowing I did not have cancer transcended any inkling of regret or displeasure for the turmoil and the surgery. I felt no discontent, I felt release and lightness. I was a human soul set free. The feeling Dr. Troost's report gave me was probably not so much that of someone being told, "We have the wrong person: you may step down from the gallows now," since with my biopsy there was not a certainty that I would die soon, just the threat. My feelings were probably more those of one being released from the Gulag's mines into the clear, clean daylight of freedom. The only "but what if what I had only offered to Dr. Troost was my concern about having lost my lymph nodes". The lymph nodes would have been the best signals of any new primary that might occur eventually. He reminded me that adequate visits for exams should take care of that matter.

Within two days my staff women noticed I had the blues. Yes, I did indeed, but that was not from second-guessing the events of the month, but because of the frustrations caused by my wound, such as the difficulty finding a comfortable position for my head and neck in bed and the anesthesia hangover. It would happen again two months after my April surgery, when I got the flu for the first time since finishing radiation therapy in '89. With it came that other illness, melancholia and the plague of a disorder I'll call "Untamed Imagination Syndrome". "Is my immune system, the mortar and bricks of life's fortress against invasion, crumbling?" I wondered. "Am I going to get pneumonia and die? Am I that fragile?" My sore throat was cancer, my cough was pneumonia, my hoarseness was cancer again-disgusting examples of letting oneself be tormented by a flea. I felt a little guilty for this outlook, as if the Almighty, assuming He had the inclination to check into my attitude, might mistake frustration and lapses into immaturity for ingratitude.

That little sickness passed, of course, and I didn't. Post-op and still under the influence of anesthesia, many surgical patients imagine the mind and body to have their usual capabilities before the requisite recuperation time. But if I'm typical, most cancer patients tend, for the rest of their lives, to envision the worst with every little nuisance-for-a-day illness. They see the end of life through a telescope and need a reminder that it isn't quite so close. They visualize relapse and its shadow of death with any new symptom, even when they know better professionally. When these little incidents and their attendant fears are recognized as fancy, they are replaced by embarrassment or even a tinge of shame for having harbored such creature figments.

When serious illness threatens to remove life's goals and loves from the sufferer's grasp, the best response is to try to hold them in the mind. If there is recovery, most probably prefer to salvage "positives" from the experience. I would summarize these as a reorientation of one's inner life-earthbound loves and spirituality and one's outer life-relationships with others and priorities pertaining to goals. After Dr. Troost's announcement I felt life-renewed. I can give no clear definition of the human soul. The best I can do is to describe it as that inner place that is reached by certain things, such as sublime music and the beauty of nature. That's the inner place that I felt was liberated, with power over the now trifling annoyance of surgery and recovery, even if my face divulged the day's cares. For a while I did have some thoughts that the surgery might not have been necessary, but, after all, probably was. The spirit of someone who has been told to go on living dwells within the sphere of Gratitude and Receptivity. By "receptivity" I mean being open to living by a creed that views life as an unearned favor and calls for living with some sense of obligation, recognizing the proneness for a backslide when the day's graffiti devils paint a sorry face. "Obligation" to what? Well, to living with gratitude for life.

A week after surgery the swelling was noticeably less, which means the blood and lymph leaving my head were doing their best to build new channels. There were still symptoms such as considerable laryngitis and its hoarseness, trouble getting comfortable on the pillow, restless sleep, and the occasional hint of a headache, and probably some intellectual obtuseness. But there were hints of improvement within all these. Two weeks post-op I felt well enough to go swimming and would have if my staples had been removed, but they were still holding my neck together.

Anyway, improvement in energy was definite. I turned on my word-processor, even though the one in my head wasn't fully operational. I had been trying to write a reference book when this interruption began, and it was a pleasure to revisit it. Now maybe writing could move from distraction to focus.

Through May and the early weeks of June I gained strength and my neck gained flexibility. My mood improved lockstep and even overtook my physical improvements. Recovery was fully underway. Some months later, I felt I had more energy than most my age. I'm still addicted to exercise. I'll always be subject to those fears lurking inside the heart of the cancer patient, who sees the bumpy road of any petty illness turning at the fork toward Life-Threatening Disease. But when the body is up again, so is the morale. Life can be beautiful; it is bountiful, if not always materially, and it is brief. Everyone should try to fix his or her helm on gratitude for life and its blessings, but to do so takes a wakeful watch.

POSTSCRIPT

The damage to Charles' throat and neck, caused by surgery and radiation, resulted in such difficulty eating that, over time, he lost weight and eventually lost his life. But he never lost his desire to write about the great variety of interests that filled his bright mind. At the time of his death, Charles had completed the Latin Thesaurus referred to by Dr. Capages in the Foreword to this book. He was also working on a book about the history of symphonic music and great opera when he passed away.

Charles never, to my memory, harbored an evil thought about another person and maintained a positive, objective view of everyone. My brother Stanley would say that Charles' legacy was his humility, his sense of humor, his concern for others and his love of family.

O.K. "Kay" Armstrong Jr.

ABOUT THE AUTHOR

Dr. Martin Capages Jr. was born on August 28, 1944, at Fort Sill, Oklahoma, the son of Marine captain, Martin Capages of NYC and Helen Elizabeth Powell Capages of Millington, Tennessee. As a Marine "brat", he attended elementary schools all over the US along with his three younger sisters. When his parents settled in Missouri in 1956, he attended Dora junior high school and Dora High School in 1958. The family moved to Springfield, Missouri in early 1959 and Martin attended Parkview High School where he was an honor student and lettered in football, graduating in 1962. He attended Missouri State University on a Regent's scholarship until 1964 when he transferred to Missouri Science and Technology in Rolla, Missouri, where he graduated in January 1967 with a BS in Mechanical Engineering. At Rolla, he was a Resident Assistant, Distinguished Military Student and Cadet Commander of the Army ROTC Brigade.

After receiving his Commission as an Army Ordnance Officer but prior to reporting for active duty, he joined Boeing Aircraft in Wichita as an Associate Engineer working on the new 737. He reported for active duty in June 1967. Military service during the Vietnam era took him to Aberdeen Maryland, Redstone Arsenal, Fort Knox, and southern Japan where he served as the Officer in Charge of the Kawakami Ammunition Storage area just outside Hiroshima, Japan.

313

After completing active duty, Martin joined Exxon in Houston, Texas, with assignments throughout the U.S. and Europe. He left Exxon in 1984 to join Kerr McGee in Oklahoma as Manager of Engineering until 1992 when he left the petroleum industry to start his own professional structural engineering consulting firm in Springfield, Missouri. He continued post-graduate studies in Civil Engineering and Management receiving an earned Doctorate in Engineering Management in 2002. He retired from full time practice in 2012. Martin began writing political commentary in 2009. In 2017 he authored *The Moral Case for American Freedom*.

Martin is married to Pamela Kay Capages. It was the second marriage for both and between them they have five children and seven grandchildren. Both Martin and Pamela are active in their Church and are members of the Gideons International and Auxiliary.

DISCLAIMER

This biography has been authorized by the immediate family and heirs of Dr. Charles Lindbergh Armstrong. The opinions and positions are those of Dr. Armstrong. The biographer, Dr. Martin Capages Jr., and publisher, American Freedom Publications LLC, are not offering it as a factual accounting of events.

While best efforts have been used in preparing this book, the biographer and publisher make no representations or warranties of any kind and assume no liabilities of any kind with respect to the accuracy or completeness of the contents and specifically disclaim any personal references to actual individuals mentioned by Dr. Armstrong. This book is not intended as a substitute for the medical advice of physicians. The reader should regularly consult a physician in matters relating to his/her health and particularly with respect to any symptoms that may require diagnosis or medical attention.

Neither the biographer nor the publisher shall be held liable or responsible to any person or entity with respect to any loss or incidental or consequential damages caused, or alleged to have been caused, directly or indirectly, by the information contained herein.

REFERENCES

Anadarcia Sirianni, was a University of Florida graduate student, completed her 1992 master's thesis titled *Orland Kay Armstrong: Writer, Educator, and Public Servant: A Thesis Presented to the Graduate Council of the University of Florida in Partial Fulfillment of the Requirements for the Degree of Master of Arts in Mass Communications.*

J. M. Roberts CBE was Warden at Merton College, Oxford University, until his retirement and is widely considered one of the leading historians of his era. He is also renowned as the author and presenter of the BBC TV series *The Triumph of the West* (1985) and *The History of the World*, Sixth Edition by J.M. Roberts and O.A. Westad. He died in 2003.

John Kirk Singlaub (born July 10, 1921) is a highly decorated former OSS officer, a founding member of the Central Intelligence Agency (CIA), and a retired Major General in the United States Army. In 1977 Singlaub was relieved from his position as Chief of Staff of U.S. forces in South Korea after criticizing President Jimmy Carter's decision to withdraw U.S. troops from the Korean peninsula in an interview with the *Washington Post*. Less than a year later Singlaub was forced to retire after publicly questioning President Carter's national security policies. In 1979 Singlaub founded the Western Goals Foundation, a private intelligence network that was implicated for supplying weapons to the contras during the Iran-Contra affair. Singlaub has contributed to several books, as well as writing an autobiography.

Harry G. Summers Jr. (May 6, 1932 – November 14, 1999) is best known as the author of the neo-Clausewitzean analysis of the Vietnam War titled, *On Strategy: A Critical Analysis of the Vietnam War* (1982). Summers was an infantry colonel in the United States Army and had served as a squad leader in the Korean War and as a battalion and corps operations officer in the Vietnam War. Colonel Summers was also an instructor and Distinguished Fellow at the Strategic Studies Institute at the U.S. Army War College in Carlisle, Pennsylvania, and served on the negotiation team for the U.S. at the end of the Vietnam War.

Charles Augustus Lindbergh
https://en.wikipedia.org/wiki/Charles_Lindbergh

Dust Off by Luis P. Carranza

http://history.amedd.army.mil/booksdocs/HistoryofUSArmyMSC/page306.jpg

Letter from Dad to Kay

1307 BENTON AVENUE
SPRINGFIELD. MISSOURI

Sunday, April 28, 1946

Dear Kay:

It is Sunday night, and I have been so busy for weeks that I could not write you. At any rate, that is the excuse, and believe me, I've been working night and day on several articles and trying to finish the LeTourneau book. It is almost done. I leave Tuesday for the east, to see the *Digest* crowd and to lay plans for more work. Never a dull moment.

Now, I really got a kick out of the account of your fight with that guy. You did exactly right. Never pick a quarrel or a fight. But if some fellow jumps on you, under the false impression that you are yellow, then give him the works. Some men, unfortunately, can learn no other way. They do not have sense enough to let peaceful men alone, and they mistake other men's peaceful actions for weakness. They have to have sense pounded into them, and the process is painful. I am sure you handled yourself with credit. Keep in good condition, and remember it was Theodore (the Great) Roosevelt who said, "Trust in God and take your own part."

Boy, howdy, everybody has been thrilled over the stuff you've sent back. That last consignment of linens, hand-kerchiefs, etc., was grand. It came while the ladies of the missionary circle were here, and mother displayed the stuff for them. They were google-eyed. The little boys have a fit over it. They took one of the Jap flags to Sunday school this morning, and Charles began waving it in church. It almost broke up the meeting.

I plan to go to the S. Baptist Convention, way down in Miami, Florida. I ought not to take the time but can take a lot of work with me. I want to put through some resolutions. You may have seen my story in the May issue of the *Digest*. I am hearing from it widely.

This afternoon, the Drury band put on a concert of original music from Prof. Rockwell. It was good. Some of it slightly corny, perhaps, but on the whole, he has whipped that Drury band into a good outfit. The other night Mother and I heard the H. S. orchestra. Boy, what an outfit that is No better than when you were there, however. I do want you to get back to the clarinet. By the way, it seems that you may be coming back. Good work! Don't get impatient or worried about it. My guess is that it will be late summer. The longer you stay, the longer your G. I. education. But hurry home soon as possible. I may drop into the Navy in Washington this coming week and ask some of my friends there the lowdown.

Do keep well, and love from all, --Daddy.

Letter From Charles To Kay (with note from Mom Louise)

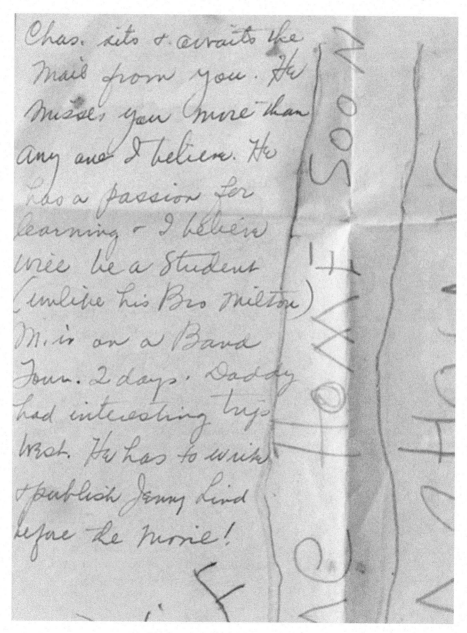

Chas. sits & awaits the mail from you. He misses you more than any one I believe. He has a passion for learning & I believe will be a student (unlike his Bro Milton) M. is on a Band Tour. 2 days. Daddy had interesting trips West. He has to write & publish Jenny Lind before the movie!

INDEX

The Armstrong Family's favorite hymn. Sung at Charles' memorial service and interment at the Missouri Veterans Cemetery on Southwood Road, Springfield Missouri.

Beulah Land

CPSIA information can be obtained
at www.ICGtesting.com
Printed in the USA
BVOW09*0941230418
514170BV00007B/63/P